Advance Prais
Creating a Life of

"Gail Stark, in a voice that is intelligent, witty, and disarmingly candid, recounts her year-long study with her teacher, Joseph Goldstein, of the integrity factors of personal and spiritual development. In so doing, she firmly extends the line from the liberating teachings of the Buddha in the forests of India 2,700 years ago into the middle of business venues in the twenty-first century. Every minute of every day, given mindful attention, becomes an integrity choice. Undertaking this practice, as laid out here, is demanding and thrilling. We can lead worldly, engaged lives and be happy."
—Sylvia Boorstein, author of *Happiness Is an Inside Job*

"If you thought Buddhism was only meant for laid-back meditators, Gail Stark's *Creating a Life of Integrity* shows you how the Buddha's teachings can become essential operational guidance for high-performing leaders and executives. Part passionate memoir and part practical how-to, the book captures the essence of a special teacher-student relationship and translates perennial insights into accessible, resolute action. An invaluable resource for business people on a path of purpose and impact."
—William Rosenzweig, founding CEO, The Republic of Tea; recipient of the Oslo Business for Peace Award

"Whether you are an experienced Buddhist practitioner or simply want to know more about Buddhism, *Creating a Life of Integrity* is a great book to add to your collection. First, the author is in conversation with one of the most renowned, insightful, and compassionate teachers of our time: Joseph Goldstein. The Buddha's teachings come alive in their spirited talks. Second, the book takes the reader step-by-step along a path that leads to what we all aspire to—a life of purpose, joy, and contentment. *Creating a Life of Integrity* gets my highest recommendation."
—Toni Bernhard, author of *How to Wake Up: A Buddhist-Inspired Guide to Navigating Joy and Sorrow*

"In *Creating a Life of Integrity* the reader receives personal lessons and practices for true well-being from the ultimate wisdom coach, the renowned mindfulness meditation teacher Joseph Goldstein. Gail Stark has written a fun, engaging, yet genuinely profound guide for living in alignment with your highest values. I highly recommend this gem of a book."
—James Baraz, coauthor of *Awakening Joy: 10 Steps to Happiness*; cofounder of Spirit Rock Meditation Center

"Reading this book was like actually being present with Joseph Goldstein, a person of exceptional integrity, as he shares down-to-earth yet profound wisdom with the author, Gail Stark. Different parts of my mind and heart were opened to new possibilities because of her unique way of expression. Creating personal integrity is the deepest kind of respect and care we can have for ourselves and others. This book is deeply reaching medicine, *leading to inner calm* and inviolable *peace*."
—Kamala Masters, guiding teacher and cofounder, Vipassana Metta Foundation, Maui

"*Creating a Life of Integrity* is a delightful duet between Joseph Goldstein, a Western meditation master, and Gail Stark, his student and friend. Joseph's teachings are candid, practical, and humorous. Gail carries them out and reports back with a charming blend of honesty and good cheer. Want to level up your life? These two make the journey accessible and inviting."
—Guy Armstrong, author of *Emptiness: A Practical Guide for Meditators*

"Gail's clear and insightful words guide us through the perplexing world of ethics. Drawing on centuries of Buddhist wisdom distilled by Joseph Goldstein, Gail's refreshing and personal accounts of putting these teachings into practice show us all how to live a life of integrity that creates a genuinely happier life."
—Mark Coleman, author of *From Suffering to Peace*

Creating a Life of Integrity

In Conversation
with Joseph Goldstein

Gail Andersen Stark

Foreword by Joseph Goldstein

Wisdom

Wisdom Publications
199 Elm Street
Somerville, MA 02144 USA
wisdomexperience.org

Library of Congress Cataloging-in-Publication Data
Names: Stark, Gail Andersen, author. | Goldstein, Joseph, 1944–
Title: Creating a life of integrity: in conversation with Joseph Goldstein / Gail
    Andersen Stark.
Description: Somerville, MA, USA: Wisdom Publications, 2020.
Identifiers: LCCN 2019049581 (print) | LCCN 2019049582 (ebook) |
    ISBN 9781614292791 (paperback) | ISBN 9781614293033 (ebook)
Subjects: LCSH: Religious life—Buddhism. | Integrity—Religious aspects—
    Buddhism. | Reliability.
Classification: LCC BQ4302 .S73 2020 (print) |
    LCC BQ4302 (ebook) | DDC 294.3/444—dc23
LC record available at https://lccn.loc.gov/2019049581
LC ebook record available at https://lccn.loc.gov/2019049582

ISBN 978-1-61429-279-1   ebook ISBN 978-1-61429-303-3

26 25 24 23 22
6 5 4 3 2

Cover design by Jess Morphew. Interior design by Kristen Goble.
Set in Warnock Pro Light 10.5/15.

Printed on acid-free paper that meets the guidelines for permanence and durability of
the Production Guidelines for Book Longevity of the Council on Library Resources.

Printed in the United States of America.

Please visit www.fscus.org.

I dedicate this book to my teacher and dear friend, Joseph Goldstein, who patiently listens to my stories of woe and then responds, "Perhaps you could try . . . ," and I am struck silent at the sheer brilliance of his offering. Sometimes, yes, I will argue a point, and then stop, suddenly understanding the profoundly simple wisdom in his words. Oh to be in the world with such clarity and ease.

To my husband, Ron, my rock, my partner on the path, and for teaching me how to laugh in the midst of it all.

And to each of you who choose to live your life with integrity. Thank you.

Contents

Foreword by Joseph Goldstein | ix

Preface | xi

Introduction | 1

1. Generosity | 15

    Instructions: We Start Where We Are

    Working with Generosity: Julie

    Check-In Conversation: Push That Edge

2. Virtue | 37

    Instructions: The Peace of Non-Remorse

    Working with Virtue: A Refuge for Mice

    Check-In Conversation: Investigating with Interest

3. Renunciation | 55

    Instructions: At Peace with Our Piece

    Working with Renunciation: Everything Passes

    Check-In Conversation: Reframing Deprivation as Non-Addiction

4. Wisdom | 75

    Instructions: Anything Can Happen at Any Time

    Working with Wisdom: What Is Creating Suffering in This Moment?

    Check-In Conversation: The Causes of Suffering and Happiness

5. Courage | 97

    Instructions: Warrior Work

    Working with Courage: Exploring Our Distractions

    Check-In Conversation: The Valor of Truly Being Present

6. Patience | 117

    Instructions: Short Moments, Many Times

    Working with Patience: Floating Downstream

    Check-In Conversation: Practicing the Mind of Letting Go

7. Truthfulness | 139

    Instructions: Not Fooling Ourselves

    Working with Truthfulness: The Antidote to Self-Delusion

    Check-In Conversation: What's Surprising Is How Difficult It Is

8. Resoluteness | 157

    Instructions: Buddhists with Biceps

    Working with Resoluteness: Set an Aspiration and Ask What Is Needed

    Check-In Conversation: A Vision of Where We Are Heading

9. Loving-Kindness | 179

    Instructions: Don't Throw Anyone Out of Your Heart

    Working with Loving-Kindness: What Obstructs Our Loving-Kindness?

    Check-In Conversation: Am I Getting More Loving?

10. Equanimity | 199

    Instructions: Path to Peace

    Working with Equanimity: We Ask, What Just Happened?

    Check-In Conversation: The Essence of the Path

Conclusion: Final Thoughts on a Life of Integrity | 221

Acknowledgments | 229

About the Author | 231

Foreword

I have known Gail Stark for many years, both as a student and a friend, and I was delighted when she proposed the idea for this book on qualities that lead to a life of integrity. We decided on examining what in the Buddha's teachings are called *paramis*, or perfections of awakening, and had monthly conversations about how each of these qualities might be practiced off of the meditation cushion. These themes are eminently timely—as they always are—and Gail's unique combination of life experience, deep Dharma practice, and a willingness to push the edges of what it means to "walk the talk" highlights the challenges and joys of living as impeccably as possible.

Her very loving nature and incisive investigation brought her into close contact with the wide range of beings inhabiting her world, from her Dharma-buddy husband, Ron, to friends and business colleagues, to people on the street. Each one provided opportunities to explore what generosity, patience, renunciation, and the other paramis might mean in the context of daily life. What made this exploration so fruitful was the strength of Gail's mindfulness and the intensity of her interest as she tracked her own impulses and responses to the practice of these qualities. Her reports on each month's investigation were always a joy. Her enthusiasm was infectious and we both learned a lot in the process.

In the midst of these challenging and often confusing times, I hope that this engaging book will be an inspiration for many others who would like to actively engage in refining the understanding of integrity and how that can express itself in the busyness and complexity of our lives. This one overarching value can be a healing balm both for ourselves and for the world we all share.

Joseph Goldstein
Barre, Massachusetts

Preface

At different times in our lives and meditation practice
we may get glimpses of something
beyond our ordinary, conventional reality,
touching a space that transforms our vision of who we
are and what the world is.
These intimations give passionate meaning
to questions of ultimate truth,
because although we may not always be living
in that space,
we understand it to be the source of everything we value.
—JOSEPH GOLDSTEIN, *ONE DHARMA*

Many books have been written about happiness lately. Good books. Not so many on integrity. Perhaps this is because the whole notion sounds . . . dull. Also prone to failure. We stumble here, frequently. And yet integrity is a crucial and often overlooked ingredient in the happiness mix. Like yeast in bread making, living with integrity lifts our spirits. When we do or say the right thing, we know it. We feel touched, better about ourselves. The happiness from that effort is threefold: we are happy when we act on an ethical impulse; we are happy to witness the results of that good intention; and we are happy again later, remembering the act and its results. Those are a lot of good feelings we may be overlooking in our mad rush to stake out our piece of solid happiness in the shifting sands of life.

Buddhists call the pleasure that arises from one's ethical conduct "the bliss of blamelessness." Enticing? After many years devoted to improving my own integrity, I can confirm the authenticity of those words. Strengthening my integrity has profoundly altered the trajectory of my life, bathing it in a rich contentment. Surprisingly, I discovered contentment was precisely the component of happiness I had been seeking when I began this work.

———

I have been a businesswoman for most of my adult life, taking some time off to write this book. When I returned to work and colleagues asked where I had been, I would tell them I had written a book. Inevitably they would respond first with surprise, then with interest.

"What is it about?" or "What is the title?" they ask.

"Integrity," I say.

"Oh, we certainly need more integrity now" is the most common response.

"Yes. I feel we each have our own sense of what integrity is." Inevitably, heads nod in agreement.

"And when we don't live up to or act on our own sense of integrity," I continue, "we feel lousy." Again, the heads nod vigorously.

"But where is integrity taught? How do children learn about integrity? So few of us attend places of worship now. The book lays out ten components of integrity and shows how we can work with each one separately to actually improve our own integrity."

"Can I find it on Amazon?" is, honestly, the next most common response.

———

Integrity is perpetually underrated in our moment-to-moment choices for well-being. Instead we are often preoccupied with considering how to obtain more of what we want or how to avoid what we don't want. And yet the value and importance of integrity is universally acknowledged.

Trustworthiness is a highly prized trait in friendship, business relations, marriage, and parenting. We want our spouse, friends, associates, and children to be honest with us. And we expect the same from ourselves in regard to others.

Many of us feel we could be living with more integrity, generosity, kindness, and, consequently, more joy. We want to be happy and live honorably. We want others to be happy and live honorably. We just go about it haphazardly. The Dalai Lama says, "Our part is to bring a cheerful mind and heart to a suffering world." But how do we actually accomplish this? Most of us don't walk out our front doors (or in them!) with an intention to be unkind or dishonest. But life slaps us. We react. It is not always a cheery enterprise.

The repercussions of a disingenuous life can be staggering—to ourselves, to others, to a world flirting with madness. We suffer from acts of insincerity—our own and those perpetrated against us and against others. Over time we may forget an indiscretion. We move on. But do we really? In a quiet moment we can find remorse arising over a past misstep: passing by an outstretched hand with averted eye, not calling the friend who needed us, harsh words. A non-ethical response can be subtle, and that small indiscretion can also tug at our hearts and minds for years.

Not feeling worthy feels lousy. Many of us wish we would act and speak with more decency, largesse, and nobility of spirit. Not doing so takes a serious swipe at our peace of mind. We smudge our integrity and we—not to mention those who could have been helped by a more skillful response from us—suffer. Living without integrity crushes the spirit, tramples the heart. Even seemingly harmless burps of non-integrity are relentlessly eating a hole in our happiness, like sour stomach acid. Simply stated, general well-being, contentment, and happiness rely on a clear conscience. We can all do better—we wish we would and we need to. But how?

Creating a Life of Integrity is your personal trainer for strengthening the integrity muscles. It will push you. Urge you to stretch more. Caution you against laziness. Needle you. Soothe you. Praise you. And like a challenging session at the gym, you just may emerge from this training invigorated, glowing, and firmer, the better for having pushed yourself to do more than you thought you were capable of.

The hidden jewel here is that just knowing you hold an aspiration for integrity is softly and immensely gratifying. It is the sweet secret you pack with you for nourishment every day that you sally forth. You pay close attention to your motives, make mistakes, make corrections, re-choose words, and rethink actions. Throughout the day, every day. But once your bottom line—as we say in business—is integrity, you have already won. You are on your way, soaring. With integrity as your chosen destination, the particulars are merely passing landmarks. The plane has departed and your GPS, programmed for integrity, is correcting in flight.

You may also find, as I have, that this aspiration comes with a bonus gift: freedom from self-slander. We no longer need to negotiate with ourselves or delude, defend, rationalize, or scold ourselves. Imagine a pilot arguing with her GPS. Pointless. (Yes, I was once a pilot, soloing in a seaplane on San Francisco Bay.) An airplane on autopilot is *continually* making minor adjustments to stay on course.

Simple, though not always easy. But just knowing we are working on improving our integrity really does help banish the disappointment that arises when we slip. Over time we learn how to avoid our particular potholes, our wisdom and resolve strengthened by previous falls from grace. The good news? Our ability to be in the world with truthfulness can improve dramatically and swiftly. It is awesomely grand and gloriously uplifting to experience this. Integrity is a worthy road map for life, a lifelong endeavor eminently worthy of our daily mindful attention.

We will work together to keep your commitment strong. Dog-ear the following pages, underline passages, and write in the margins. Try meeting with a group. It can be fun to share the insights, and mishaps, of this journey. I have taught this work in groups. The stories brought back to share can be life-altering. And work with it alone, deep within the silence of your own heart's yearning to give back more, to make a difference.

The pursuit of integrity is a rich mulch—a many-layered, lifelong dig. It is work that has profoundly redirected my career, my marriage, the company I keep, and the words that tumble less heedlessly out of my mouth these days. I can still wrestle with integrity when buffeted by the strong winds of my particular sirens: haste, overwhelm, and weariness. But I can truthfully say, and this is amazing to me, that I trust myself now to do and say the right thing. The first instinctual response is one of integrity. It is a completely satisfying commitment, and a lovely and much-needed path to walk.

———

Creating a life of integrity. *What does this mean?* Living up to our own aspirations for ourselves and for a full and honorable life. *How does one go about it?* Relax. The following chapters contain more suggestions than you'll need. *Why would one want to?* Because we feel lousy when we don't. *It doesn't sound like fun.* No, but sappy as it sounds, when we commit to living with integrity, the world really will be a better place for our having been here. And knowing that gladdens our hearts immensely. *What if we don't feel the need to challenge or improve ourselves?* Then don't read this book. It will alter that notion. *No one else seems particularly concerned about it.* Doesn't matter. You know it is important, and once you understand, you cannot go back to apathy. *What if we are more-or-less, depending-on-circumstances, honest?* Living with integrity is a dividend-paying investment. We get back much more than we contribute. But we need to contribute. *No thanks. I'm good enough.* Does anyone really aspire to be *good enough*? In every moment we are presented with a tantalizing choice to speak and act with integrity, or not. Our choice. Go for it or disappoint yourself, and others you love, not to mention the planet, again.

So, *why is integrity important?* Because when you begin doing the right thing even when no one is watching, even when no one will know unless you tell them, *you will know.* You will have arrived, and you will write me and thank me for turning you on to the 2,600-year-old secret called the "bliss of blamelessness."

Introduction

Morality brings us the peace of non-remorse.
—Joseph Goldstein

The Ten Components of Integrity: How Do We Get There?

In Buddhist technology, the ten components of integrity are referred to as the *paramis*. It is taught that these ten qualities of mind and heart, when perfected, can result in liberation from our suffering. *Liberation from our suffering*. Practicing them, strengthening them, slowly purifies the mind and heart. They are the path for crafting a life of integrity. And as promised, they are our path to the bliss of blamelessness. Here are my own definitions of the paramis:

1. Generosity: Responding to the world from a sense of abundance, sharing freely of one's resources in gifts, actions, and words.
2. Virtue: Honoring the preciousness of all life through a steadfast commitment to not harming ourselves and others.
3. Renunciation: Letting go of the habitual behaviors, thoughts, and emotions that cause us, and others, to suffer.
4. Wisdom: Attaining clear comprehension, deep understanding, and a purified, open heart and mind through mindful investigation of one's life.

5. Courage: Perseverance and vigor in a mind that does not retreat from, but rather relishes, difficulties.
6. Patience: Being tranquil and welcoming with things as they are.
7. Truthfulness: Seeing the world, and speaking and acting in it, with a mind and heart unclouded by greed, hatred, or delusion.
8. Resoluteness: Carrying through on our deepest aspirations with tenacity and wisdom.
9. Loving-kindness: Relating to the best in others and ourselves with an open heart, free from attachment or aversion.
10. Equanimity: Impartially embracing whatever arises with a non-reactive, compassionate heart and mind.

In *Pay Attention, For Goodness' Sake: The Buddhist Path of Kindness*, Sylvia Boorstein writes that she loves knowing that all of these qualities are the natural, built-in inclination of the human heart.

The good news is that we can develop these ten natural, innate qualities just as we might strengthen weak, neglected muscles at the gym. The result? A well-toned mind and heart that serve and support us, like a fit body does. Over time, not unlike endorphins arising in a physically toned body, happiness begins to arise spontaneously as we pursue a more wholesome lifestyle. With a cleaner mind, our load lightens. We are more relaxed. We are kinder, more mindful, more trusting of ourselves and of others. We see more clearly what is occurring, what is important. Same circumstances—different perspective, different response. Perhaps a different outcome.

These ten ingredients of integrity are the nitty-gritty part of life—where the rubber meets the road. They are pervasive, in your face, messy, relentless, insistent. And perfect for seeing what needs to be done and fixing it. Perhaps the most enticing aspect is that these ten components of integrity are practiced in daily life, not on a meditation cushion. Daily life will be our meditation cushion for mindfully improving our integrity.

Real estate has been my livelihood for many years, and it can be a 24/7, on-call occupation. When I began this work years ago, I was in the habit of beginning the day with an early morning meditation. (I still do.) I would often rise from the meditation cushion feeling tranquil, open-hearted. Then my phone would ring. Emails would begin arriving. Client problems, staff problems, traffic problems. Suddenly I was rushing, brusque with my husband, my kind heart and good intentions left behind on the meditation cushion. I would leave home already feeling off-center, lousy. I had begun the day with such noble intent, and yet again, so quickly, I had stumbled. Often by midday I had given up my loftier goals. Tomorrow I'll begin again, I would decide.

How does this happen? Ask yourself: *Where and how do I habitually go astray? What might I do differently here the next time?*

As we begin to study the individual components of integrity, we discover there is an inherent order to the process. Each component naturally leads into the next one, like a set of stairs. Each supports the one that follows. This is an important understanding. By focusing on just one component of integrity at a time, in their natural order, the task becomes significantly easier, less burdened with discouraging setbacks. This is not tackling the entire concept of integrity, as in, "Just try to be kinder today, Gail." Instead, working with each component separately and deeply, we begin to see genuine, trackable progress. Again, the synergy of this approach is similar to working each muscle on a different machine at the gym. And just as each step on a stairway transports us to a different elevation, a different perspective of the same terrain, so too this work will slowly and steadily transpose you to an empowered place of clarity, strength, commitment, and, consequently, more joy. This is how I describe that stairway process, beginning with the first parami:

Path to Peace
Being *generous* makes us feel happy.
We aspire to live with more *virtue*.
We investigate and *renounce* unskillful habits.
Wisdom blossoms.
Energy blooms.
Now *patience* is needed.
Slowed down, we discern and speak with more *truthfulness*.
We grow increasingly *resolute*.

Loving-kindness becomes our first response.
Now, with *equanimity* as our guide,
the bliss of blamelessness arrives.

The work that follows is a process of inquiry. We will work with each component of integrity individually in a separate chapter. These chapters will help clarify our underlying, unrecognized motivations, thoughts, and emotions, so that our effort leads to a purification of what is specifically not working for us. Every chapter begins with a series of questions to ask ourselves in specific situations we encounter every day. These are not instructions on what to do or how to do it. Instead, we explore each situation as it arises naturally in our lives, asking ourselves questions, observing what works and what doesn't in alignment with our own intentions. What follows are tough tools with which to dig into deeply rooted, often unconscious habits and reactions that are arising in every moment. We may be seeing many of these habits and reactions clearly for the first time. *What is really happening here? What are we feeling and why are we feeling this way? Why did we just react as we did? What were we thinking? What was the deeper intent behind those words?* Over time it becomes abundantly clear where we can trip and fall from our noble intentions. We begin to successfully craft our own path of integrity, avoiding our own particular potholes. This has been a remarkably transforming journey, one that continues to deepen and bring profound clarity and joy into my life. I am confident it can bring the same results to you.

This work is about crafting the life many of us yearn for. And so this book is a workbook, with very practical, easy-to-handle tools you can continue to utilize for years. You may not want to read through the whole book now. Instead, you may want to read up to and through the generosity chapter and stop there. Work with the generosity instructions for a time. Then approach each subsequent set of instructions, until each individual component of integrity transforms gradually from an exercise to a spontaneous and natural inclination of your heart.

You can work exclusively with one component for a month and then move on to the next, as I did in the period recounted in the book. Or perhaps you will decide to read through the book and then, like the Burmese people often do, select just one parami to work with for an entire year! This is a purely personal quest. If you are mindfully attentive, there is no way to fail, regardless of what nastiness you may uncover. We all have ghosts in our closets. The secret is remembering they have no substance.

We must continually ask ourselves, are our lives leading onward in any way? Of course, we also need to find the line between being impeccable and being rigid, so that we refine our understandings with a light heart.
—JOSEPH GOLDSTEIN

Joseph Goldstein, Integrity Coach: I Want What He Has

We are committed to improving our integrity. We have selected a set of tools. Now, what about a coach? Here's how I knew I had found mine.

It's twenty-five years ago. My new boyfriend, Ron Stark, his friend Joseph Goldstein, and I are driving up from San Francisco to the mountains surrounding Lake Tahoe for a ski vacation. Joseph Goldstein is an internationally revered Buddhist scholar, teacher, and author, and I am surprisingly nervous about meeting him. I want our first time together to go well. (I had no experience with Buddhists and could not imagine myself chatting casually with a famous one.) Ron is driving, Joseph beside him, and they converse easily, catching up. I am content to sit in the back and listen.

Even without the 6'3" height, Joseph is an imposing presence. He has the manly jaw of a cowboy, a large head, and dark hair. As he speaks, thoughtfully and with long, contemplative pauses, he occasionally gestures with his hands, which are also large. What's surprising to me are two things: his voice, a deep baritone, is gentle and resonant, and his smile, when he turns to include me in the conversation, engages and softens his prominent features. His is a wide smile—playful, infectious, its shadow already well-etched into his face. This is not the serious, soft-spoken, and reclusive Buddhist scholar I had been imagining. Ron, who once did stand-up comedy, is the funniest man I know, and Joseph, clearly, is enjoying matching wits. There is much laughter and playful kidding as we drive toward the mountains. I relax, genuinely relieved to discover that Joseph Goldstein is remarkably human, likable, and even fun!

Two hours into the drive, in the foothills near Auburn, California, white flecks of snow begin appearing on the edges of the windshield and on the tips of pine trees lining the freeway. We continue to climb. Heavier snow is now piling up on the sides of the road and drifting across the pavement. Soon the road, trees, and windshield are white. It is seriously snowing. We pass a neon freeway sign flashing: "Heavy Snow. Chains Required. All Vehicles." Ron decides to exit and stop at a small mountain gas station. He had been told our rented SUV with all-weather tires would be sufficient for any road conditions. Now he is not certain they will allow us over the pass without tire chains.

As we exit, a highway patrol vehicle suddenly appears out of the dense white fog and follows us. The untraveled exit ramp is buried deep in snow, the frontage road a dark cavern of swirling drifts. I suddenly remember Ron telling me he grew up in Miami! Visibility extends to about the end of our noses. Ron is leaning forward, peering intently through a fogged, iced-over windshield. I imagine he is also rehearsing what he will say to the officer: explain how we are just now on our way to buy chains. The car glides silently through the blizzard. With nary a fishtail or skid, we finally come to a stop before a small convenience store with "Chains for Sale Here" in the window. The highway patrol car stops at the gas pump behind us. Ron's shoulders slump, and I reach forward to massage them.

"Good work!" I say, and Joseph agrees. Ron suggests Joseph and I go into the store to see about purchasing tire chains. He is going to speak with the patrolman, now fueling his patrol car.

Inside the small shop my relief at our safe arrival is heightened by the bright lights and gaily colored packages on overstocked shelves. I smell coffee. Joseph turns to me, grinning. "A snack perhaps?" he asks.

"Sure," I say.

We start with a couple of coffees from a machine, giggling as we try to direct the coffee and foaming milk into the tiny cups provided. Then, sipping our coffees, Joseph leads us to the snack aisle. I learn that Joseph and I share a fondness for cookies. We are discussing our options, holding several boxes, when Joseph's head swivels. I follow his gaze. Sandwiches with a "Freshly Made" sign are enticingly displayed in a glass cabinet. He looks back at me, eyebrows raised.

"What do you think?" he asks. "A sandwich, then the cookies?" I follow him into the third aisle, but now I am uncomfortable, thinking, *Wait, we had a purpose here. What about the chains?*

Juggling cookie boxes and steaming coffees, we lean in to look at the sandwiches. Suddenly Joseph starts chuckling, low and deep. He straightens up and turns to me, grinning. "This," he says, resuming a conversation we had been having in the car before the weather changed, "is Wanting Mind."

"Buying chains, I see," Ron says, laughing, as he walks up to us. He tells us he has learned we do not need chains and soon we are on the road again, the three of us munching cookies and laughing.

Years later I would ask myself why I still remember that day so vividly. Joseph doesn't! But of course he wouldn't. For him it was an everyday experience. For me it was decidedly extra-ordinary. This is the mind caught in desire, he was showing me, and most of the time we just unconsciously, habitually follow wherever desire leads us. This I understood only too well. I had felt the desire arise immediately in response to the store's bright displays—an excitement, then a longing, then a craving for something, anything. But it was the difference between our responses that was so startling to me. Joseph recognized what was happening and then was actually enjoying having caught himself midstream in a snack seduction. To him it was a delight! He seemed to be welcoming the recognition of his craving as if seeing a dear friend standing there in the cookie aisle. "Why, look who's here! It's Wanting Mind. Come, let me introduce you. Or have you met before?"

And as he pointed out what he had just seen in himself, he was laughing! He was *embracing* his sudden lust for coffee and cookies.

Laughing at himself. The contrast between my mind and Joseph's was a game-changing moment for me. Something was missing from Joseph's response, from Joseph's mind, that was clearly not missing from mine. Sure, I was enjoying myself in the store, beginning to feel at ease with this prestigious teacher. But I was also feeling uncomfortable about having fun with Joseph, drinking coffee and selecting cookies while Ron stood outside in a blizzard negotiating with a policeman. I was anxious about checking into the tire chains. I was thinking, *No, really, I don't need to be eating a bunch of cookies now.* And I really wanted those cookies. In that moment, when he paused to point to, and laugh at, our foolishness, I was totally lost in distracted and conflicted thoughts that did not include thinking kindly about myself. In contrast, Joseph's mind seemed so carefree, delighted, playfully chiding himself. Subtle but strikingly, profoundly different.

Watching him I could see clearly that Joseph was not *in* his mind. Somehow he was outside his mind, laughing at it as one would do with a misbehaving child. He could watch the cravings arise in his mind without owning them, without taking them as "Joseph's craving." It was simply a mind caught up in wanting, acting out old habitual responses to the enticingly displayed goodies. Seeing it and catching himself as if he were a small child, he could laugh, turn the child away from the temptation, and just move on. I am not my mind? I can laugh at it when it misbehaves, then re-choose my response? Tell me more!

I want that, I thought. A surprising, compelling, and totally new yearning arose for Joseph's carefree demeanor, a desire now much deeper than the previous lust for coffee and cookies. How different might life be if I was as present and welcoming as Joseph. Something strikingly profound was playing out before me, and although I didn't understand precisely what was happening, I suddenly felt a deep longing arising. It was a taste of *that* sweetness that I truly craved. I am not my mind?

And so in that moment Joseph Goldstein became my teacher as well as my friend. He and Ron, now my husband, and I have played and vacationed together for many years. He still is the wisest *and* the most humble person I know. And after twenty-five years I now understand what it takes to get to where and who Joseph is. That carefree lightness is actually the hard-won result of many years spent observing his mind, combined with a steadfast commitment to live with razor-sharp integrity. The root of that unburdened sweetness is a guilt-free mind. We have our integrity coach.

———

A teacher, guide, and spiritual friend can be of inestimable help on the path. Such a person can reveal what is hidden, point out the path, and inspire our highest aspirations.
—Joseph Goldstein

———

A Format for Training in Integrity: And So We Begin

Immediately after that first ski trip with Joseph twenty-five years ago, I did my first ten-day silent meditation retreat with him. At the conclusion, as our small group gathered in a circle, I surprised myself. When it was my turn to speak, I pledged aloud the aspiration to live a purer life. This had only just occurred to me as something I deeply yearned for. I was inspired by the time I had spent with Joseph, and also by the fierce dedication I had observed in those around me all week. I had never been in a group like this before. There was so much love and gaiety in the room, I felt like the Tin Man who had suddenly acquired a heart. I could taste my own goodness rising in a sweet resolve to live with more awareness and kindness.

I had no idea I wanted a purer life, nor could I remember even feeling it was lacking. If asked, I don't know that I could have elaborated on what a purer life for me might look like. In fact I was so surprised at this sudden burst of longing, just shared with a roomful of strangers, that I did not know what to say next. Thankfully everyone nodded and smiled and seemed to understand the yearning I had just uncovered in myself. And I left that first retreat with no idea how to go about actualizing my shiny new hope.

I once attended a talk on Buddhism given to a large group of non-Buddhists. The question was asked, "Why does Buddhism always talk about suffering?" Perhaps you have wondered about this also. I did when I attended that first meditation retreat. I kept hearing that one's suffering can be what compels one to explore, question, and reevaluate. *But I'm not suffering*, I had thought. "'Suffering' is one translation [of the word *dukkha*] from the Pali language of the ancient Buddhist texts," the Zen teacher Lee deBarros answered. "Another translation could be 'dissatisfaction.'" Ah, suddenly heads nodded all around the room. Dissatisfaction—*yes, we certainly experience dissatisfaction*, I could sense us all thinking.

Dissatisfaction is a big part of the difference between Joseph's carefree mind and ours, befuddled and laden with conflicting desires. As we begin paying attention to what we are thinking and feeling, saying and doing, we may begin to notice that much of the time we are dissatisfied. We are either resisting something or desiring something. Sylvia Boorstein calls this "the insatiable need in the mind for other." It is the mind perpetually avoiding or wanting. And this rampant, but often quite subtle, dissatisfaction is indeed suffering, even if it appears only as a background shadow to our perceptions. This longing for something different than what is right now is what prevents us from experiencing the lightness and joy in the present moment that Joseph so beautifully demonstrates. It was precisely that dissatisfaction that propelled me into this integrity work.

I once heard a Tibetan teacher say that he often had to encourage Tibetan students to generate more energy but that he often had to advise American students to slow down, not try so hard. We know this fierce drive well, ardently pursuing what we perceive will bring more happiness or success. What I have also seen, after years of mindfulness, is that we might work incredibly hard at something without first taking adequate time to deeply consider the direction undertaken or the motivations driving that intention. We just follow the popular consensus of what constitutes a successful life. We might achieve a goal and then be surprised by the lack of the good times we had envisioned would come packaged with it. Sometimes the pleasure in the desired object or outcome can be fleeting. Disillusioned by the hollowness of a victory after a vigorous pursuit, we may begin to question the time and effort invested.

A few years ago, having founded, built, and then sold a very successful real estate company, I found myself exhausted in mind and spirit. I asked Joseph if we could work together monthly. He agreed and suggested we work with the Buddhist teachings on integrity. I had heard of the paramis but could not have listed them, nor told you why they were important. It didn't matter. I trusted whatever Joseph thought would be best.

The profound, life-altering effects of that work now permeate every aspect of my life. The idea to make our work together a book came early on from Joseph, who was enjoying the process as much as I was. Joseph would begin by giving me specific instructions to work with each month. At the end of the month I would report back, taping those conversations as we discussed the results. Each of the chapters that follow is organized into three sections on a single component of integrity: Joseph's instructions, my experience working with those instructions, and our taped conversation discussing those experiences.

Joseph has a knack for translating ancient Buddhist teachings into clear, useful, timely concepts we can work with today. You need no prior experience with Buddhism to undertake the work that follows. What is unique to this book is that Joseph has taken each parami and devised a way to specifically and precisely work with it in our daily lives. And he adapts this training to the challenges we face today, often including his own successes and failures as examples: How do we find balance? How do we resist temptation? How do we respond with integrity and kindness when confronted with dishonesty, when harried, disillusioned, or in despair? How do we keep our hearts open when they are continually flooded by so much suffering and need, in ourselves and others? How can we welcome our challenges? How do we pick ourselves up, dust off disappointment, and start again after we fall?

As I became increasingly delighted and profoundly altered by our work together—in how I conduct myself, treat others, communicate, and hold myself accountable—I was moved to write this book for friends and for colleagues in business who are not so inclined to pick up a Buddhist book nor attend a silent retreat. There is much timely wisdom in the ancient teachings of the Buddha, as His Holiness the Dalai Lama has so gracefully demonstrated.

Have you ever encountered a group of Buddhist monks or nuns? I saw a small group of monks once at a seashore. They were wading into the surf on thin, pale legs, maroon robes hoisted up above their knees. Splashing and being splashed by the waves and their companions, they were giggling and laughing. Why do so many monks and nuns generally appear to be happy? They too have jobs to do and conflicts that arise. They have noisy neighbors and bodies that age and fall ill. Monks and nuns can act frivolously, you may say, because they are not facing losing their home. Their children's education will not bankrupt them. Their livelihood is assured. But I suggest it is a sense of their own integrity, expressed continuously with mindfulness and vigor, that is the source of such carefree joy. The power of one's integrity is what the monks, nuns, and Joseph understand, and what we, perhaps, have temporarily forgotten. The fruit of a commitment to live with integrity is abundant, deeply satisfying contentment. This is the bliss of blamelessness. Mere sense-pleasure gratification pales in comparison.

In the chapters that follow, the teachings come from the Buddha, with Joseph interpreting. We will take you deep inside those ancient teachings and work alongside you as you explore your own successes and failures, highs and lows, crashes, midair recoveries, delusions, and insights. Over time your experiences, like roadside caution signs, will help alert you to impending obstacles we inevitably encounter on our journey. One of my favorite caution signs is the mountain roadside warning: "Caution: Falling Rocks Next Three Miles." I think it is a perfect warning for what lies ahead and interpret it to mean:

Look up. Look down. Look around.
Listen. Stay alert. Pay attention.
The terrain ahead may not be as solid as it appears.

And yet perhaps Joseph's most powerful teaching is watching him move through each day with wisdom, compassion, integrity, *and* humility. Throughout this book, you too may discover how well these ancient teachings still work.

So we begin.

1 Generosity

For many people generosity is the easiest parami
to appreciate and develop because it brings
such immediate delight to our lives.
—JOSEPH GOLDSTEIN

The First Parami: Generosity
The Pali word *dana*, which we translate as *generosity*,
is used to designate the first parami in Buddhist
texts. It means sharing with others and includes
nobility of mind, magnanimity, and graciousness.

Instructions: We Start Where We Are

"Let's begin working with the paramis by talking about generosity," Joseph says. "There is one story, I think from the Buddha's time, about a monk whose generosity was very undeveloped. So the Buddha said to take a stone in one hand and practice giving it to the other hand. Just go back and forth, practicing giving the stone to one hand, and then giving to the other hand. Begin to train in what the movement of giving is like."

"And it worked?" I ask, laughing.

"It worked. Gradually he got used to the notion of giving, of letting go, even on that most basic level. So we start where we are."

For this first instruction, Joseph and I have scheduled an early evening phone conversation. It is just after dinner on the East Coast. Joseph is in his home on the grounds of the Buddhist center he founded, the Insight Meditation Society, in Barre, Massachusetts. And I am seated on a bench outside the San Francisco Ferry Building, gazing over the bay. I have an hour before the ferry taking me home will depart. Sunlight glitters on the tops of boat wakes like scattered sequins. The breeze off the bay carries with it a salty rustle of excitement. A seagull poses for tourists on a railing post. People in business attire are eating oysters nearby, calling out to one another across a long table and laughing. A dozen pelicans glide overhead in formation. I feel happy to be sitting in this beautiful setting, starting on this new venture with Joseph as he shares his wisdom. I am filled with gratitude . . . and also a bit distracted! Next time I shall choose a less enticing location.

"So we start where we are," begins Joseph. This idea that we can *work* on our generosity is intriguing, inspiring. Many of us tend to be quasi-generous, our generosity sporadic, unplanned. Sometimes we may be dismissive when an impulse to be generous arises, other times genuinely magnanimous. I much prefer the magnanimous Gail. She is happier.

"One of the great benefits of the practice of generosity," Joseph continues, "is that we get to see the whole range of our motivations. Often we can think that our motivations are very pure, but then sometimes if we look more carefully, we see underlying motivations or mixed motivations.

"A good example of this is when I was in India in the open market bazaar," he continues, "just buying some fruit." (Joseph studied and lived in India for seven years.) "There was this little Indian beggar boy standing by my side. I should say, wherever one goes in India, there are hundreds and hundreds of beggars, and living there you learn, in one way or another, how you choose to relate to them.

"So I was at the bazaar, and I had bought some fruit and he was just standing there. Without thinking about it—it was not some great moment of generous feeling, it was just a spontaneous moment—I took a piece of fruit I had just bought and gave it to him. What turned out to be surprising was that after I gave it to him, he just took it and walked away. There was no response. There was no smile. No nod. There was not *anything*. No acknowledgment whatsoever.

"And it was striking to me not because I had expected some effusive thanks," he says, laughing. "It was just an orange. I didn't *think* that I wanted anything in exchange for it. But when he just walked away, without any acknowledgment whatsoever, it revealed to me that there had been at least *some* expectation of something in response. It revealed a level of expectation and motivation in me that I hadn't even known was there. And so in moments of generosity, and in the practice of it, it is helpful to be watchful of what we think our motivations are for doing it. To notice what inspired us, and then to watch it through the whole act, and to pay attention afterward to see what's going on, because it can often illuminate some hidden shadows."

"I can definitely feel that if I did that, I would be expecting him to give something back," I say.

"Yes," Joseph says, "a smile perhaps." We are quiet.

"I'm thinking now about all the homeless people I see every day," I say slowly. "I passed several walking to get here."

"That would be a good place to begin."

"But there are so many."

"Just try it. My first suggestion to you for working with generosity is each time the thought to give arises, act on it. Then notice what happens." He chuckles—that low, deep sound that puts me on alert.

"What?"

"This practice can be very revealing" is all he says.

Joseph then gives the instructions that follow below for working with generosity over the next month. We say our goodbyes and I walk to the ferry, my mind whirling.

Buddhists casually categorize people into three types, none of which is particularly flattering: the *deluded* type, whose positive attribute is equanimity, is someone who can be ambivalent and somewhat casual about details, time, and appearances; the *aversive* type, whose positive attribute is discernment, is someone whose first response can be one of resistance or aversion; the *greedy* type, whose positive attribute is faith, is someone who can be motivated, basically, by desire. Of course we all have aspects of all three tendencies arising at different times, but we may also have a predominant inclination, a habitual first response to new stimuli. Joseph and I are classic greedy types, and we often kid each other about our shared propensity.

I am on the ferry now, gliding across San Francisco Bay toward a sun that is slipping behind the Golden Gate Bridge and letting us all know of her departure with a riotously colored show. Some folks sitting with me in the front cabin are also gazing out, sipping a wine or beer. Others are reading or working on laptops. This is the quiet cabin. I am soothed by the ambience as I sit contemplating the idea of strengthening one's capacity for generosity. Can we really do this? You may be thinking, as I was then, that the practice of improving one's generosity may not be easy. When I began this work I didn't consider myself to be overly generous, especially in contrast to other magnanimously generous people I knew. This recognition in ourselves can feel tight, and disappointing, like a shield constricting the heart. Most of us would truly like to change this automatic response of scarcity, of holding back. And so, together, we will begin wherever we are, and then begin again, and again. But this time we have a set of instructions and a gentle, wise coach for guidance.

———

In my experience, generosity never leads to remorse.
—JOSEPH GOLDSTEIN

———

Joseph's Instructions: Working with Generosity

Weakness or lack of generosity can give rise to greed, desire, craving, and lack. Strength in generosity develops and manifests in much happiness. There is happiness in planning the generous act, happiness in the actual giving, and happiness in reflecting later on your generosity. I suggest:

1. Whenever you have the thought to be generous, *just do it.*
2. Notice what happens next. What feelings arise? What thoughts arise?
3. Then pay attention *as* you give. What feelings arise? What thoughts arise?
4. Finally, *after* you have been generous (or after you have not been generous), investigate. What thoughts arise? What feelings predominate?
5. Try exploring other arenas, other ways to be generous. Make a list. Every day there is some way of being of service to others.
6. Pay attention to everything. Look closely for subtleties, for that which is not at first apparent.
7. Ask: What is the motivation underlying this moment of generosity?
8. Then—this is important—watch throughout the day for what undermines the motivation.
9. Have fun with this. Remember: awareness doesn't have to be grim.

Generosity becomes stronger and more
delightful the more we engage in it.
—Joseph Goldstein

Working with Generosity: Julie

Day One: I am sitting at my desk at work, writing birthday wishes in cards for two of my nieces. Because they are older now, instead of a gift I send cash. I tuck a twenty-dollar bill into each card. Then I think, *What can a teenager buy with twenty dollars?* And because it is my first day strategically practicing generosity, and because I have had the thought to do it, I add another twenty-dollar bill to each card. This is more than I usually send. They will be thrilled. I am thrilled anticipating their delight.

At noon I walk out to mail the cards and have lunch, still pleased about my generous act. Just before the restaurant I pass an older man, panhandling. I smile. He smiles, then breaks into a song. He has a beautiful voice and I tell him so. Others walk past. No one is putting money in the top hat he has placed on the sidewalk. He sings parts of another few songs for me, grinning. I open my purse to give him a dollar. He leans over, peers into my wallet, and suddenly begins to cry! He tells me he has just lost a close friend. He is hoping to earn enough money to attend the funeral, traveling by bus to Seattle. "That twenty would sure be helpful," he says.

1:00 p.m. Back at my desk, I check in with myself, as Joseph has instructed. I still feel happy. And generous. Also poorer: $80 to my nieces + $20 to the street singer = $100, my entire month's budget for cash. Enthused and pumped up with the intention to be generous, I have just given it all away in an hour on day one! Now some deflation occurs, tempering the enthusiasm. Doubts join the gathering clouds preparing to rain on my parade of good intentions. The man on the street may have just been telling me a story. It doesn't matter, I argue with myself. He asked; I gave. The Buddha said, "There is no spiritual life without a generous heart." But he could be buying liquor right now with the twenty dollars. I imagine him pouring drinks into plastic cups for all his friends on the street from a bottle in a brown bag. Confusion arises about this idea to act on every generous impulse. I have to be more discerning, right? But that thought feels like a piece of the old, less generous tendency. Well, I obviously can't call Joseph on day one. So, somewhat confused but still determined, I decide to continue stretching my generosity, no holding back, and watch what happens. I am curious to see how this is going to play out. Which will I run out of first—my cash or my heart's measure of generosity? I also notice I am still feeling a quiet, soft peace as I reflect on the gladness I feel I have just brought others. Small efforts, but in the moment I did respond generously, at least more generously than I think I would have responded yesterday. Happiness arises . . . then doubts . . . happiness . . . second-guessing . . . happiness. This continues at intervals all afternoon. On the way home I stop at an ATM and withdraw another hundred dollars. Begin again.

Still determined to be generous *whenever* the opportunity arises, I now focus also on how I am giving. Is it grudgingly or is it with delight? Am I giving the best I have, the most I am able, or am I holding something back?

To get to work I often take the ferry from Sausalito to San Francisco, then walk many long urban blocks to my office. I pass, on average, half a dozen folks sitting on the filthy sidewalk with various signs, all asking for my generosity. I try to honor my first instinct, which I am happy to discover is almost always to be generous. Still, I do not always act on that initial impulse to give. Why *is* that? So I begin paying attention to what happens when I don't give. I make a list of why I sometimes choose not to be generous.

My list: I notice there are times I just don't want to make the effort. It's not convenient to stop and rummage through my bag for my wallet. The person asking annoys me or follows me or keeps pressing. I am tired. I am cold. I am rushing. I am cranky. The light turns green as I'm still rummaging in my bag. My shoes hurt. I don't have any dollar bills. I just gave to three people before the one now asking me. I don't feel this one looks needy enough. I look ahead to see how many more pleading faces I will walk by; my heart sinks to see them ahead. I make detours. I pretend to be distracted, look at something else as I pass. I tell myself it is OK to pass by just this once, then notice this is not how I feel after I have passed by.

All this awareness may be a sign of progress, but I feel the discouragement and I fear I'm sliding back. When I tell Joseph I have made a list of why I sometimes choose not to be generous, he asks, "Is it a long list?" And yet, each morning I awake inspired to hit the streets again with new resolve. This is something that I am beginning to feel I can change. Today. So I just begin again, mindfully. Don't judge others, don't judge myself. This morning I almost walk past a young man needing ninety dollars to pay his rent, or so his sign says. He appears to be healthy and sane. My first thought is, as has been my habit, *But he looks like he could be working.* I almost pass by. Then I think, *Actually, these days, there is a good chance he could not find work.* I stop walking. I am delighted to feel my old habit of rating who is worthy of my generosity slipping. Everyone I pass who asks, is asking *me*, and if someone is asking me, I will give. I open my wallet to get a dollar bill but have none. He talks me into giving him a twenty-dollar bill. We are both grinning as I walk away. On the way home I stop at a bank on Market Street and get twenty dollars' worth of one-dollar bills, which I fold and slip into my coat pocket, not my wallet.

And so I continue watching and trying hard not to judge or talk myself out of my initial motivation of generosity. Today I'm surprised and delighted to notice the desire to be generous is quickly becoming the first response to arise. Seeing that natural instinct of goodness arising fortifies me. That impulse, sometimes but certainly not always, can be immediately followed by rationalizations. As Joseph suggests, I can choose to believe these thoughts, or I can choose to let them float by, like the insubstantial clouds they are. I can ignore them as if they were someone else's thoughts blown down the crowded city street and into my head. I can't (yet) seem to stop those old patterns of thinking from arising, but I *can* choose not to listen. I *can* choose for them not to be the motive I act on.

As I continue my walk to work, spirits buoyant, I recall Don Terner, who died tragically in a small plane crash while on a humanitarian mission in Nigeria. Don founded a San Francisco company that is now the largest builder of affordable housing in the country, BRIDGE Housing. When he walked the streets of San Francisco, he would stop before every street person, greet them (often in the middle of a conversation he might be having with a companion), and give them a dollar bill from a wad he always kept in his pocket for just such occasions. A wad!

Joseph is like this. In a coffee shop, at the overnight free ski kiosk, on the shuttle bus, and especially walking San Francisco streets with me, he has money out and offered often before I even notice that we are being asked. He seems to have an early radar system, and he *always* gives when the opportunity presents itself.

In the third week I begin looking for other opportunities, other ways to be generous. Not limited to handing out dollar bills, I have fun just trying to bring a smile to someone's face. I bring dinner to a friend recovering from surgery, offer unsolicited kind words and compliments. I do those little inconvenient acts that can seem so trivial, so easily dismissed, and yet can bring such gladness to others and to myself. I discover there are many inconvenient acts I routinely talk myself out of doing. Acknowledging another person's good qualities (a personal favorite). Calling on an elderly neighbor. Offering encouragement. Withholding a criticism (a big one). Smiling at, acknowledging, thanking all those who serve: cashiers, bus drivers, waiters, clerks, ticket takers, office cleaners. Their often surprised smile of delight and thanks cheer me immensely. Such small gestures, but such heartfelt connections.

As the generosity month is waning, I am in downtown San Francisco. It is Saturday, and I am off work. All morning I have been feeling relaxed and curiously, softly content, despite all I have to do today. It is noon. I have finished all my errands and still have time for a quiet lunch outside at a sidewalk café on Maiden Lane. I carry my lunch tray outside. It is one of those delightful, rare days in San Francisco that is warm enough, with no wind, to do this enjoyably. I am just about to sit down when a woman, clearly a person living on the streets, approaches asking for money. I feel an initial irritation. It passes quickly. I set my tray down on an empty table and reach for one of the dollars I have loose in my coat pocket. As I hand it to her, I look into her creased, leathery face. We exchange greetings. Then she asks if we can talk. I am momentarily taken aback. When I say yes, she sits down at the table!

CREATING A LIFE OF INTEGRITY

Still standing, my buoyant spirits now sink. This is not the leisurely, tranquil meal I had been looking forward to all morning. I see other patrons, some with kids, staring at us. I also see a waiter start forward from the café doorway. A shiver of fear brushes me lightly, probably shared by some of the diners watching us. I hear Joseph's voice reminding me to look closely for subtleties. What *do* I fear here? I fear that if I open up to the disadvantaged waiting on every city street corner that they will burden me with their sad tale and ask for more and more. I fear I am out of my comfort zone and don't know the proper response. Perhaps most acutely, I fear not knowing how to extricate myself once we begin. All this is arising. But she is seated at the table now. This is the month to investigate *and expand* my generosity. So my fears and I sit down, trepidation and reluctance joining us. What a crowded table this has suddenly become.

We begin to talk. She speaks softly. She tells me her name is Julie and that she is forty-eight years old. She looks sixty-eight. She tells me she is grateful that I was willing to speak with her and tears up as she says this. I do, too, imagining the isolation, loneliness, and invisibility of a woman living on the streets. This is something I had not really considered before. She is wearing several layers of clothing, topped with a long red wool sweater, even though it is quite warm. The clothes seem clean but are patched, wrinkled, unraveling. There is grime beneath her fingernails. Her hands are chapped, red and large-knuckled. She is thin, with rounded shoulders. A gray wool ski cap with dangling tassels covers her head. Her eyes, set deeply into lined cheeks, are a brilliant pale blue.

I am hungry, my full plate untouched before me. I ask if she is hungry. She rummages in a crumpled brown bag and shows me a Starbucks package with a partially eaten chicken salad sandwich and says she is not hungry right now. So I begin eating and talking, but mostly listening. As I listen, I can feel myself slowly relaxing. I actually physically feel my heart opening. Compassion arises, quite spontaneously. Julie is very lucid, and I am increasingly interested in knowing her story, how she got to where she is and what it is like to actually live on the streets.

First, however, we do the traditional dance. She tells me if she only had twenty dollars, that would buy her two nights at a shelter. I give her the twenty. Then, after carefully pocketing the bill, she looks down as she says, "Now, if only I had forty dollars . . ."

I reach for another twenty, then look up, smile, and say, "Oh, now, enough of this game."

She stops, looks up at me intently, then throws back her head and laughs surprisingly robustly. "OK," she says nodding, and we bump knuckles across the café tabletop, grinning at one another. I am quite certain people around us are shocked, but now Julie and I are tight. And I give her the second twenty.

Over the next hour we laugh. We get teary. I am delighted to discover she is as interested in my life as I am in hers. I ask her bunches of questions, and she asks them of me in return. At one point she wants to know what brings me downtown. I say a hair appointment and show her the gray hairs I am going to the salon to get colored. She whips off her knit cap to show me her gray hairs and we grin at each other, shaking our heads. I learn it is alcohol that has taken her down, although she says she no longer drinks. She tells me in two months she is going to get her own apartment. This she glowingly describes in much detail. She has been accepted by a City of San Francisco outreach program. She will also receive money every month, which she can hardly imagine. She tells me she has requested they dole out the money in small portions so she won't get into trouble again.

At this point the waiter approaches. He has continually watched us and is, I believe, shocked to see us continue sitting together. "Will there be anything else?" he asks me. Julie asks if she can have a Coke, and he pretends not to hear her.

"Please bring my friend a Coke," I tell him. He returns with the Coke in a can! Julie requests a glass with ice, and reluctantly he brings it. After he leaves, Julie leans in and whispers. She tells me how important and good it had felt to her that I would speak up for her.

We talk about relationships. She was married for fifteen years, she tells me, until the drinking and fooling around finally brought down the marriage. I ask what she did for a living before landing on the streets, and she proudly describes working in construction. We talk another thirty minutes, lingering long after I have paid the bill. Finally, reluctantly, I glance at my watch. Almost immediately she begins gathering her things, clearly not wanting to detain me. I am touched at this gesture from her.

We rise, and as we walk away from the table, she asks for a hug. There on the sidewalk outside the café, with patrons watching, we embrace—a long, tight hug. The waiter emerges from the café, sees us, and laughs. It doesn't bother either of us. We look into each other's eyes, holding hands. "Thank you," she says. "I hope to see you again."

"Yes," I say. "I hope so too." She turns and walks away down Maiden Lane, past upscale boutiques. I turn and walk in the opposite direction.

————

Generosity weakens the tendency of attachment
and grasping and is intimately connected
with the feeling of loving-kindness.
—JOSEPH GOLDSTEIN

And we are all held back at times, but I think
what is important is to acknowledge it, to
remember this is a practice, and understand
that at times we can just . . . *push that edge.*
—JOSEPH GOLDSTEIN

Check-In Conversation: Push That Edge

For my check-in conversation with Joseph at the end of the month, I am home alone on a Sunday. The house and the neighborhood are quiet, much fewer distractions than when we spoke at the beginning of the month. I take a few deep breaths, look one last time through the notes I have accumulated all month, and dial Joseph's number. This is the first of our monthly taped conversations, and he is expecting my call.

"Hello," he says, and I can hear the smile in his voice. I relax. After exchanging quick pleasantries and checking in on each other's health and recent activities, I dive in.

"So, Joseph, I am appalled at the magnitude of my selfishness. I can't believe all the rationalizations and judgments." I describe my experiences walking the streets of San Francisco. "And when I felt I was suffering—you know, when my shoes hurt, for gosh sakes—I was even less compassionate, less generous. It is terrible to see that, and so discouraging."

"Yes, but remember, the practice is to investigate, not to judge."

"Investigate, not judge. It is so easy to forget that broader perspective," I groan.

"Yes. I think that the main part of this is really making it an investigation and also not assuming that it's always just one simple thing. We can act spontaneously but then take an interest, asking, 'OK, what really happened here?' We sort out what are the pure motivations and what are the motivations that are not so pure. This is what makes it so interesting—and ultimately purifying. Because if you don't see what is unskillful, then you can't see what needs more work."

"I understand. And I do notice that after I give, I always feel good. And I notice when I don't act on the impulse to be generous that arises, I am always disappointed in myself. But I also observe how quickly the bad feeling dissipates. It seems I can dismiss it so easily."

"Dismiss what? The impulse to be generous?"

"Well, yes, that too, but more the regret, feeling 'I should have' after I don't act on the impulse to give."

"Yes. That is a big one to investigate."

"Any suggestions?"

"Well, one of the practices I do—or I try to do—is when I recognize the impulse to give arising, I try to make it a practice to act on it. *Just simply act on it.* And it's not perfect, but I follow through on the generous act much more often now. And I really enjoy this, because it takes you over the hump of laziness or perhaps a bit of apathy, because you have it in your mind that this is a *practice.* This is one way of practicing generosity. And it's beautiful. It's really beautiful.

"In some teachings it is said that you should give without regard to the outcome, without regard to the need. If there is an opportunity to give, you give. And so for me my practice has been if I come into contact with a situation where there is an opportunity to give, I don't think about what kind of person they are or even what they are going to do with the money. It's just a spontaneous act. It is about not letting those opportunities pass by."

"Yes, I see. I understand the difference. That simple commitment is quite powerful."

"I have also found it interesting to play with generosity on varying levels of largesse. In other words, you could have the impulse to give a dollar to someone on the street, or twenty dollars, as you describe, or . . ." He pauses. "Or you could have an impulse to give a thousand dollars to a friend who you think really needs it. And this is something that you would not normally do. But the thought might come, and with something like that there could also come a lot of second-guessing."

"Oh, I definitely have experienced the second-guessing."

"And I think that this could also be taken to an extreme that might not be skillful, where you just give everything away and then you're living on the street. I'm not suggesting that. But I think there is a very wide range within which we can be unusually generous and have it not be to our detriment, even financially. And again, watch the motivation behind it. You can give the best of what you have, which is called 'royal giving.' But if you are not delighted to do so, then that would not be considered royal giving. I guess you could call that 'princely giving,'" Joseph says, laughing. "The important piece is to notice on which level you are giving. But it is also important to remember that even beggarly giving is better than giving nothing."

I am quiet for a few moments, letting this boundary-stretching concept settle in. Then I speak. "OK, so now another question. I know this can be tricky because you and I have talked about this before. Generosity, giving, makes one happy. It really does. But if we are doing it to feel happy—if we're feeling glum and think, *I'll just pass out dollar bills to everyone on my way to work and then I'll feel better*—is that beggarly giving? Is that motive impure?"

"Well, again, as with almost everything for those of us who are not yet fully enlightened, our motivations will often be mixed."

"Oh. Mixed. Right."

"So it's not to expect that we'll necessarily always have completely pure motives. But I think to the extent that we're honest with ourselves, that we see what's going on, that we're not deluding ourselves, then we can *give emphasis* to the more skillful aspects. Even if other conflicting thoughts are arising in the mind, we can let them come and we can let them go rather than have those thoughts be the main motivation."

"I see, even with beggarly giving, you're still giving."

"Yes, absolutely. And I've played with this quite a lot, both ways," Joseph says.

"You mean sometimes you've acted and sometimes you've talked yourself out of it?"

"Exactly!" He laughs, then becomes quiet.

"But even when it feels like something significant relative to my resources," he says softly, slowly, "I have *never ever* regretted doing it. Which is itself something to learn."

"Yes, I understand that." We are both quiet for a few moments before I continue.

"When I began this work I would walk down the street making judgments—*this person looks like they could get a job, this person is harassing me*, or whatever. And it is so encouraging now, only a month later, to discover that I may still have one of those thoughts come up, but then I'll have another thought, *Well, maybe he couldn't get a job.* Or, *maybe she didn't have a place to sleep last night.* And, you know, it doesn't matter. They are asking, and at this moment they are asking me, so I will give."

"Right. And maybe this is their job."

"What?"

Joseph laughs. "That's what I say to myself. *Maybe this is his job.* This is what they have chosen to do for a job."

"Oh, my God, Joseph . . . that's crazy."

"So, I really like that," Joseph says. He begins chuckling.

"What?"

"It's not a job that I would want to do." This makes me laugh.

"So his job is . . ."

"To sit there and ask for money."

"And, I guess, also help us to expand our generosity?"

"Well, yes. And it gets even further complicated. There is a lot in this, and that is why the whole practice of generosity is so rich. Of course the fruit, the benefit of the gift—beside the obvious benefit to the receiver—is enhanced by *not wanting* the benefit."

"Yes. I understand that."

"It must be given in a really spontaneous and genuine way. So it is all of these aspects. This is what makes it such a rich practice. There are many dimensions to it—many dimensions to look at and to examine within oneself."

I'm beginning to understand the richness and complexity to this practice, levels I had not observed. I am quiet again as this new understanding sinks in.

"Now this may sound silly," I say finally, "but I did notice that even cooking felt like a gift of generosity."

"Oh, yes," he says. "As you well know, I love it when you cook. Anytime anyone cooks a meal for me, I feel they are being generous. Especially for those of us who don't cook, or who don't enjoy cooking for ourselves." Joseph doesn't cook much. As a bachelor he has created the perfect scenario: an easy stroll through the woods from his house to the Insight Meditation Society dining hall.

"I also love being generous when no one else knows," I continue, "like preparing dinner and giving Ron the best of whatever it is I've prepared. Something about that tickles me."

"And the shadow side of that is . . ." Joseph says.

"Now what?"

He pauses. "To see if there's some ego gratification in that. And there could or could not be. Again, it's not with any judgment, because so often our motivations are mixed, remember. So it's all by way of exploration."

"Well, it's interesting you say that. It's true. There is ego gratification. It does make me feel good about myself. How could it not?"

"Right, but again . . ."

"That's not my only motive?"

"Right. Think the mix."

"Oh, the mix. That is so good to remember, Joseph. We all can tend to think either/or. We have to remember that. Not either/or. I can so easily get stuck here."

"Yes. For example, in giving the best piece of food, that generosity could be combined with a genuine feeling of *mudita* for Ron's enjoyment" (*mudita* is a Pali word meaning "sympathetic joy" or "wishing another well").

"It is."

"And, on the other hand—which I think it's probably not, but maybe a little—mixed in with feeling good about yourself for having done it."

"Yup. That too."

"So then, that's different than *mudita*. That mind moment is not wishing well for another; it is not *mudita*. That mind moment is not generosity."

"I understand totally. So now a question that can be kind of juicy. We have spoken about this before. Being generous to oneself. For the greedy types, this can be very . . . sticky." He laughs. "You know? It can be hard for us to discern wholesome and unwholesome generosity for oneself. What could you say about that?"

"Oh, well, I'm in the same boat, as you know!"

"But you're farther along. You've been rowing a lot longer than we have—you can see the shore!"

Joseph is quiet for several moments. "I think a useful question, just to make us more aware, might be to ask, 'Do I need this?' Of course need can cover a wide range of things," he says, chuckling. "But at least asking the question stops the mindless forward momentum. And then at times I might think, *No, I don't really need this.* And then at other times I may think, *I don't really need this, but I'm going to do it anyway.* Or it might be, *Well, in a way I need it,* you know, *it will do this, this, or this for me.* So I think there's a whole range of responses to that question. But at least in asking the question it makes one stop and reflect a bit."

"Yes, that's good, and I have worked with another similar idea I got from you, which is asking, 'Will this lead to a simpler life?'"

"Right. That's also a good one. Something else I do sometimes . . ." He laughs. "I'm assuming it's a good thing to do. There may be some undertones that are not. But sometimes, if I'm doing something for myself that feels a little extravagant, I'll make a not always comparable but significant donation or gift to some place or person that I feel really needs it. It's kind of the sense of, well, if I'm doing this for myself, I ought to do something like this for others."

"Oh, I really like that idea. I don't know if we've talked about this before, but probably we have. Interesting. I can feel what you're saying, that it can be hard to discern if it's totally wholesome."

"I think the point of interest here is to see if one is doing this out of guilt." We both laugh.

"Yes, I think that's what I was just feeling arise," I say.

"But that can be sorted out. Generally, I think it's a good thing to do."

"Yes, because as you said, there are often mixed motives. Guilt might arise, but it might not be the motivation you act on. The one you act on could be the feeling that if I'm doing something nice for myself, I would like to do something nice for someone else too. Spread the joy."

"Right."

"I like that. Then it feels like it's a little more OK for oneself!"

"Yes," he laughs, "so it's that complexity that is interesting to keep observing."

Finally, I relive the sweet, deep pleasure of the afternoon with Julie as I describe our lunch together to Joseph. "And I didn't feel I was holding anything back," I say in conclusion. "In fact, it felt almost like I, Gail, wasn't there. I was so focused on Julie that compassion was just arising spontaneously and flowing through me. I seemed always to know just what to say or just what to do. It wasn't strategic at all. I wasn't trying to get anything or accomplish anything or be anything. I was deeply relaxed, clear, open, and interested. Only after, in reflecting, did I understand that this was certainly my purest experience of generosity yet. I gave respect, inclusion, genuine interest, and caring as I would with a close friend. And it was remarkable to watch and feel the results as Julie opened and trusted and shared herself."

"Yes," he says softly. "Yes." Again, we are quiet for a few moments before he speaks.

"What I really like about that experience—and it might be delicate to figure out how to say this in the book—is the notion of the practice extending beyond what might appear to be a comfort zone of generosity, as was the case for you here. When the impulse or a situation arises, we can practice with not letting our comfort zone be a barrier, because then that experience really can enlarge one's capacity, as you found. And it's also not only about giving money or material things, as you discovered. It can also be about doing things, about how we relate to another. And that's how so many of the great people who go out into the world can do these tremendously generous, compassionate things, because they're not held back by a view of 'Oh, that's too much.' I think that's a beautiful, inspiring example. And we are all held back at times, but I think what is important is to acknowledge it, to remember this is a practice and understand that at times we can just . . . *push that edge.*"

After we complete the call, I remain sitting still for some time. If generosity brings us such happiness, why do we feel pressed to erect fences around ourselves, our natural inclinations, and our resources? Together we can resolve to continue exploring those boundaries and stretching a few deeply ingrained but perhaps no longer useful or true beliefs we are secretly hanging on to about what we are really capable of doing. Congressman Tim Ryan says, "The deepest part of ourselves is not at peace with the suffering in the world."

Now I try always to have dollar bills handy and receive much joy in sharing them. How about you? Can you report more generosity now than before you began this practice? Seeing this in oneself is surprisingly uplifting. Our generosity muscle can indeed be toned and strengthened. Acting on an impulse to be generous can begin to feel less like an exercise and more like our naturally arising inclination or even our preference. Rationalizations, doubts, fears will still arise, but they become much less relevant. Recently I pledged significant gifts to two local philanthropic groups working to ease the suffering I see much more clearly now. The initial impulse surprised me both times, but not my acting on it. The gifts stretched my resources, and yet a deep satisfaction arises each time I remember. Giving the best of what we have also need not be confined to money. We see opportunities everywhere. We stop to talk with the person crouched on the sidewalk. We volunteer, even while feeling protective of limited free time. Royal giving. And when we don't do the generous act, later we begin to find that we wish we had. We notice. We remember. Sometimes for days a selfish response may bedevil us. But we have crossed a line, and although we may feel we have surely not arrived, we also understand, deeply, that there is no going back. Continue widening your vision to the profound need all around you, and the impulse to respond with generosity will arise naturally, and joyously. More attuned to need and lack, we spontaneously become more mindfully compassionate in response, and delightfully and surprisingly and profoundly more generous. Trust me.

Once you have tasted and retasted the joy and fulfillment that comes from your generosity, you will lose all interest in turning away.

———

Even though my mind entertained all these other
thoughts and feelings and motives, I could always
come back to that first moment of pure motivation.
—Joseph Goldstein

2 Virtue

Meritorious actions hold the key to happiness in our lives.
They are the seeds of happiness of all kinds,
both temporary worldly success
and all spiritual accomplishments.
—JOSEPH GOLDSTEIN

The Second Parami: Virtue

The Pali word *sila*, which we translate as *virtue*, is
used to designate the second parami in Buddhist
texts, where it is defined as purity in speech, action,
and livelihood. It means moral excellence, right
thinking and action, and goodness in general.

Instructions: The Peace of Non-Remorse

"There are so many good stories of working with the parami of virtue,"
Joseph says as he begins his instructions on virtue. "One that is coming to mind happened when I was living in India, and we would go up
to the mountains in the summer to practice. We rented this house—a
very primitive house in a beautiful setting. And there were these huge
spiders on the ceiling. You know . . . really big!" He laughs. "I was practicing the precept of not killing, and I also really didn't like the spiders

in the house. But they were much too big to just scoop up and put out. You didn't want to get that close to them."

"So what did you do?"

"Well, what I noticed is that they just hung out on the ceiling. So after a while I thought, *OK, if they're staying on the ceiling, perhaps I can just coexist with them.*"

"Oh, no . . . really?"

Joseph laughs. "Well, yes, and it became very interesting. Once I had made and was following that commitment not to harm, and had decided not to try to humanely remove them, which would have been OK too, I found that it really was fine, actually. They had their space. I had my space. We just coexisted quite happily. And it was interesting to me because," he chuckles, "it's not my usual mode, of course, to live with giant spiders. So that is just one example of trying to apply the precept of non-harming in a situation where, without that intention, one might just kill them."

One of the unfortunate by-products of this attention to living life with impeccability is that not only do your current transgressions become increasingly, painfully clear, but memories of past general bad behavior can also arise. It can be sobering.

Joseph's story reminds me of a vacation to a similarly rustic (cheap) resort in Mexico with a girlfriend. I was twenty-two years old. After many hours traveling, bone-weary, we open the door to our charming little bungalow, come in, and dump our bags on the floor. My friend goes into the bathroom and suddenly shrieks. Standing in the open doorway, bleary eyes now wide, she points. I peer around the corner and see a spider on the closed lid of the toilet so large its thick hairy legs reach completely from one side to the other. We both race out of the room and around the grounds yelling for help.

Naturally when we return with a gardener, who does not speak English but is willing to follow us, there is no spider on the toilet cover. We point into the bathroom. Neither of us will go in there. We make spider-like gestures with our hands. He seems to understand, rummages around, and then smiles, shrugs, and points to the ceiling. In horror we now notice the open-air gap between the top of the wall and the slope of the thatched roof. I am sad to reflect that all I wanted was to see a very dead spider being escorted out of our bathroom. I surely wished harm to that spider. I guess we did coexist with spiders that week in the tropics, unseen, but I am also clear we would not have lived with them visually hanging above our heads.

"OK, so now before you give the new instructions," I say to Joseph, "I have a basic question. I have seen this second parami translated as 'morality.' And you introduce it as 'virtue,' which I've also seen. Are both of these translations the same?"

"Yes. I think they are referring to the same thing. Other phrases that I sometimes like to use are the ethics of non-harming, or ethical conduct. The essence of all of them is that one's actions are *non-harming* of others or of oneself. That is the core meaning of the second parami."

"It seems to me that the word 'morality' can also have a heavy tone these days."

"Yes, well, it can. All of these terms can be used, but there may be certain modern-day connotations to some of them. So it's helpful to understand what their general meaning is; again, it's really, simply about non-harming."

Joseph's Instructions: Working with Virtue

Virtue is the practice of not causing harm. I suggest for this parami that we work with the Buddha's concept of the five precepts. The precepts are five components of a virtuous life, a life of non-harming. They are:

1. To refrain from killing (non-harming).
2. To refrain from stealing (taking that which is not freely offered).
3. To refrain from sexual misconduct (harming another or oneself through sexual actions) and instead giving the gift of trust to another.
4. To refrain from wrongful speech (unkind or untruthful).
5. To refrain from using intoxicants (that which clouds the mind).

To begin, you might select the precept that most entices you or the one you might feel you can struggle with. You can work with a different precept each week. You can also work with one precept for the entire month. Again, there is no wrong way to proceed. Remember, this is an investigation. The instructions that follow apply to all five precepts.

1. Consider how you might refine the definition of each precept for yourself.
2. Investigate everything. Look for subtleties not immediately apparent.
3. What attitude arises when you are abiding or refraining?
4. What attitude arises when you slip up?
5. After a skillful or unskillful act, what reflections or emotions linger?
6. Continue to monitor and refine your understanding.
7. What are the positive aspects of adhering to this precept?
8. Is compassion arising for yourself, for others?
9. Explore the motivations before, during, and after you speak and act.
10. When considering words or actions, ask, "How does this serve?"
11. Ask yourself what you are trying to escape from when you indulge.
12. And when resistance arises, notice the attitude in the mind.

One final suggestion: As you go from the habit of breaking the precepts to the habit of honoring them, consider:

- What ramifications arise from this new habit?
- What benefits are you seeing as you refrain from acts of harm to yourself and others?
- What gratification and joy, or sorrow and remorse, do you notice as you do or don't follow your new intentions?

Suffering reminds us to investigate: What's happening?
How can I understand what's going on?
—JOSEPH GOLDSTEIN

Through our commitment and practice of non-
harming—in actions of body, speech, and mind—the
suffering of regret, which can be a powerfully negative
force in our lives, does not agitate our minds.
—JOSEPH GOLDSTEIN

Working with Virtue: A Refuge for Mice

My first few retreats with Joseph were at the Angela Center in Santa
Rosa, California—a lovely, serene Catholic nunnery. My fourth-year
retreat took place at a summer camp in the middle of winter. The accom-
modations were very rustic: wood cabins deep in a thick redwood forest
alongside a river. My assigned sleeping space was a tiny office, with a cot
for a bed, adjacent to a big dorm room with bunk beds. I was happy for
the private room, even if it had been a closet.

On that first night, as with every first night of a Buddhist retreat,
we chant the five virtue precepts together, proclaiming aloud our intention to live together for the next ten days in a community committed
to non-harming. Later, drowsy and snuggled happily into a sleeping bag
in my cozy little room, I gaze around . . . and freeze. A giant spider is
walking along the opposite wall, maybe five feet away from my nose.
Instantly my gut begins churning in terror. Oh-so-slowly I slide out of
my comforting, toasty warm bag, eyes never leaving the spider, and feel
around the floor for my shoe. My heart is pounding so loud I am sure
the entire camp can hear it. Sweat runs down my armpits. I am shaking.
Did I mention I am terrified of spiders? For some time I just stay there
crouched, shoe in hand, truly, insanely petrified. Perhaps sensing dan-
ger, the spider stops and waits. Time elapses. It is very late. Bad karma
(the result of one's harmful intentions or actions) is accumulating here
as the minutes tick by. My intention, clearly, is to do harm. If it comes at
me, I will have to kill it. If only there was an empty bed in the adjoining
room. But no, Joseph's retreats are always full. Well, I can't sleep with
this thing in here. I will make amends. I will meditate all the harder during the retreat. Slowly I make my approach, shoe raised, arm shaking.

Something catches the corner of my eye, and I shift my gaze. The illumination of a lamp outside, shining through the window's thin yellow curtain, casts my shadow on the wall beside me: a giant with raised arm and weapon, poised for battle. It is a horrific image. I see myself reflected as the killer that I am clearly about to be. The seriousness of my intent suddenly overwhelms me. Yes, I also have the thought, *What if someone else were to see me right now, just after we have pledged aloud our intention not to harm?* But this is not the thought that lowers my arm. Frightening as the spider (unfortunately) still appears to me, I also suddenly understand I will not kill this living creature. This is the thought that lowers my arm. I will not harm him. I will not. We will coexist, like Joseph and his giant spider roommates.

Did I sleep that night? Not much. Did that spider crawl across my face and through my dreams? Many times, or so I imagined. Was he there the next morning? No. Did I look for him each and every time I returned to my little room all ten days? Yes, but never again with the intent to do him harm. And I have not intentionally killed a spider since that pivotal night many years ago.

And so I begin this month working with the second component of integrity—non-harming of myself and others. It is November, and I am beginning to see what look like mouse droppings. We have lived in this house twenty years and have never had mice. The occasional but persistent droppings are outside an old, built-in cabinet that extends from the floor to the ceiling of the garage. I notice the cabinet's plywood doors are warped. Plenty of space between the bottom of the doors and the base of the cabinet for a mouse to squeeze in. With some trepidation I open the cabinet. Uh oh. I remember now. The bottom shelf is filled with bags of yarn, old blankets, and towels. Cozy. Warm. Inviting. Quickly I close the cabinet, unwilling to investigate further. It is a wet, cold November. If they stay in the garage, just for the winter, on the bottom shelf . . .

A few days later a terrible smell permeates the house. I need to find someone who can trap and relocate mice. I investigate my options and turn up "We Care Pest Control." I am elated. We live in Marin County. Of course there is a green, compassionate solution available.

I leave a message at We Care Pest Control indicating I am interested in someone coming out to humanely trap and relocate mice we may have in the garage. They do not call back. The next day I call again, and this time a man answers. "Oh, hi," I say. "I'm so glad you're there. I left a message. I'm looking for someone to trap and relocate some mice."

"I don't talk to you people," the man says, interrupting me, and hangs up! I am shocked. Then amused. "You people?" Who could he mean? And then I notice I'm feeling honored to be included in the group wanting to let mice live.

Unfortunately, the smell persists. Three days now. I can't help but wonder, *Why is this happening just as I am beginning to work with an intention of non-harming?* (I swear this is true!) I want to do the right thing. But I can't live with mice in the garage *and* this smell, can I? I am determined the mice will live.

I try again. "Bio-Pest." I don't like the "pest" part, but "bio" sounds promising. I reach someone on the phone immediately. He informs me the first step is confirming the problem, and we schedule an inspection. He suggests leaving a few walnut pieces out before the inspector comes to determine if it is still "an active infestation." Then he says, "Good chance it's rats, you know, ma'am. Lots of rats in Sausalito, being on the water and all." Rats? I hang up, suddenly understanding that my compassion may not stretch to include providing comfort from winter rain to rats. The next morning the smell is gone, the walnuts untouched. I relax just a bit.

Bio-Pest inspects. Nice guy. "No rats," he says. "But definitely mouse droppings. You had mice recently. Can't say if they are still around." He tells me where to buy a trap to relocate the few mice we might still have. He says the smell was probably a mouse dying. Could have been an old mouse coming in from the rains, or maybe one that had fallen! He informs me that mice are not good climbers.

With the smell gone (and the knowledge that mice are not good climbers), I feel no immediate sense of urgency to buy a trap. Periodically I sweep up a few droppings. I am glad no mice have been killed and am now, honestly, grateful I can offer them dry refuge in the garage from a miserable winter. When the rains eventually stop, so does the task of sweeping up mouse droppings. I quickly throw out everything stored on that bottom shelf, and they have never returned. I will add that I am now an expert at escorting spiders back outside.

Next I select wise speech from the five precepts to work with. I keep the Dalai Lama's description of the five components of right speech with me as I begin work:

- spoken with a kind heart
- spoken gently
- must be true
- must be beneficial, useful, and uplifting
- spoken at the proper time

The first morning, driving to work, I am thinking about an upcoming meeting with difficult clients. I soon find I am rehearsing what I will say—to the clients, to their agent, to my developer client. After a while it suddenly dawns on me that I am replaying various scenarios, because each time I am adjusting the facts, recasting them ever so slightly *in order to* steer the participants in a direction I think is best. I am surprised and then also dismayed to discover this motivation behind what I had thought was simple rehearsing. Fortunately I have a long commute. I actually say aloud in the car, "Well, I guess it is pretty tough to speak the truth when I am rehearsing lies!" And then I laugh.

But I am aghast. So simple, but definitely not always obvious, clear, or easy, this strengthening of one's trustworthiness, in this case with words. I consider how much simpler and honest it might be to just be present with no hidden agenda. Listen. Respond thoughtfully, honestly. Speak only what I believe to be true from what I observe. And then be open to hearing what others observe, what others might believe to be true. As I have this thought, my shoulders drop. I feel the release and then the ease immediately. I don't need to direct the world. I certainly don't need to mislead it. I need only to listen and facilitate. And so that is just what I do. The meeting has warmth and is governed by a spirit of everyone thinking together, out loud, to craft a solution that, quite amazingly, also works for everyone. Simple; not always easy. And I leave with a deeper understanding of how much easier it is to maintain a commitment to honest speech by predominantly listening!

In any business, truthful speech can be a tricky, sticky edge. Ultimately business is about achieving results. The bottom line. But when we box ourselves and others in with an expectation or a desire for a specific outcome, we can sabotage our most important intent, which is to bring both kindness and integrity of motive and words to the negotiating table. This applies equally to a real estate transaction and negotiating with your twelve-year-old on homework time. We may feel certain a particular resolution is best. But we are not the only ones making the decision. Business and life really do operate most effortlessly when structured to facilitate discussion, with all participants arriving at a solution that is the best they all can stitch together. The process itself becomes the answer we were seeking.

Did my sterling moment's revelation in the car change the rotation of the earth, never to return to its original path? Not totally. But now I catch myself mentally rehearsing. And when I do, I eavesdrop! Often it becomes quickly clear what small and subtle white lie I am contemplating, fabricating. It might be a dialogue wrapped in righteousness that I will (hopefully) never have. It might be, as I found that day, enhancing a position, padding the facts to make my idea more persuasive. When we catch ourselves and see clearly, this is a profound opportunity for understanding that this behavior is neither kind, gentle, true, beneficial, nor uplifting. Gradually I have found I can change course and let it go, quite willingly, easily, its darker intent so clear now.

Quite often during this week's exploration of speech, I feel like an undercover agent. I will be chatting casually with someone while also watching for motivations and attitudes—both mine and my companion's. I feel like a spy, my subjects clueless both as to their being studied and also, sadly, to their failures at right speech. It is easier to see another's faults than one's own, isn't it? Of course, I also watch for my own motivations and attitudes. I have two exchanges where my motive is askew. In both instances what I say is true. In both instances it is also not beneficial, particularly useful, or uplifting. I feel the other's reaction and am immediately saddened and disappointed at my thoughtlessness.

Sometimes I find this investigation into my speech to be picky and tedious. It can irritate me. But as I investigate, I also come to understand that on some level, just as with my practice of generosity, I know what I am doing. I understand I can choose a more compassionate response, even if that clarity comes only as a flash, too late to stop the words. *I knew.* It could be when I catch myself rehearsing, or when I speak in haste and see another's reaction to my words, or when I recall a less-than-ideal interaction. Those reflections, just like remembering a non-generous response, cannot so easily be swept under the rug. I know that crud is under that corner of the carpet. Someday I will trip over that bit of wrongdoing, and it will bring unhappiness as I recall my unkind words or actions. I imagine my heart like a red paper valentine. Each time I see the virtuous choice but act or speak otherwise, I take scissors and stab a jagged hole in it and cut out a piece of my peace.

So much suffering in the world comes from lack
of attention to the words we use. It is possible
to make choices about what we say: words need
not simply tumble out of our mouths.
—JOSEPH GOLDSTEIN

VIRTUE

All the moral precepts are rules of
training, not commandments!
—Joseph Goldstein

Check-In Conversation: Investigating with Interest

For my reporting this month we are again speaking by phone—Joseph in snowy Massachusetts and I in still-rainy Sausalito.

"Well, November turns out to have been a good month to focus on non-harming," I say, laughing, after telling him the mice story. "But then, also for the first time, ants began marching in the back door. So I purchased a soft shoe brush and dust pan, like you once had recommended, and escorted them periodically out the door. It does work surprisingly well. The ants are very much alive as I leave them outside. And just as you described, after several days they gave up and moved on. As I escorted them out or swept up the mouse droppings, focused on my aspiration of non-harming, I found happiness periodically arising, unexpected. My acting with impeccability, certainly in ways I would not have before, did at times feel like the bliss of blamelessness."

"Right," Joseph says. "Meritorious actions hold the key to happiness in our lives."

"Ah, but then, 'This too shall pass'—that gentle reminder that both challenging times *and* good times move on. So I'm still feeling good about my efforts when I notice tiny sawdust piles on the living room windowsill. I call still another inspector. And this time it's termites! Eating their way into our dry house. And termites, I decided, painfully and sadly, we cannot coexist with, right? I almost called you. The day they shot the orange oil into the beams, Joseph, I cried. I swear I could feel their panic, their terror."

Joseph is quiet for a while. "Well, the first thing that comes to mind—this goes to another piece within the understanding of morality—is that it is better to do something that's unskillful knowing it's unskillful than to do it not knowing."

"What? I don't know that I've ever heard that."

"Because sometimes we do things that we know are unwholesome, for whatever reason, or whatever justification, as you did with the termites. But it's better to do it with the knowledge that it's unwholesome, even as we're doing it, than not to acknowledge that it is unwholesome. Because in the former case, at least there's a seed of wisdom in there. If it germinates into some further reflection, it opens up the possibility of some future restraint. Whereas if we don't know that it's unwholesome, then there's never any motivation to even consider what we're doing."

"I would think it would be the opposite."

"No. But it is somewhat counterintuitive."

"So somebody who would call up the exterminator without questioning their motive is worse than somebody who would make that call while understanding the ramifications of that choice? And that is because then maybe, for that person, when it comes up again next time they may reconsider and choose differently?"

"Right."

"Wow. That is interesting. Is that true working with all the paramis?"

"It is true with all unwholesome and unskillful acts in general. If one is going to do them, it is better to do them knowing they are unskillful than not knowing."

Just like with my practice of generosity, continually holding the intention of non-harming begins to starkly illuminate all my shortcomings, rationalizations, defeats. I can humanely trap spiders and mice and mosquitoes, but the termites had to go, right? My life savings are in these old wooden walls.

"So now moving to the second precept, to refrain from stealing, from not taking what is not freely offered. I didn't choose this one to work with yet, but I did watch for it, especially with the little things. Like a page I wanted to take home and almost tore from a magazine in a waiting room. Others had done so, but I did not. A pad of paper and a few pencils from the company storeroom. Not freely offered. I left them there. More important, I began considering the idea, *Am I taking more than my share?* I began feeling that this also is a form of stealing. Why do I get to live lavishly compared with so many others? Our circumstances are relatively modest, but in comparison to most of the world, a modest Western lifestyle is opulent. What is the measure for excess? What about working at something we do not enjoy just to accumulate more money to buy more things?"

"Yes," Joseph responds, "in working with this second precept, a helpful question to ask might be, 'Are we consuming more than we actually need?' We can ask ourselves what feels like excess. This investigation can have subtle and not-so-subtle ramifications in many areas of our lives." We are both quiet for a few moments.

"OK, Joseph, so then, sexual misconduct. I had a hard time coming up with anything at all. I mean, I have memories from when I was young and certainly didn't always behave as I should. Painful memories. And regret. But I was clueless!"

Joseph laughs. "Well, yes, I've had some of my own!"

"So what can be said now?"

"I think that it goes back to the question, 'Is this action causing harm to myself or others?' And then you can explore different ways that harm is caused by different actions. Certainly when there are acts of deceit, it undermines the relationship. It breaks the sense of trust. You know the old song." He starts singing, *"Love me or leave me, but please don't deceive me."* I am laughing. "It just came to me a couple of days ago actually, about that song being a good teaching. You know, 'OK, just love me or leave me . . .'"

". . . but *don't* deceive me. Oh, I agree. I think most people would want that."

"Yes."

"OK. Good. Let's move to the juicy one: right speech. So, Joseph, I watch you in conversation—like at dinner when a bunch of us are together. If the conversation strays into gossip, or judgments, or unkind bantering, you don't participate. You just kind of brush it off. You're very good at unobtrusively not participating. I'm becoming more aware of that dynamic now, so that at least I notice when it's going on. Even if I don't always stop myself from joining in, at least I'm *thinking* about doing it differently. I might change some words or, as you do, change the topic. But it can be so slippery."

"Yes," he says again and then nothing more.

I sigh aloud. "OK, right speech report. The new CEO, the man we sold the business to, will walk through our offices occasionally in the early evening. When he finds someone at work late, which is often the case with real estate agents, he will offer us a little glass of a good port that he keeps in his office. This is usually at the end of the week or the end of a long, complicated day. It's a cozy ritual. So this month, when he entered my office, without thinking, I smiled, indicating I was willing to be interrupted. He placed the glass on my desk, poured, and I gestured for him to join me. He sat, poured a glass for himself, we toasted, settled back, and began chatting.

"Now, I like this man. I enjoy chatting with him, especially like this at the end of a long day. But, soon, inevitably, the talk veered to other agents. And here is where it began to get slippery. He began to gossip, and I didn't know what to do. It's such a fine line. This man has a large heart. The talk is not mean-spirited. In our shared managerial roles, it is perfectly normal to discuss different agents, their transactions and difficulties. But now of course I am watching my speech closely, and it does not feel acceptable to slide into a few snarky comments and laughs about someone's attire or latest girlfriend. And I suddenly understood that this type of exchange is a common pathway to bonding in casual business conversations.

"But of course now I was finding it difficult to continually not respond to his friendly but gossipy comments. I tried changing the subject. But the repeated deflections definitely began to put a damper on the flow, the laughter, and the bonding. It actually became a bit awkward, and he soon stood up, mumbled something about forgetting a call, and left. And with other, similar work exchanges I've been dismayed to see how often this bonding piece is a component of forging connections. I saw how quickly one can slide into treacherous and unkind chatter! And then I'd fall right off the cliff of my best intentions into the compelling swampland of wrong speech. So difficult."

"Yes, it certainly can be. And you are describing another good thing to look at with the precepts," Joseph says. "Another place of investigation, especially when we may notice we are up against particular, familiar habits, is to ask, 'What are the specific conditions that arise that then lead us to break our intention?'"

"What conditions are giving rise to my unfortunate lapses? Ooh, that is interesting."

"Is it because we're tired? Is it because we're depressed? Is it because, as you describe, we want to connect with an associate? Whatever it might be. We each have different conditions that can tend to lead us to break one or more of the precepts. And it's really helpful to see and understand what they are so we can become more aware of them."

"If you can be aware of those conditions, then when they arise, they arise with a red flag waving!" I say, laughing.

"Exactly," he says. "For example, I notice for myself that I'm more likely to cater to the unwholesome when I'm tired. And I'm not speaking necessarily about going out on mass murder sprees! But, you know, plop down in front of the TV, or have a glass of wine that I really didn't need or particularly even want. It's just for me, when my mind is tired, I lose that certain quality of resolve. There's no need for resolve when I'm not tired."

"You just don't want it."

"Right," he says. "You don't even want it."

"Yes! I know exactly what you're saying. So what do you do?"

"Well, it depends on how mindful I can be. Can I understand that it's the tiredness that's motivating me? Because when I am mindful, then it gives me a little more space to make a choice. And then sometimes I still go for it! Just plop down on the couch." I laugh. "And sometimes I don't!" he says.

"Evenings. Oh, I agree. I can be lazy then. I can be lax. Whether over a glass of port with a colleague or relaxing at home. Absolutely."

"Yes, well, so it is good to remind oneself at those times that this is an ongoing process. We have a lot of habits here that are very easy to fall into and not so easy to recognize quickly as they are arising. I see this as just another part of the practice. We are simply practicing, working with and improving our dedication to right speech, one of the paramis."

"You make it all seem so clear—and easy. Sometimes I hear your voice clearly saying one of your reminders, and then I wake up just before I might do something I have promised myself not to do." He laughs.

"It's true. OK," I say, fumbling with notes. "What was the last precept? Let's see."

"Intoxicants," Joseph says, chuckling.

"Oh, right. Well, when we discussed it you suggested, ever so lightly, that I might just try not drinking for a while."

"Right."

"You didn't tell me to do it, but after a few days I decided I would try it. And I only lasted a week and a half! I went to the opera, and I had the thought, *I deserve this glass of champagne with my friend.* And then I sat through the entire opera with regret! I was experiencing a hangover," I say, laughing, "but it didn't have anything to do with the glass of champagne. It was a virtue hangover! It was because I had set up to do this one thing for a month, and I had reneged on that simple intention so quickly. It seemed like such a small thing, but when I broke it, it didn't feel like a small thing. I really felt lousy, and that was interesting to me."

"Yes. Right. This also ties in to a discussion of renunciation, which is, naturally, the next parami. And one of the challenges in working with renunciation is that we make a commitment to not do something, we are honoring that commitment for some time, and then we just break it. So then, is there guilt? Is there remorse? How do we reestablish and begin again? All of this is the practice. These things really need to be understood as aspects of training. And in all of that there should be some exploration for ourselves of the idea that in certain situations we are able to honor that commitment perfectly. But more often, in other situations, we are not."

"Oh, yeah."

"So then, how does one handle not doing it perfectly? What is the mind state, and how do we recommit? Again, we are working with that distinction between guilt and remorse, which we talked about."

"Yes, back in generosity we talked about this. For a week or two, all I could see were all the ways I wasn't meeting my own intentions. And I got really discouraged. But then you reminded me that the goal is not to judge but to investigate. To just keep investigating whatever is coming up . . . *with interest.* That is the piece I find can be too easy to forget. We just need to keep on noticing with curiosity. Now remorse is arising. Now it's this, or now it's that. It's not good or bad, necessarily. It's also not solid. It's just moments. And I found there were a lot of clear, unencumbered moments between those moments of feeling discouraged, but if I was labeling the whole experience as 'failure,' it was hard for any new feeling that might arise to get recognized."

"Exactly."

Joseph gives us one final bit of advice. He suggests reflecting at the end of the day:

- Have I done anything that has caused harm?
- Have I done anything that was helpful?
- Was there a time where I almost harmed but stopped myself?

Non-harming leads to tranquility of mind. Ultimately and simply, to live a virtuous life is to live a life of non-harming.

"When I am around monks," Joseph tells me, "I appreciate the level of purity that exists there from years of practicing and living a virtuous life. Even for someone not knowing anything about Buddhism or its wisdom, with monks one can feel the heart of the teachings. It is an uplifting feeling. And it becomes a motivation to consider refining our own efforts. Certainly for myself this is true."

———

The guide for our actions should not simply be
whether something is pleasant or unpleasant right
now, but whether wholesome qualities of mind and
heart are being strengthened. It is those qualities
that are the source of our more lasting happiness.
—JOSEPH GOLDSTEIN

3 Renunciation

It is possible to understand renunciation in a way that
resonates more deeply within us. We can begin to see that
addiction is a burden, and that not buying into it is freedom.
—JOSEPH GOLDSTEIN.

The Third Parami: Renunciation

The Pali word *nekkhamma*, which we translate as
renunciation, is used to designate the third parami in
Buddhist texts. It means restraining desires, giving
something up voluntarily, often at a sacrifice.

Instructions: At Peace with Our Piece

We begin work with the third parami, renunciation, by considering two
basic questions: Why rein in our desires? And how? Our first thought
might be that renunciation of indulgence rings true as a key component
of one's success at strengthening skillful intentions. But . . . *ugh*, right?
The prospect of a month's work on our renunciation skills just does not
sound like fun. We may intuitively understand why this is the next component of integrity, as they build on each other. We may also feel we
need work here. And yet we still feel unenthusiastic, perhaps resistant. I
was. Denying oneself does not sound like a fun way to spend a weekend.

Generosity was fun. Virtue was insightful and memorable, significant. We felt genuinely uplifted by our generous acts and kinder intentions. Anticipating renunciation, the task can appear daunting—familiar patterns of failure and resistance can be woven deeply into our nature, our inclinations. We are tempted. We indulge. Sometimes we regret it later. Many times we do not. We genuinely enjoy indulging—ourselves and others. We crave that rush of pleasure from a new object, a shared fun activity, a tempting sweet, even while understanding the pleasure is fleeting.

And yet at times we can also feel like the one consumed instead of the consumer. A desire arises, evocative, then unrelenting, pulsating with promise until we capitulate. This is an interesting edge worthy of our investigation. There can be unskillful head-in-the-sand behavior here. Also rebelliousness as we struggle with conflicting intentions. How motivated are we to change or even investigate? And this is curious because we also understand we suffer here when we can't have or don't get what we want, perhaps even what we feel we *deserve*. Attempts to rein in desire by setting resolutions, then breaking them, can be a discouraging and debilitating cycle of hope and regret.

Are we willing to consider unpacking this virtually universal blind toppling forward into sensual desires? Just how deep does our desire for freedom go? We all get caught here, repeatedly—slammed, shackled, driven, then stuck-like-crazy-glue to the notion there is something better awaiting us: a better-suited partner, the perfect pair of shoes, a deeper meditation, more money, an answer we are groping for, a stronger will, more compassion, a new couch, a different job, a better self. One thing we can say for certain is that our attachment to the belief "I would be happier if . . ." is the source of bucketfuls of dissatisfaction and much suffering. I want. I want. I want. So enchanting; so exhausting. But how do we turn off the faucet of incessant longing?

———

Joseph is about to give the instructions for renunciation.

"So I'm happy to be continuing this work," I tell him, "but I have to say, the first thing that comes up about this next component of integrity is . . . renunciation, *ugh.*"

Joseph laughs, "Well, you're right, you know. When people hear the word 'renunciation,' it feels like deprivation."

"Exactly!"

"And so our response is that we don't usually greet it gladly. What helped me a lot was to reframe it. Instead of thinking of it as deprivation, try framing it as *non-addiction.* I think we can more easily relate to the obvious suffering of addiction, where the inner workings of the mind compel us to act on our desires. Framing it as non-addiction contains within the language the idea, and the understanding, of freedom. We *want* to be free of an addiction. And we do this by basically recognizing and then breaking the unskillful habits that we might have."

Surprising relief arises as Joseph speaks. It's like a door has opened and suddenly I am aware of how stuffy the air in the room was as fresh air rushes in. *Addiction.* That is precisely how I feel when I am gripped by a desire that won't let go. It is amazing the difference one word can make in one's perception. Joseph is very good at articulating these subtleties of understanding. I am now enrolled in releasing addictions.

Joseph's Instructions: Working with Renunciation

Insatiable wanting is the cause of much of our suffering. Desire arises from habit. So we begin by investigating the power of habit, which is easy for the mind to establish and not so easy for the mind to let go. This exploration of habit has a thousand implications. Most of what we do is habitual. Watch for the tendency to perform a certain action or behave in a certain way without even thinking about it. It is a very interesting arena to explore. Although habits are not the same as addictions, they may feel almost as difficult to break.

1. What are our compelling, familiar habits?
2. Then we explore the workability of our habits: Which are skillful? Which are not serving us? Which habits might be up for some letting go?
3. We investigate further: What is the mind state from which each habit arises?
4. Once we have seen the power our habits have over us, we can begin working with letting go of the unskillful ones. When you have an impulse, try not following it. Ask yourself if there could be a way of doing it differently or of not doing it. Practice letting go of a moment's desire, then watch closely for what arises, what happens next.
5. How do you feel in the moment when the habit of craving slips away? This can be a very rich, very revealing opportunity to see the power of the wanting mind and feel the relief of its release.

———

Habit is habit, and not to be flung out of the window
by any man, but coaxed downstairs a step at a time.
—MARK TWAIN

———

"Joseph, I have a quick question on the instructions. You said it might be interesting to investigate what mind state is present from which a habit arises. Can you give us an example of that?"

"Yes," Joseph replies. "There's an easy example, a very common experience that people have. We're feeling tired, or depressed, or something like that, so we eat. We go straight to the refrigerator or the nearby store. And really, it is just a way of relieving the unpleasantness of that mind state. So we investigate. Instead of just being mindful of that moment, try looking more deeply for the mind state that is driving the habit of going to the refrigerator. If you notice you are tired, for example, then that becomes a red flag, as in, 'Pay attention here. I am tired now, and the habit when I am tired is to go straight to the refrigerator.' We recognize, 'Oh, this is a mind state from which I might be inclined to do something unskillful,' whatever our particular habit might be. For example, with some people it might arise out of the mind state of boredom. They might turn on the TV. It's the same process."

Simplicity. Renunciation. Could this actually be fun? This is not about denial. It really is about freedom. In that moment, in every moment we are gripped by a desire, if we catch it, while we watch it, we have a choice. The clear and lightly teasing tone that says, "No thanks," and moves on. In every moment we can just step out of the paralyzing, blinding grip of desire. When we do, we may feel a physical sigh of relief from the heart. Yes. Let's get on with the authentic business of life. How much of this, really, do we need?

———

Ask yourself: Is this leading to a simpler life?
—Joseph Goldstein

We discover that everything passes,
including uncomfortable desires.
—JOSEPH GOLDSTEIN

Working with Renunciation: Everything Passes

So we begin by paying attention to habits. Easy? Yes. Revealing? Also yes. Just as Joseph promised, it is alarming to see how much of what I do is from habit. Like little robots, many of us roll through the day according to instructions programmed so long ago no one remembers why or by whom. Each time I catch myself doing something the same way twice, I make a mental note: How do I get out of bed, what do I do next, then next, while commuting to work or sitting at my desk? What happens next? If you are being mindful, you may begin noticing that pretty much everything you do is from habit. Mindfully watching myself moment after moment, I progress from curious to appalled, to feeling it is all very amusing, to claustrophobic, to bored, bored, bored, to itching to shake everything up, to deep dismay at how much of the time I am not very present, to wanting to scream when I catch myself doing something *again* exactly as I did yesterday, to fear about what this all means, and back again to curious. And after only a few days, not surprisingly, the observations totally rally my previously lackluster enthusiasm for working on strengthening my renunciation skills.

These are some of the habits I notice in the first week: Saying "I'm tired" when I arrive home from work each day and then (surprise!) feeling so. My husband has the very same habit. Incessant planning, especially for a rosier future. Yearning for simplicity, then not acting in a way to support it (buying more things, accepting more invitations, scheduling overloaded days). Wanting other than what I have, other than what I'm feeling, other than what I'm doing in that moment of noticing. Reaching for a snack when mentally weary. Accepting a glass of wine upon arrival in most every social situation. I continue making insane and impossible to-do lists, then feel disappointed when I don't accomplish them. My final, sobering discovery after all this observation occurs to me as

I review my notes. Really, it is so amazing to me that I keep forgetting to notice wholesome endeavors. I have not noted one wholesome habit! What the heck is that about? This is a revelation. What about you?

Many of us yearn for a simpler life. And then we continue making choices that do not support that wholesome desire. The entry hall in a friend's house is remarkable. No coat closet, just a shelf, wall pegs, and a bench. There is one coat, one hat, a pair of flip-flops to wear indoors, and lots and lots of nothing else. A tranquil welcome. Yet I keep making choices that are not headed in that direction. Why is that? I want to investigate the "I deserve this" mind state that continues to fuel all this wanting, especially when I am overworked and stressed. Habitual wanting is not skillful, is not serving me, and is definitely up for some letting go. As Maurice Sendak once said, "There must be more to life than having everything."

By the second week I am fully engaged and actually eager to renounce purchasing anything new for the next thirty days. I limit myself to replenishing only: healthy food and house necessities. Nothing more. I know I am not alone in this yearning for a simpler, more contented and connected life. Many ads now capitalize on this yearning for less stress and a simpler back-to-basics lifestyle. Addressing our dissatisfaction, they entice us with more ways to fuel dissatisfaction and ramp up the wanting mind! Romanticizing simpler times, the ads speak to this growing dissatisfaction with our consumer-driven, but still ravenous, American culture.

———

Day One: Easy, fine, no worries. No temptations; no purchases. (I stayed home.) Day Two: I purchase a CD while browsing at intermission in the opera gift shop. I am on automatic and don't even remember to remember! Feels like a small failing. *I still failed.* But oh, I loved that opera. *Begin again. It is not about the CD.*

Day Three: I resist another "reasonable" purchase of a sweet treat Ron and I like while in the grocery store to pick up a couple of necessities. I turn away and practically run to the check-out counter. Insight: Browsing is a big source of temptation. But this time I do resist; a win.

Day Four: On my run I discover I am mentally compiling a shopping list. I shake the list out of my head, look up at the trees. Gold star. Day Five: Find myself dreaming/planning what I will buy on day thirty! Arrgh.

Joseph once said to beware of "catalogue consciousness": quietly browsing—a catalogue, a shop, a website—*looking for something to want!* The ads are subliminal, cunning, rampant. A mind filled with desire doesn't stand a chance at successfully resisting. Three current ads promising that inner fulfillment is just a purchase away:

A beautiful young woman sits cross-legged on a plateau overlooking a serene mountain lake; the caption: "Found inner peace 100 feet from an amazing spa."

A handsome young man with backpack stands beside another serene mountain lake; the headline: "Find Meaning. Guidance by Garmin."

A car ad: "To be one with everything you need one of everything."

The Buddhists have a wonderful image of the hungry ghost, a creature with a big, empty stomach but a mouth the width of a thread. There is no way to satisfy this eternally hungry spirit. And yet we persist, in spite of our misgivings. We swallow external pleasures as fast as we can stuff them in, yet remain curiously hungry for more. This mindless pursuit, against our better judgment and the urging of our hearts, extracts a heavy toll. The Buddha said this misguided striving to satisfy our never-ending craving for sensual pleasures is the source of all our suffering. *All of our suffering.*

As the week progresses I am beginning to notice *how much time* goes into just planning for acquiring, not to mention the actual pursuit. I am starting to settle in. I notice a significant diminishing of the push to run errands or check out favorite websites—which equals browsing, which equals wanting, which equals purchasing.

You know this mind state, urging us to purchase an item just because we want it, just in case we may need it. This is capitalism's dark side. This is twisted consumerism. Many of us recognize this is not making us happier nor our lives simpler. Certainly it is not providing more joy, peace, or contentment. It is also not helping preserve the planet's limited resources. As Americans we consume more than our share in contrast to developing countries struggling to feed and house their citizens. We know this, and even while understanding that the promise being peddled is neither sustaining, nourishing, or even true, we persist. We are addicted. Why *is* that?

One night I drive by the mall on my way home from a frustrating, lonely day at work. It is brightly lit. Lots of cars in the surrounding lot. I feel like a teenager with no date on a Friday night. Everyone is out having fun but me. But I do keep on driving by, because after I feel the excitement arise, I notice the longing that accompanies it. I look for what is fueling it, see through its momentary allure, recognize the illusion, and say pleasantly, "No thanks." And I keep driving because the ease and quiet with which I am simply driving home, honestly, is more satisfying. Wow. Big win.

I begin to notice I have more free time now with no purchase errands. Surprising and lovely. I read a book over two long evenings. As I reflect on my efforts, I am pleased with my performance. I feel like I am making a small but important effort on behalf of the planet. I like thinking of myself as a renunciate. I love the free time, the ease, the contentment. But can I really go thirty days? Sylvia Boorstein says, "I get to say, each time I avoid temptation, 'Thank you very much, but I have everything I need.'"

One morning I catch myself once again mentally creating a list of what I will buy at the end of the thirty days, but this time my first reaction is to laugh at myself! Now *this* is progress. Renunciation is settling into the beginnings of a new habit. This is cause for celebration. No extraneous purchases for three weeks now. I am indeed forging new habits, skillful habits that support what I truly yearn for. I am feeling, as Joseph describes, strong, wholesome, and also good about myself. I feel I am doing my part for humanity and the planet, and ripples of the bliss of blamelessness again arise.

"Good Enough" is my new mantra, but with an entirely new slant and attitude. When I look in my closet, I really do see the abundance there. It most certainly is good enough. More than good enough. I honestly feel content, which is a definitely altered perception.

As the month continues, like a stone dropped into a still lake, the first ripples of a strong desire are still powerful enough to rock my boat. Gradually, though, when I can be patient and observant, the ripples ease then recede. Cravings move on when I don't continually feed them with compelling fantasies. And when I watch a desire slide away, I feel lighter and eventually forget about it altogether. This is a new approach to working with renunciation—seeing clearly the nature of its intrinsic impermanence and just waiting for it to pass instead of resisting, then succumbing, if only out of fatigue.

———

We need to keep going and to continually begin again.
—JOSEPH GOLDSTEIN

It doesn't matter to what we don't cling.
—JOSEPH GOLDSTEIN

Check-In Conversation: Reframing Deprivation as Non-Addiction

"I love the story you tell about the cup of tea," I say to Joseph as we begin our check-in. I am seated at my desk at work. Everyone is gone for the day, and I am leaning back in my chair, feet up on the desk. This is something I would not do with others around, so I feel deliciously at ease. I am looking out at a maze of slow-moving brake lights in a beautiful pink dusk sky. Sometimes staying late at the office alone can feel soothing. This is one of those times, especially as I watch the sea of commuters and feel happy not to be among them.

"You once described doing a self-retreat at home and watching as the desire arose for a cup of tea. And the desire stayed with you, *cup of tea, cup of tea,* until you suddenly found yourself, in an unconscious moment, in the kitchen preparing a cup of tea!" We both laugh. "And I just had a similar experience. I was driving home (a three-hour drive) from the mountains alone. Before leaving I had prepared a bag of snacks for later, then hit the road. Maybe five minutes transpired, and the desire arose for a cookie. I have a strong habit of snacking when I drive alone on trips and even to and from work. So I started to reach for the bag, and I was not even to the highway yet! So then I thought, *Ah, good opportunity to practice saying no to this habit of craving.* 'No thanks,' I said aloud. Maybe five minutes pass. *Cookie.* I can taste its buttery richness on my tongue. 'No thanks.' Again. 'No thanks.' Again. You know? I had just had lunch! I wasn't even hungry, and it was *cookie, cookie, cookie.* Such a little thing; such a strong habit."

"Right." He is laughing.

"And I was saying 'No thanks,' as a way to indicate I had a choice, instead of just saying no from exasperation, but even the 'No thanks' was beginning to have an edginess to it."

"Well, in addition to the 'No thanks,' sometimes I find it helpful to practice with saying 'Not now,' because some things are not inherently bad, but they may not be helpful in the moment."

"Like cookies?"

"Like cookies," he says, chuckling. "Or like so many things. It's just another way of reinforcing that intention of renunciation."

"Hmm. I have used 'Not now' with thoughts that arise. They can slide away. But with the snacks . . ." I laugh. "I don't know, I guess I'm still stuck here. I drive; I snack. Definitely a habit up for some attention. I will try using 'Not now.' But it just felt like a kid having a tantrum. I just kept insisting, you know, wailing and pounding my hands and feet on the floor of the grocery aisle, so to speak! It was debilitating to feel the strength of that one desire!"

Joseph is laughing. "It *is* amazing. And that itself is a very interesting insight—to really *see* the force of desire, the power of habit, in oneself. And to really appreciate that this is a powerful force. The object may be insignificant, but the nature of desire, that energy of habit, is not insignificant. It is really deeply rooted."

"Yes," I say after a few moments. "Yes, it is."

"OK, switching to another uncomfortably familiar habit. I am feeling deeply mired in this habit of too much stuff. And I am really weary of it. But when a desire arises, it doesn't just feel like *a* desire, it feels like *my* desire." I sigh. "You know?"

"Oh, yes."

"Well, why does it seem so . . . sticky? Why do I persist, even when understanding, on some level, it is not leading to more freedom?"

"I think you're framing it the wrong way."

"Oh, good. I love your reframing. Say more."

"It's sticky, as you describe, because the habitual force of desire is a very deeply conditioned force in the mind. So it's not that this is *Gail's* problem," he says, chuckling. "This is the problem of *samsara* (a Pali word for endless realms of suffering). It's not surprising that it's so strong. But that doesn't mean we have to personalize it. We can see the tendency as personal, but we can also see the deeply conditioned energy of it in the mind. And that's all. So you are seeing it. You are acknowledging that it's strong. But—and this distinction is important—you are not taking it to be you. It's not *your* desire. It's just desire."

"Just desire; not mine. Wow. I can actually feel how holding it as mere perception creates so much space around it. Space for another, perhaps different, response."

"Exactly."

"I like that! OK, so now switching topics to another discouragingly familiar habit. As you suggested, I've started a thirty-day no-new-purchases aspiration. It's only been a couple weeks, but already it's juicy."

"Oh, yes."

"First I noticed how much time I spend planning for purchases. The mind loves it, you know, *Oh, we could stop now and get that loaf of cinnamon bread,* or *Let's look here for that jacket.* And then I would remind myself, *We're not doing that now.* And sometimes the next thought would be, *OK, we can wait thirty days!*" Joseph laughs. "Then I think, Hey, if I wait thirty days, it's still a lot better than I was doing before. Maybe I won't want it in thirty days. Probably I won't. In fact, there's a good chance I won't even remember I wanted it," I say, laughing. "And then I also tried doing something differently, like trying to fix something instead of just heading out to buy a replacement."

"Yes. All that is great. It is right effort in the service of simplicity."

"And that's the crux of it for me. Simplicity is what I yearn for, from the bottom of my toes, and yet most of my endeavors and purchases are all reinforcing the opposite! That is just so amazing to me, to watch that counterproductive dance. You have said that in any moment we can disengage the power of desire. But what about the next moment and the next moment and the next?"

"Well, Tulku Urgyen (Joseph's Tibetan Buddhist teacher) used to say, 'Short moments, many times.' And this is important to see. It's not the idea that I'm going to do this a few times and the habit of desire will be gone. But we *can* do it for short moments. That *is* within our power. So we just cultivate the habit of doing it for short moments many times. That becomes a more wholesome and achievable habit."

"That is encouraging, actually! I feel the lightness of it."

"Yes."

"Here's another example of my getting caught. I went to the grocery store, and there was the perfect doormat on a little rack by the front door. And I had recently searched all over because our doormat had disintegrated, and I finally just bought something after looking for a while. And now here was the perfect mat! Only $29.00. But I had just bought one! So I said, 'No, remember it is renunciation month.' And the next morning I walk out to get the paper and I see the mat, then imagine the other one and think, *Only $29.00. Such a small thing.* And this has gone on over the course of the last three days!" Joseph laughs. "And it's still going on! And so I just wonder," I sigh. "Gosh darn it! I alternate between 'Gail, it's only $29.00,' and 'Wait a minute! It's part of a pattern that goes really, really deep.'"

"Well, it *is* a pattern that goes deep. Bhikkhu Bodhi (a contemporary Buddhist monk and scholar) spoke about this kind of craving and called it a 'craving for aesthetic pleasure.' And that's what this is. You think it will be more beautiful."

"Oh, absolutely. Trust me, it would be."

"And he described this as attachment to perception. I have that same thing, as you know," he says, chuckling. "In a big way. But when he described it as attachment to perception, it really became an insight into what was actually happening in that moment. And so this brings it down to a very subtle meditative experience. One can really see how, when you look at the old doormat, there is a moment of perceiving—which is recognizing the form and the color and the shape—and then the implications of what one is perceiving. If there's an attachment to one perception rather than another, this will lead to craving. For me, just seeing that certainly didn't remove the desire for beauty. But when I found my mind obsessing about something that I knew was rather ridiculous, just recognizing *Oh, this is attachment to perception* was helpful."

"This is so good, Joseph. So helpful. Yes, I understand. Perception. I can change the lens. I can look at the old through a lens of 'good enough' or 'abundance,' and actually watch the desire dissolve."

I am gazing out at an evening sky of lights and pink haze. This is the time of year when the skies are thick with abundance. I have a mental image of my home now, around which yellow clouds of finches are swooping and singing. Red-breasted robins perch like ornaments in the naked locust tree next door. Sea birds cry, swirling low over the water, while raptors on their migration path glide silently above. And I think I need a new doormat to be happy?

"I do have to say here, Joseph, that balancing all three paramis is becoming a bit of a chore. At times I can feel myself backsliding into the abyss of . . . convenience. Denying myself, being generous—there are more homeless on the streets this time of year—watching my speech at all the holiday parties, and now still more stretching of my goodwill. It can feel overwhelming, like it is all too much. Integrity overload. But then, even disillusioned, I also can feel the strengthened generosity and virtue urging me on. I can say I am uncovering some deep habitual patterns, like feeling overwhelmed at this time of year, like giving in to convenience even when I know, as I do so, that it is not good enough. Not only am I asking more of myself now, I am expecting it."

"Sometimes I talk about this particular parami," Joseph responds, "in terms of the balance of the value both in our practice and in our lives. It can be an investigation of the aspects of *yes* and the aspects of *no*. Often in meditative circles we talk a lot about acceptance and opening, saying yes to things. This is of course very valuable, especially for an aversive or judgmental mind. But it is equally valuable to learn how to say no *without aversion*. To say no with the understanding that 'I don't have to do this. This is not skillful. This is not so helpful.' And we do this with as much freedom in the *no* as there is in the *yes*. When we understand it like this, it gives impetus to our being willing just to pay attention through the day. Before we act on every habit of desire, we can ask, 'Is this something worth doing or not? Is this helpful or is it not?' Then, at the appropriate time we can practice saying no, which is really a practice of renunciation."

Joseph is holding the *no* so much more lightly than I, holding it as a practice, not as a club with which to clobber oneself.

"I understand. And, you know, I feel like I am slaying one siren but I am facing a whole platoon of sirens coming at me! Desire after desire after desire. And here I can rationalize: What difference does this one little purchase make, especially when it is only a doormat?"

"Well, here is another way to consider it. This goes back to the story of the Bodhisattva (Buddha before his enlightenment) under the tree on the night of his enlightenment. He is being attacked by Mara, the evil tempter. Some of the images Mara is assaulting the Buddha with are delightful. There are many delightful things to tempt him, not just fearsome things to frighten him. And with both he just sat there with an unmoving mind. So in those moments when I can see that kind of desire arise—and it can be with something little . . ."

I laugh. "Oh, yes."

"But the desire is arising quite obsessively. In those moments I just hang in there, using some of the tools we've mentioned. And then, sometimes at least, the desire actually does go away. The Buddha said, 'Learn to let go. That is the key to happiness.'"

Joseph continues after a moment, "And so sometimes, when that desire actually goes away, I feel, 'OK, I've let go of that.' And in that moment of letting go, I've started celebrating!"

"What?"

"Celebrating in the sense of, 'I've just won!'" Joseph is laughing. "Yes. 'I've just won!' And it's really like a sense of winning the battle with Mara, the tempter, in that moment. And that recognition casts one's aspiration in a larger context. For example, it's not just about the doormat. It's about whether we are *addicted*, whether we succumb. Are we strengthening that quality of saying no? Are we strengthening renunciation? Are we letting go? Whichever words one uses. In the moment of doing it, if we pay attention to that moment of renunciation, the mind feels very strong, very wholesome. And so we celebrate it." He pauses, then begins to chuckle. "Not by going out and then buying something." I whoop aloud with laughter. "But by appreciating, 'Oh, we've just won a battle here.'"

"I love that, Joseph. I really do. You have once again successfully reenrolled me."

Another good reminder Joseph has given me in the past is to continually ask, "What in this moment is truly lacking?" He also casually suggests I extend my thirty-day intention of not purchasing. I decide I will. More important, I decide I can! Working with these pithy reminders, inspired, I come up with a new habit: lean. Lean eating, lean browsing, lean buying, lean planning, lean schedule, lean entertainments planned, lean chores, lean expectations, lean to-do list. Everything is up for investigation. I feel amazingly fresh.

"The trick is," Joseph continues, "one wants to use all of this to reinforce the understanding of the wholesomeness of it, not to reinforce acting out of aversion. It is helpful to have the right attitude with it. With the right attitude, it becomes like a game."

Yes, I have seen that, I think happily, especially with not purchasing. It is not about denying myself but about releasing myself from addiction, from the feeling that I continually need something new, something else, something different to make me happy.

"You also have spoken about paying attention to the moment when craving slips away," I say. "And I have noticed that can be a very revealing moment! I feel like I am in a vice grip and then, poof, it's completely gone. But then sometimes I can also feel how tightly I was gripped by it just moments before. The contrast is startling."

"Yes."

"And I know from past experience that a month from now I probably won't even remember what I wanted so fiercely. Or if I do, I'll wonder what all the fuss was about."

"Exactly."

"The perception will be that my mat looks just fine. Which it does now, actually. Wow. This is all so rich." We are quiet for a few moments before I speak again.

"And finally, one last question: you talked about the three arenas of clinging. These were good for me to work with. I notice how familiar I am with the habit of doing everything and anything I can think of to maintain pleasant moments and avoid unpleasant moments." I hear the frustration in my voice as I say this.

"I think that's almost everybody. But the greedy types have a particular propensity here," he says, chuckling. "And I think I say this a lot in Dharma talks: that's why the teaching of the Buddha is really such a wake-up call. He says as long as there is attachment to the pleasant and aversion to the unpleasant, liberation is impossible. And I find that so challenging. It cuts right to the heart of things. It can become one's motivation to work just with that. But again, it is also important we're not seeing giving up the addiction to pleasure as some burdensome activity. We are seeing it more on the playing field of freedom. In any moment we can experience equanimity that is not attached to pleasant or averse to unpleasant. It's not that the objects are important or not important. It's the understanding that *here is where freedom lies.* We're understanding the practice in its largest context. And when we can remember that, that's what's inspiring. Of course," he says, chuckling again, "we often forget it."

I laugh. "I have found that. Yes. I discovered it was helpful to also pay attention to *how* I asked the questions," I say. "You know? Not bludgeoning the desire that was arising! That didn't really work well. It gave rise to my very healthy rebellious side. But if I remembered that it's a choice toward more happiness, that it's a choice toward something I want, something I long for, actually—when I could see it as bigger than this one thing and understand that it's not moving away from something I want, but toward something I really want—then that felt like a very important distinction for me to make."

"Exactly."

"So now I'd say I'm in the habit of trying new habits."

Joseph laughs. "Yes, there are a limitless number of wholesome habits to cultivate. There could be the habit of the practice of each of the paramis, as you are doing. That itself is a wholesome habit—the practice of generosity, the practice of renunciation. All of those could be translated into new habits. And then as we practice any habit, it becomes much easier because it becomes our natural way of being."

"Yes, like with generosity, you described how that continues to be your habit. You continue to work with it. It's your natural way of being. And it's up for me a lot more now too."

"Exactly. And this is a strong habit in you already: the habit of seeing the good in people rather than focusing on what's bad. You can apply this to anything. You can go through any of the paramis, or the wholesome mind states, and reframe them as the practice of a habit."

Suddenly Joseph starts laughing and says, "Just make sure in the manuscript that there's no implication that I'm a master at renunciation."

I whoop aloud. "Oh, I'm glad I'm still recording," I say, laughing. "That's good, Joseph. I'll make sure I make that note in the text. This has been big fun. Renunciation fun. Who knew? Thank you, Joseph."

A desire does pass away. It is so. Every desire passes. Many habits are beginning to feel less solidified just as a result of their being noticed. I am beginning to not blindly follow every desire thought that arises. I look again. Consider. It could be an old, unskillful habit no longer serving me. It may just be passing through on its way south for the winter.

The next morning I go out to get the paper. I wipe my feet on the mat. Remember the other one. Imagine it there. Arrgh. Then I remember, this is not just about more stuff. This is about untethering myself from the addictive grip of rampant desire. Life is about every one of these little choices, these little, insubstantial—and huge—choices. Small moments, many times. OK. No new mat. I hone my renunciation skills. I wipe the desire from my feet on my surely good-enough mat and go indoors with a lighter step. I actually feel a sweet release, this small moment of renunciation giving rise to gratitude and contentment. When I resist the siren call of wanting mind, just let it blow through me and pass on, it is replaced by a surprising blast of expansiveness. I am released into acknowledging all the abundance present right now. I would like more of this contentment. I would like to sit in my living room and notice how beautiful it really is instead of seeing the faded wood chest and thinking again how I need to get a blind installed on the skylight.

Simplicity. Renunciation. Could this actually be fun? This is not about denial. It really is about freedom. The lightly teasing tone that says "No thanks" and moves on. In every moment I can just step out of the paralyzing, blinding grip of desire. When I do, I feel a physical sigh of relief from my heart. "Yes," she says, "let's get on with the authentic business of life." What do I really need? I say silently and often, "Keep it simple. Just this now."

———

As we do consistent, patient zazen (practice) we begin
to know that we are nothing BUT attachments: they
rule our lives. But we never lose an attachment by
saying it has to go. Only as we gain awareness of its
true nature, does it quietly and imperceptibly wither
away; like a sandcastle with waves rolling over, it just
smooths out and finally—Where is it? What was it?
—CHARLOTTE JOKO BECK, *EVERYDAY ZEN: LOVE AND WORK*

4 Wisdom

Finally, a great liberating mantra arose in my mind,
reminding me of the truth of things:
anything can happen anytime.
Changing conditions are not a mistake.
It's just how things are.
—JOSEPH GOLDSTEIN

The Fourth Parami: Wisdom

The Pali word *panna*, which we translate as *wisdom*, is used
to designate the fourth parami in Buddhist texts. It means
insight into the three characteristics: impermanence, the
unsatisfactory nature of phenomena, and selflessness.
More commonly, the term refers to the ability to judge
rightly and follow the soundest course of action based
on knowledge, experience, and understanding.

Instructions: Anything Can Happen at Any Time

Wherever we are on vacation with Joseph, we begin each day with meditation. At the beach or in the mountains, at his home or ours, we and
whoever else might be with us gather. Sometimes if we are lingering
with coffee, chatting in the kitchen, Joseph will begin. He will seat himself on the living room floor, cross-legged, a blanket over his shoulders.

He will place his watch on the floor in front of him, then close his eyes. This is our clue. This is his gentle way of letting us know it is time. Quickly we assemble ourselves around him, on the floor, on chairs, on a couch. With pillows and blankets we make ourselves comfortable, burrowing into our surroundings, then ourselves. Eyes close. The room becomes still. Then very still. We meditate together until Joseph's voice calls us back. "May all beings be happy," he will say, indicating our time of meditation is over.

Often the contrast between our previous caffeine-fueled kitchen conversations and the postmeditation stillness is sweet, soft. We will stretch but remain seated, gazing softly at one another, silently floating in a warm bath of tranquility. We may slide into a Dharma discussion. Someone will ask a question of Joseph or share an insight they had while meditating. For a while, the rest of the day hangs suspended. The Dharma conversation can go on for some time, especially when there is a group of us. Even as snow falls or sunshine and sea beckon, we linger, sharing our thoughts, reflecting, questioning. Then the mood will gently shift and the talk move to planning the day. Soon we are gliding down the mountain or into the ocean with clearer vision, softened hearts, open minds. This is wisdom at work.

I am very much looking forward to working with wisdom this month. Wisdom seems such an integral piece to the puzzle we are assembling as we choose and craft a life of integrity. But it also seems vague. How do we "do" wisdom?

This morning I pass by the guy offering a "free" copy of the *Streetscape* newsletter without making a donation. As I do so I am aware that in that passing by, eyes averted, I have chosen not to be generous. And then, suddenly, I understand. Continually observing and then understanding the impact of our unskillful actions is possible because we are utilizing the wisdom component of integrity. And strengthening that skill, that ability to catch the moment before I have walked by, is a moment of wisdom. Yes, wisdom is indeed another important ingredient to enhancing and strengthening one's ability to live in the world with sterling integrity. We don't *act* wise, like we might act generously, virtuously, or with renunciation. We are *becoming* wise as we use mindfulness to stay present to truthfully observe what is happening. Wisdom is the component that is strengthened by right action and that then becomes our trusty companion. As we forge these new habits, wisdom arises as our new habit, gently urging us, providing clarity for a response grounded solidly in integrity. So again, this idea that we can skillfully hasten the process of becoming wise is intriguing. Working out our wisdom muscle in the gym of daily life is definitely appealing. Who wouldn't want to hone their wisdom? Who wouldn't want someone to point at them across a sea of heads and say, "Talk to her. She's the wise one."

Joseph's Instructions: Working with Wisdom

1. Another word for wisdom is "understanding." Wisdom is the investigating factor of the mind. Wisdom is understanding on all levels: the mundane, worldly arena and the realm of Dharma, the path of truth that leads us to liberation. Similar to our work with generosity, it is equally important, as we undertake the investigation of wisdom, to do so with the deeper understanding that this investigation, this enhanced understanding, is leading to the purification of our hearts and to our enlightenment. So we begin by paying attention in our daily lives in different situations as they naturally arise.

2. Hold the intention, periodically throughout the day, to pause and ask yourself, "What do I understand here?" Let this be easy, not forced. Let the wisdom come to you.

3. Explore different areas of your life—thoughts, emotions, actions, speech—and ask, "What do I see clearly here in this situation?" Be specific. For example, you could ask, "What is creating suffering in this situation? What is driving it?"

Next we explore more deeply, beyond worldly mundane happiness. This is an investigation of what in Buddhist terminology is referred to as the *three characteristics:* (1) impermanence, (2) the unsatisfying unreliability of phenomena, and (3) selflessness.

1. Investigating the first characteristic: impermanence.

    • Go beyond the abstract concept of impermanence to look for examples in your life. Ask: "How is impermanence present in this moment of craving?"
    • When and where are our views of things conditioned by some sense of permanence?
    • Also notice when you *are* in touch with impermanence, when there *is* understanding. It is important to recognize this as well. For example, "What is creating happiness right now? Why does it arise here? What is driving it?"

2. Investigating the second characteristic: the unsatisfying unreliability of phenomena. This includes all conditioned things, everything that arises then passes away; bodily sensations, thoughts, and feelings are all classified as phenomena.

    • A good area for investigation: You are cruising along, then suddenly you experience a glitch. What is the attitude in the mind that is causing suffering in this situation? Be pragmatic, not philosophical. With planning mind, for example, as we plan, are we overlooking the understanding that everything is arising and passing away? This understanding can help to bring some balance.

As you get comfortable and accustomed to pausing and checking in, try going deeper. Don't settle for the first thing that comes to mind. Use that as a doorway into further investigation. For example, you can ask yourself, "What else do I have going on in my mind right now that might not be true?"

3. Investigating the third characteristic: selflessness.
    • Ask yourself, "What am I identified with here?"
    • Watch for those moments when we categorize what is happening by labeling it "me" or "mine," "I versus others" thinking.

- Be especially attentive to your speech. Sometimes it is easier to catch the selfing there: "I am tired. I am angry. I am hurt. I am right."

One final suggestion: You might try this as a new habit, following on last month's work with renunciation and skillful/unskillful habits. Try taking moments, when you are tuning in to the wisdom parami, to notice the difference in the quality of the mind when you are just paying attention to whatever is arising and when you are lost in the content of your thoughts.

For example, you are observing a hummingbird. Are you just watching, or are you lost in some story about the hummingbird and you? If so, contrast and investigate the difference in the quality of the mind state in each of those instances. Play with switching it. And keep observing. This is an experiential way of working with wisdom and can be quite illuminating.

A couple of days after receiving the wisdom instructions, I have lunch with a former business associate, a young man I am fond of and also respect. We have a lot of catching up to do, but he is more intrigued by this work I am doing on integrity. He asks many questions, expressing a strong belief in the world's need for more integrity. He says it feels to him like integrity has become discounted, overlooked, buried beneath busy lives. As I listen to him, I feel his hunger. "Where is integrity even taught now?" he asks. He wants his two young daughters to grow up understanding and embracing its significance. When I mention that integrity is a key ingredient in one's happiness, that we know when we don't act according to our own integrity and then feel lousy, he tears up. "Yes," he says with a seriousness incongruous with the sun-drenched waterside bar setting. He already understands the first question, "Why be good?" But the second question, "How?" stumps him. He admits to no sense of how to teach it or improve it in himself.

I am nodding in agreement when it comes to me, suddenly, that I am no longer yearning. I connect with his longing. I understand the restlessness and dissatisfaction. But I *do* know what to do to strengthen my integrity . . . and I am already hard at work on it! The difference is I have had the good fortune to be given a gift, a glimpse into the under-pinnings of this dis-ease that is the cause of so much of our deep and unrelenting suffering. After a mere three months, I am digging my way out. I am hard at work crafting my own path of integrity, and I am mak-ing progress. I have tasted the bliss of blamelessness. I understand there is no going back from this point. Often my efforts have felt small, but I suddenly understand that I have actually made some progress here. I am already wiser, if only for seeing clearly the work to be done and embrac-ing it wholeheartedly. Wisdom is already blossoming. I just hadn't noticed the tender new shoots popping up between thick old habits.

This is when, sitting at that bar eating mussels and kettle bread with my friend, I first understand the significance of this work with Joseph. *I know a pathway out of my suffering, and I am on it.* As I listen to him grapple with the issue, the contrast with my own new peace about it is striking. All the small efforts now suddenly seem lofty and significant. We need to remember this when we are discouraged and seeing only the work still to be done. This is wisdom at work.

At different times in our lives and meditation practice
we may get glimpses of something beyond our
ordinary, conventional reality, touching a space that
transforms our vision of who we are and what the
world is. These intimations give passionate meaning
to questions of ultimate truth, because although we
may not always be living in that space, we understand
it to be the source of everything we value.
—JOSEPH GOLDSTEIN, *ONE DHARMA*

> Wisdom is that force in the mind that illuminates
> how things really are, so that we see clearly.
> —JOSEPH GOLDSTEIN

Working with Wisdom: What Is Creating Suffering in This Moment?

In the first week of working with the integrity component wisdom, Ron and I go out for Chinese food, and this is the fortune I receive: "Seek out the significance of your problem at this time. Try to understand." A good omen, I decide, for a month's exploration of wisdom. It also makes me laugh, so I tape it to my computer—partially to bring a smile and partially to help me remember that what I am doing this month is investigating and deepening my understanding.

Ah, but doesn't life seem to work this way? Lest my impression of my measure of wisdom get too lofty, the very next day provides fertile ground for observing its lack. Saturday morning errands. I start early for an hour drive through San Francisco and beyond, to South San Francisco. Wham! I round a curve to enter the freeway and slam on the brakes. A long line of stopped cars stretches between me and the on-ramp. Early Saturday morning? Quickly there are cars stopped behind me. No way to turn around and try another route. Just stuck.

My first response? Resistance. *No! This can't be happening now! To me? I purposely left early. I don't deserve* . . . Foolishness. OK. Second habitual response? Distraction. As if to sidetrack a disappointed infant, I am already reaching for the radio, pushing preset buttons until I find something I like. This helps. Then it doesn't. I reach for my phone, of course. Now the part of my mind I lovingly refer to as "the narrator" takes center stage. *Why is this happening to me? Now? The morning began so joyously. I have a long list of errands on the seat beside me.* Still we don't move. *This could be an hour or two of wasted time.*

Wasted time? And then, finally, wisdom arises. I am sorry to report it is a while before I think to investigate, with wisdom, as I sit feeling helpless and victimized. I reach for a small pad of paper

I have in the door side-pocket, plus pen, and write "Wisdom" at the top. I look around. Nothing has changed. Under the heading I write, "Sitting in stopped traffic. What do I know is true here? Frustration arising, and arising, but not passing away; now aversion and also *why me?*" Sigh. I discover I am very familiar with this bucket of emotions. "Traffic congestion habituated response" is what is true here. What else?

Habituated response? I stop writing and look again out the window, this time at the equally inconvenienced inhabitants of the cars around me. We have all turned off our car engines. Most seem to be either looking down at their cell phones or talking on them. Oh yeah, I'm not the only one inconvenienced here. Then it comes to me. What is actually creating suffering in this situation? Resistance to what is happening right now plus the desire for things to be different than what is so right now—these are the actual causes and total source of any suffering going on in this car. I sit still with this for a moment.

And beneath that, still digging deeper, I am not resisting and craving. Habit is. This is simply a long-standing first response to sitting in traffic. In any moment here I have other choices. I am not only my unskillful habits, even if they are the first responders and deeply entrenched. Each and every moment offers up a new opportunity for a new choice. The choice to suffer here, or not, is completely mine to make, and make, every moment. In this sudden moment of clarity, the wisdom of this insight completely dispels any lingering "poor me" thoughts.

Now I am curious. Rather than distract myself with more music, writing, or smartphone possibilities, I just sit still and ponder, considering this. I am in congested traffic nearly every day. What other more skillful choices could I be making that eventually might become the new habituated response? I take a deep breath. Another. The situation is completely and totally out of my control. All I *can* do, truthfully, is relax into it, let it be just as it is and then notice what happens next, and then next. Understanding that impermanence is one of life's characteristics, I suddenly also understand that I can rely on it! This too does change. The revelation is game-changing.

Eventually engines start up, we begin moving. A tow truck tries to maneuver between and around us on this old roadway with no side lane. Over an hour later (but who's checking now?) we are directed around a stalled airport shuttle, big pieces of tire strewn alongside. I am pleased to note my first thought is for the occupants of the shuttle. *Are they OK? Did they still make their flights?* I am just delayed, a gentle reminder to limit my errands list. A missed flight can be a genuine inconvenience. Really seeing wandering thoughts as the source of suffering, watching as habits arise, and doing my best not to get entangled in their lures. These seemingly small insights are wisdom.

I remember hearing once that if you were to stop folks on the street and ask them if everything changes, most would agree this is so. Ask those same folks if they operate their lives with this principle in mind and the response would be quizzical at best. How does one live with that understanding in daily life? For me on that pivotal day, first recognizing and then understanding the truth of impermanence allowed me to (eventually) let go of the tight hold on resistance and desire for something other than what was there. In that moment of letting go, the peace that took its place was both unexpected and amazing. Once again, I had successfully flexed the wisdom muscles in the gym of life.

A week later I am walking in Sausalito. The city is hosting a small bazaar where local artists have their work displayed for purchase. I browse. I don't intend to purchase, but I want to support the event by attending. I also begin to feel a strong desire to be generous arising. I love supporting other artists by buying their handiwork, especially if they are amateurs following their passion. As I slowly browse the tables and speak with the artists, I pay close attention to thoughts and feelings arising and passing away. Impermanence. I buy a CD from musicians who just performed on the small stage. They smile as they sign the cover and give me a schedule of their upcoming gigs. I see a handcrafted silver necklace with large pink stones. It matches my sweater. The artist insists I try it on and beams as others admire it on me. I buy the necklace. Now, several days later, the CD is still wrapped in cellophane and the necklace is in a drawer. How quickly the impulse of desire passes away. Again, impermanence. Yet curiously, what lingers is the joy my generous acts brought to the artists. Yes, desire was present. But I am clear that generosity was the primary motivation preceding both purchases, which were also modest. I paid close attention through the entire thought stream, which definitely felt like a wisdom exploration.

As the month continues, I decide to also investigate happy, easeful, contented moments. First I learn that I don't commonly investigate happy, contented moments because that is how I believe it always should be! I am somehow entitled to a happy life. I also discover that I believe *I am doing it right* at those times, so why investigate? (Big slice of wisdom cake here.) I don't want to screw it up by meddling in my good fortune, looking too closely and then watching it all unravel! I don't want to rock the boat and have all the goodies topple out. I feel the resistance arising as I ponder this, but now I fear the happiness will dissipate just as angst can disappear as one investigates more deeply. And I discover, not surprisingly, that I have absolutely no interest in causing moments of happiness to slip away. There appears to be some resistance here to seeing the impermanence of pleasurable moments. I am definitely more attached to and own the pleasant experiences—"I did that." Ah, but when they pass, as they inevitably do, having been attached, I suffer. Now I want more of what just was, not what is here now in a new moment. And on top of that I discover I also can blame myself when the happiness dissipates! I think, *Oops, I must have done something wrong here.* We should just simply remain happy, right? Don't you find yourself thinking that, or feeling that, as happiness dissipates? Now I consider how foolish this resistance really is and, no surprise, how much suffering it can cause us.

Suddenly one day we have an earthquake. The way I know it is an earthquake is that things in my bathroom, where I am standing, that do not normally rattle are suddenly rattling. Bottles on shelves, pictures on the wall. Places inside me begin rattling, buzzing. Suddenly I have the most amazing thought, as if the shaking has rearranged certain assumptions I have always held dear. *If I am not the cause of my happiness or my discontent, if everything is arising out of certain conditions (like this earthquake) and passing away (hopefully like this earthquake), if I am not the one constantly craving or resisting, if there is actually no me inside wanting or resisting so fiercely, if I can really see the arising thoughts and emotions as not mine and impermanent, at least in this moment . . . might I not be better equipped, and wouldn't it be so much easier, to just pause for a moment or two and let them pass on by like this earthquake?* I stand still, waiting. Sure enough, the rattling stops. The wisdom does not.

My five siblings and I grew up as military brats, our father a pilot and squadron commander. He was often away. One summer day, probably in response to a houseful of bored kids, my mother announced an excursion. All she would tell us was that it included swimming and a picnic and it was somewhere we had never been. We were each to pack a duffle bag with swimsuit, change of clothes, towel, book, games. Wonderful aromas wafted out from behind the closed door to the kitchen. Gradually we became less lethargic, more engaged, then excited, pestering her for details. Mom was mum. "Don't forget sunscreen," she said.

The night before the excursion, she insisted our six duffles be at the front door and that we go to bed early, as it would be a long day. At dinner around our big round dining table we traded ideas as to where we could be going. The conversation was lively, filled with laughter and anticipation. My mother prepared a simple dinner, but we could see bags of wrapped goodies in the kitchen. She would only smile as we questioned her, and so we teased her all the more, delighting in the secrecy.

We awoke the next morning to pounding rain and dark skies. One by one we padded out in our pajamas and robes to find our mother calmly sipping coffee. Six glum kids collapsed onto the floor and couch, all our previous excitement now in puddles at our feet. She looked at us. "Why aren't you dressed?"

"But it's raining. We can't go swimming, we can't have a picnic now."

"Let's get going. We'll have breakfast on the way," she said, rising from the couch and clapping her hands. I remember to this day how happy my mother seemed, especially in contrast to our gloomy faces. So we did as we were told, dressing quickly and reassembling at the front door. But instead of heading out the front door, our mother wheeled around and called out over her shoulder, "Grab your duffle. Everyone ready?" Then she lead us down the stairs to the basement!

For a moment, in the basement, we all just stood there in silence. In front of the two small high windows my mother had hung a picture of a big sun in a brilliant blue sky and a beautifully beckoning seaside beach. Floor lamps made the place much brighter than it normally was. Several colorful picnic blankets lay on the hard linoleum floor, along with bunches of pillows and a few folding deck chairs. In the middle was a freshly baked coffee cake, our two plaid thermoses, and mugs. We turned to her.

"You can't stop the birds from flying over your head," she said smiling, "but you can stop them from nesting in your hair." My younger brother dropped his bag and started to walk onto the blanket. "Take off your shoes, first," my mother said. "You don't want to track sand onto the blanket." He looked at her, his eyes wide. He looked at the linoleum floor. We all started giggling, then laughing, pulling off our shoes and settling onto the blankets and pillows. We had hot chocolate and coffee cake, then lunch, then lemonade and cookies. We played games. We talked. We read. We were together all day, and I still consider that basement picnic the best picnic I have ever had.

I remember that day as I am reflecting on the instruction "You are cruising along, then suddenly you experience a glitch. What is the attitude in the mind that is causing suffering in this situation?" The attitude in the mind for all six of us was the aching disappointment of foiled expectations. And that attitude was certainly causing us suffering. Granted, we needed to be enrolled in a switch of attitude. We weren't going to be swimming in the ocean or working on a tan. But we could still have fun. And we did have fun. Great fun. We were able to let impermanent expectation and disappointment (unreliable phenomena) pass on. We overcame the glitch.

The novelty, the magic, the silliness, the closeness we experienced that day fondly lingers, transcending many other childhood picnics and days at the beach. Isn't that remarkable? It's the same as being stuck in traffic and suffering, while others around me were busy occupying themselves. Surely I wasn't the only one who felt frustration arising, but still—I had the choice to not allow the birds to make a nest in my hair. My attitude, not the situation, was the cause of my suffering. I can choose to have fun on a rainy day basement picnic or sitting in traffic.

At the end of the month I have a significant wisdom lesson in self-lessness. A dear friend, Gina Thompson, has been in the hospital for almost three months now, most of the time in critical care. She was beginning to improve. We were all encouraged. Then word of her relapse is followed, within hours, by word of her death. I am devastated. I realize how strongly I had bought into the good news and was already imagining her recovery. I am not prepared for her total departure. Everything else in my life fades out.

A small group of friends and family gather the next afternoon at her house. Gina lies on the couch. I say this sincerely: whether she is still lingering in her body, floating unseen above us, or nowhere near, we all feel she is here with us. Her husband sits at the end of the couch, periodically rubbing her feet. We speak to her. We speak with one another, softly, soothingly. We tell Gina stories. We hug. We cry. We laugh. We sit cross-legged on the floor, encircling the couch, and chant for her peaceful passing. At one point the cat jumps up and settles onto Gina's lap, purrs, then falls asleep there. We slowly climb the stairs, looking at the wall of photos of her life, her family, her many friends. We console her husband, John, and son, Chris. It is one of the sweetest, deepest, most heart-wrenching afternoons I have ever experienced. For days after, I continue to see her white, peaceful face floating before me. She was one of the most generous and kind people I have ever known. Many of us refer to her as an angel.

I experienced grief like a deep meditation. When I was at Gina's house I was simply and profoundly present, moment after moment. There are no well-established habits of thinking or being or doing to fall into when faced with death. This was something altogether precious, and we were all just simply there for Gina and her family. We had come to honor our dear friend and offer comfort where we could to family and friends. And we were also certainly witnessing impermanence up close and personal. Faced with or reminded of death, there is very little to arise that is more compelling. The shock of seeing her there, the community gathered around her, continually called me back from my own reflections, memories, and stories. I watched them rise. I let them drift by. Grief came and went, quite naturally, like waves, a soft quiet between each arising. I felt as I had with Julie, the woman I met and lunched with on the streets of San Francisco—like a wide-open conduit for compassion to be expressed and not much more. The present was startling, clear, and full. As enchanting and haunting as the memories were, I wanted even more to be right there, present for everything. Sitting with beloved Gina. Sitting with the people who love her.

One recognizes those who seem at peace with their mortality. You sense their commitment to life and feel the wisdom behind the choices they have made and are making. Joseph is one of those who sheds light on this path. There are many teachings on death on the Buddhist path. Joseph teaches us to hold the recognition of our own death lightly but with us, like a bird on our shoulder, a reminder of the preciousness of this human birth. Perhaps this is the most important wisdom piece: understanding our own mortality. Joseph also likes to say, "We're all in the queue."

One of my favorite takeaways from this month of working with wisdom is that when slammed with a challenge, I have taken to asking, "What is the gift here?" It is a reminder to myself to ease up on the aversion, to investigate not solely from a desire to have it resolved.

We are crafting a life with a growing comprehension that honors our own innate wisdom and commitment to living with integrity. May we all be as peaceful, kind, and at ease with our death as I understand Gina was right up to her last moments. May our slowly crafted lives of integrity allow us to release regrets, recognize our real needs, and embrace lives lived from the heart.

———

The more clearly we recognize the wisdom
mind, the easier it is to return to it.
—JOSEPH GOLDSTEIN

> Our awakening does not depend on clearing out
> all our past karma. It depends on the quality of our
> awareness, of balance and wisdom in the moment.
> —JOSEPH GOLDSTEIN

Check-In Conversation: The Causes of Suffering and Happiness

At the end of the month, as I begin my check-in with Joseph, I read from some of my notes. "I started by trying to pay attention more closely in common moments, pausing to ask, 'What do I understand about this situation? What do I know is true here? What do I see clearly in this situation?' And I was investigating different areas, like being stuck in traffic. I think you said, 'Let it come to you easily, not forced.' So I began calling this 'the wisdom of a happy life.' That's just a bit from my notes to get started. Is there anything you might want to add here?" I ask him.

"Yeah, I think I'd like to scrap all of that."

I whoop aloud. Then we are both laughing. "That's so funny," I tell him, "because while I was just talking I had this feeling that there was this heavy silence on your end of the line. So . . . you don't like these notes you gave me?"

Joseph laughs. "Well, I don't like the phrase 'the wisdom of a happy life.'" He is quiet for a few moments. "We need to understand that we are working to comprehend happiness in the context of freedom, not the more limited understanding of mundane happiness. The wisdom parami is not simply about ordinary happiness. It can include that, but it's more than that. In its fullest aspect it is really about the wisdom of how we free our minds from suffering, as you described while sitting in traffic. So again, as we do that, all different kinds of happiness come, including worldly happiness. But at the same time we don't want to limit ourselves by thinking that is all of what this is about. It is an important distinction."

"I think I understand. So the investigation has to be done, as with the other paramis, with the understanding that it's leading to the purification of our hearts, not merely the accumulation of wisdom?"

"Well," he pauses. "The phrase 'accumulating wisdom' is also a little funny."

"OK." I sigh. "How would you say that?"

"Wisdom is understanding on *all* levels, not simply the mundane level of worldly happiness, although it includes it. So then wisdom really means the investigating factor of the mind. We already talked about how wisdom is that force in the mind that illuminates how things are so that we see clearly. And so then it's a question of seeing clearly. What are the causes for different kinds of worldly happiness? What are the causes for the happiness of liberation? And it is helpful to have a theoretical understanding of it in the perspective of the Buddha's teachings, but then this practice with the parami is actually about seeing it at work in our lives. So for example, the causes of worldly happiness really rest on the understanding of the law of karma: that our actions have results. When we act with a wholesome motivation, happiness follows. And when we act with an impure motivation, suffering follows. So the practice is really to look at our lives in different situations. How do we feel when we're being generous? How do we feel when we're loving? How do we feel when we're jealous? How do we feel when we're stingy? So we really see for ourselves, not just theoretically, that our various actions, including our actions of mind, our states of mind, are resulting in happiness or suffering. And just as a way of making this investigation in our lives, sometimes it's easier to remember—in other words, it's easier to do it retroactively. If we're already suffering, then look back and ask, 'OK, what are the causes? Why is this suffering going on?'"

"Ah. Yes. I understand."

"And when we're happy, to also stop then and ask, 'OK, what are the causes of this happiness?' So we are actively investigating, we are not just being carried along by the conditioning."

"Yes, I see. That's really good. So then, that last question you gave in the instructions ties in here, to investigate 'What is my understanding of what is creating suffering for me in this situation right now?' That was a significantly useful question for me."

"Yes."

"Because sometimes it was clearly my *mis*-understanding," I laugh, "rather than what was actually happening, that was creating the suffering!"

"Exactly."

"That was so powerful to recognize and understand."

"So then again," Joseph adds, "we want to go beyond this being an abstract concept to really looking in our lives and exploring what these things mean in our direct experience. Impermanence is the easiest. But even though it is completely obvious and everywhere," he laughs, "at every moment . . ."

"And everyone agrees," I say.

"Yes. We rarely pay attention to it."

I sigh. "Oh, it is so true."

"We are just so caught up in the story of our lives that we're not directly perceiving the impermanence. And we can see it on every single level. It's not that it's hard to see. It's just remembering to look," Joseph says, chuckling. "And when we're happy, then to also stop and ask, 'OK, what are the causes of this happiness?' So we are actively investigating, we are not just being carried along by the conditioning. We flee from suffering and love its causes."

"Yes! And I know it. I know it even as I'm also getting swept up in it! I understand how fleeting the joy from acting on every desire can be. I can watch it rise and pass away and still can choose not to pay attention to the wisdom also present there. And then other times I felt I sorted out the different motivations arising and I had a choice. I was making a genuine choice."

"Yes. Exactly. And I think that the more we actively and directly see impermanence and reflect on impermanence, the more it becomes a habit of wisdom rather than a habit of delusion. So that is important to remember, something to look for and apply. As I said, it's on all levels. The momentariness of the sense impressions, of a desire, of a thought, of an emotion, as you discovered, in the different activities we're doing in the day—of everything," he laughs. "Everything is changing."

"Yes, and that's what I was seeing looking at all the different habits of thinking that were coming up. I was really noticing the impermanence of all of them. They arise and they do pass away. It is more difficult, often, to remember a desire is impermanent when it is arising. But then that insight, that moment of wisdom, would arise, and with it the freedom of seeing I had a choice. Each and every time I think whatever is up won't go away, I just watch as it does. Now that feels like wisdom!"

Joseph laughs. "Right."

"And so then what I noticed," I continue, "was that I was never asking or investigating when I was happy." I am embarrassed to acknowledge this. "You know?"

"Oh, yes."

"I am always investigating when there is suffering. And then, in trying to go deeper with that insight, I realize . . ." I am laughing from embarrassment. "I see clearly that I don't want to mess it up! I don't want to investigate happiness and cause it to go away! I see I have a little attachment to the idea that I had done it. And I don't want to be the reason it goes away."

Joseph is chuckling, "That is a really important piece to see."

"Yeah. It's quite amazing, actually. I just thought, of course it would make sense that I should investigate what isn't working. But when I go deeper, as you suggested, I could clearly feel the fear that is there of messing up the good times. And this is combined with the idea that good times are 'right' and unpleasant times 'wrong.' Not to mention totally ignoring the wisdom of understanding impermanence. All those things, so very interesting—and disillusioning—to see."

"Yes."

"OK. So a question about planning," I say to Joseph, cringing to hear my frustration, as if speaking through clenched teeth. "I was at work and watching planning thoughts continually arising because I had an opportunity to take the afternoon off. I had decided I wouldn't make a plan for the afternoon because by the time it arrived, I would probably decide to do something else anyway. *A hike might be nice.* We're working now. *Maybe I should call someone now.* Concentrate. *What are we going to do?* And I felt that it wasn't skillful because it was disrupting my concentration. Then I thought, *Well, it's also not bad. Can I just be with what is, with what is arising?* Planning thoughts. Working. Planning thoughts. Working. But soon I was planning how to stop planning! You know what I mean?"

Joseph laughs. "Well, I think you can simplify it by having within the recognition that it's arising—with planning or with anything else that feels inappropriate at the moment—just that simple reminder, 'Not now.'"

"Oh." I am quiet. "See now, why do I keep forgetting that? You've told me this before!"

Joseph is chuckling. "Because otherwise you get into a kind of aversive reaction."

"Yes, exactly!"

"Just a gentle reminder. The wisdom of seeing that it is not helpful now. Not that planning is bad; it's just not helpful now."

"And that's really helpful now," I say laughing. "I get it. You're not ignoring, swatting at, or resisting it. Plus, it just seems so much . . . easier."

"Yes. It is easier."

Later that day, after our talk, I think of another example of where this tendency may not be serving us: in meditation. Sometimes we may find ourselves trying to get somewhere (more peaceful) than where we are or attempting to fix some "unacceptable" mind state, even when we know better. Instead, we can continue to work on remembering that all we need to do when we meditate is simply pay attention. We are becoming familiar with how the mind is right this moment. We are becoming familiar with continuing to bring the mind back to just this present moment right now. Joseph's simple "Not now" could be very helpful here.

"So, this wisdom piece is really significant," I say to Joseph. "Especially being attentive for those moments of selfing and then asking what's driving it."

"Yes. We're really asking the question 'What am I identified with here?'"

"Exactly. And also, something you said that I found really helpful was that sometimes it is easier to catch that by listening to your speech. Like 'I am tired,' or whatever. Now I notice Ron with this habit, which I used to have. I would come home from work, and the first thing I would say when I'd come in the door, and that he now says, is 'I'm so tired.' But I remember myself doing it. Unfortunately, he probably picked it up from me, and so quickly!"

"Yes. This is really, in terms of elaborating that a little bit, a further understanding of wrong view of self. I read this in a book by Ledi Sayadaw, the great Burmese master. He went down a long list just like that: I'm angry. I'm tired. I'm sad. I'm happy. I'm this. I'm that. But after each one he said, 'I'm angry is wrong view about anger. I'm happy is wrong view about happiness. I'm sad is wrong view about sadness.' He was saying that it's the wrong view of taking it to be one's self. And he addresses just that whole list of emotions, which we all have. To watch during the day, as you described, not only in our speech but also in our internal state, whatever we are feeling. *I feel* this way or *I feel* that way. To realize it's wrong view about that particular emotion. It's wrong view in the sense that it's being taken as self rather than simply being what it is."

"And also believing that it's solid. Not remembering that it's not me and it's not permanent."

"Yes."

"Both of those I see now," I tell him, "but obviously not all the time. It's often quite humorous to me. I'll wake up, and within five minutes I'll have a decision about how the day is! Like a weather report printed in the newspaper the night before," I am laughing. "The forecast is that I am happy today or I am blue today. And then, no matter what happens, I continue to classify the entire day in terms of that original moment upon awakening. That is just amazing to me."

"Right."

"And so I'm also not the one that's craving. There's no I craving. It's just the *habit* of craving, arising in response to seeing something beautiful. It's just a *moment* of craving. And then it passes. Not mine. Not a forecast for an entire day. That is pretty freeing . . . when I can remember, of course!"

"Yes," Joseph says, laughing. "Oh, exactly. Just looking at these things and remembering—and doing it again and again so it becomes more habituated. To see it through the eyes of wisdom."

"So then, another aspect of what you're saying, but in a little different way: you talked about how planning can be a kind of extension of self into the future."

"It can be."

"And I thought that could be interesting to investigate, like when one is on a silent retreat and daydreams wonderful visions of how one will be different in the future." I laugh.

"Yes, now that is really an aspect of the defilement of conceit. In the Buddhist sense, it is the 'I am-ness.' The Buddha talked about it as 'I am, I was, I will be.' Any of those, he said, if the emphasis is on 'I' as in 'I will be doing that, or I was doing that,' is just reinforcing that sense of 'I am.' It doesn't mean that in a conventional way planning, for example, should never be done, because sometimes it's necessary. But we want to see it for what it is, not get lost in a kind of future clone."

I laugh. "Oh, yes. A future clone! I love that. Sometimes it is just that obvious. Certainly on retreat it seems obvious. But I do struggle with that one. Planning for a rosier future in intricate and glowing detail. My future clone saying and doing all the right things. Everyone behaving themselves." I sigh. "Such a pleasant fantasy . . ."

"So I have also been working with noticing the difference in the quality of mind when I am just paying attention to whatever is arising and when I am lost in the content. You mentioned in your instructions the example of watching a hummingbird. I've been trying to pay attention like that. Can you say something more about this?"

"Yes. One example that is very common and happens all the time is just in going for a walk. Notice the difference between when it's just walking and being aware of different sense doors, and when we're lost in some mental story. Really pay attention to that, don't just acknowledge that it happens. Really experience what it's like when we're present for the sights or sounds or feeling of the air on the body, and then when we get lost in a plan or reaction or some story. In those times we're really no longer aware of the present moment's experience. We are lost in a mental creation. Then we come out of it. Watch closely for what it's like in that moment of coming out. Notice what the difference is between having been lost and being awake again. And it happens, you know, a thousand times. Just in a walk!" He is laughing.

"Yeah. I experience that a lot when I'm running."

"Oh, all the time."

"That moment can feel like coming out of a tunnel. You're driving through a tunnel and all of a sudden, 'Look, there's the sky again!'"

"Yes, exactly. And it's a practice to pay attention to that moment of coming out. And this is important, because in that moment—when we just come out of it—we can see clearly what it was like having been lost."

"Like when you wake up from a dream."

"Exactly."

"And you can remember it for just those few seconds."

"Yes."

"Oh, I see now I had forgotten that part. That is helpful. Thank you, Joseph."

Yesterday I was clever, so I wanted to change the world.
Today I am wise, so I am changing myself.
—Rumi

5 Courage

Courage is not about changing anything or grasping for
some better state.
It's the valor of truly being present.
—Joseph Goldstein

The Fifth Parami: Courage

The Pali word *viriya*, which we translate as *courage*,
is used to designate the fifth parami in the Buddhist
texts. It means exertion in mental development,
energy, strength, vigor, perseverance, vitality. More
commonly, we recognize courage as an attitude of
facing what is dangerous, difficult, or painful with
valor, the courage to do what one thinks is right.

Instructions: Warrior Work

"So, Joseph, a quick question before we begin this month. *Viriya*. I don't know why, but I just love that word. I see it often translated as 'energy' but that word is just too vague and wimpy, uninspiring. I have also seen 'courage.' Is that also a good translation?"

"Well, the Pali word *viriya*, pronounced *veer-ee-ya*, is most often translated as 'energy,' but it can also be defined as perseverance, strength, courage, vigor, and vitality. The opposite of viriya is what Buddhists call 'sloth and torpor,' the mind that retreats from difficulties. So viriya has many connotations, and I would just include them all."

"I did write down several, but as I go through the month and use a word, I would use . . . ?"

"Well, you could select and use different words, depending on the context."

"Oh! It's not either/or! There it is again. Gosh darn it," I say, laughing. "Maybe by the end of this whole study I will finally remember that. It doesn't have to be either/or. If I just learn that one thing, it would be profound for me! That's a very good idea, calling up different aspects of that viriya energy as needed."

"And right here," Joseph speaks slowly, chuckling, "is an example of wisdom."

"No, it's not wisdom. It's the other. The evil twin."

"No. It's the *investigation* of the limitation of thinking either/or, forgetting that often we don't have to be limited by that. It can be both."

I take a big, audible breath and then release it. "I understand. In fact it's mostly both, if I take the time to really investigate more deeply."

Really, I'm thinking, *How long is it going to take for me to master not categorizing everything as "either/or," as either one option or point of view versus another opposing one?* Actually, there are numerous influences at play in every moment. Recognizing, understanding, and investigating the complexity as opposed to quickly categorizing a thought, feeling, or observation as either this or that, useful or misguided, is a significantly different response. And just remembering that our target here is recognition, then clear seeing, then an open-minded investigation that can lead to enhanced wisdom. Intentions and reactions are mixed and often hidden, in need of a deeper investigation, unlayering. There may be a prominent first response, but there may also be several underlying motives or responses that need a gentle hand, an open mind, to be recognized. Approaching the investigation with a curt dismissal—if it is not skillful behavior or thinking, then it must be unskillful—is so limiting. How much richer to dig a bit deeper. Perhaps there is a misconception or an old, outdated habit fueling the initial response that, with just a few moments of waiting to see what else pops up, could open entirely new understandings. The image I begin using this month, as a reminder, is that of a ninja warrior, creeping into and around with stealth and sterling purpose. This feels groundbreaking, enticing, and fun. I also make a silent promise to myself to focus on this new "What else might also be happening here?" response so that Joseph will never have to remind me of this ever again! And so this is my first successful challenge working with viriya: uncovering and banishing the old habit of either/or thinking. The aspect of viriya being utilized here: perseverance.

Joseph says that the Buddha talked about the four great instructions, which call for viriya:

1. Avoiding or preventing the arising of unwholesome states.
2. Letting go of unwholesome states that have already arisen.
3. Cultivating wholesome states that have already arisen.
4. Giving energy to arouse wholesome states that have not yet arisen.

Joseph's Instructions: Working with Courage

Viriya is *the willingness to stay with what is.* When we use it, wisdom grows. The more we use it, the stronger it becomes. As we use it, we are developing strength of mind. It is a powerful force that also needs a gentle touch. When we are strong in this way, we are *living* the practice instead of *doing* it. As with the previous paramis, challenge yourself to play outside your comfort zone.

1. We begin by exploring distractions:

   • Investigate all the different times in the day and the different ways you do something that distracts the mind.
   • You might try making a list of these distractions. Look to see if there are habits at work just beneath the surface.

- What is it you are wanting to distract yourself from? Investigate to see how the distraction might be a retreat from boredom or unpleasant body sensations, restlessness, or fear.

2. Viriya is *meeting* the difficulty. Viriya *seeks out* difficult situations. It is *energized* by challenges. It is *inspired* by difficulties and *faces them* with courage. Now we investigate further:

   - Begin noticing when in life you tend to retreat from difficulties.
   - What would it look like to meet a common moment of suffering with viriya?
   - Challenge yourself to play outside your comfort zone.
   - Pay particular attention to the quality of your effort. Again, this is a powerful force that also needs a gentle touch.

3. Finally, go deeper. When resistance arises as you work with viriya, use the moment as an opportunity to more deeply investigate the nature and power of the resistance.

   - When do you keep at it?
   - Why do you keep pushing?
   - When is there a moment of release, and why?
   - What happens next?

Joseph's instructions seem poignantly applicable to the current world situation—for example, the ever-changing landscape of world politics. Will there be enough viriya to overcome the obstacles? Is it mere naivety to hope for things to be otherwise and not wallow in despair or anger or apathy? Something more, someone new—how to know, to discern? A shining moment that becomes a turning point—or not? So much viriya needed. I think of Nelson Mandela in prison for so much of his life. How many times did he re-choose and renew that courage? The battleground lies within. Sometimes the viriya needed is more than we think we have. This month, perhaps, we will discover we are capable of much more, which is also viriya. And we have only just begun. We all are more capable, and we know it. Will we be wise and courageous when called upon? Unknown. Can we sow the proper seeds? We already have.

———

In these challenging times, may we all have the courage
to pursue the way of life we value in our hearts.
—ALAIN DE BOTTON

We each need to find what is onward-leading, rather
than what is simply habitual or agreeable.
—JOSEPH GOLDSTEIN

Working with Courage: Exploring Our Distractions

I am thinking the viriya instructions, with all their action-packed
words—perseverance, strength, courage, vigor, and vitality—sound
invigorating. A rally call to action. Time to ramp up. Ron and I call a
difficult endeavor that is worth the effort "warrior work." Attending a
ten-day silent meditation retreat, we agree, is warrior work. Continuing
daily to investigate and commit to living with more integrity is clearly
warrior work. To do this takes courage, perseverance, vigor. After focusing on what I know, and don't know, while working with the wisdom
parami, I am now enrolled in learning how to generate the wholesome
energy needed to support all the wisdom insights. I am especially fond
of the word "courage." I like thinking of myself as courageous.

So I begin with a list, as suggested, of all the ways I distract myself.
While at work: rising to get a snack, continually checking email, taking
a call, wandering the office and chatting with other agents and staff.
I am chagrined to discover I engage in similar behavior when working from home, which I always thought was a more productive setting.
Daydreaming and planning are also familiar distractions to the task at
hand. No surprise there. Gazing out the window. If I stop for a moment
to think, my eyes automatically shift from the desk to the distraction of
view. Strong habit.

As I drive home I am mentally reviewing a transaction I struggled
with today that involved an agent notoriously difficult to work with.
I stop to pick up something for dinner, and there in the nearby window of our local optician shop is the perfect pair of sunglasses. I am
still honoring my commitment of not purchasing anything other than
replacements and I am already in the store, trying on the sunglasses. My
current old ones are, well, old. Is this replenishment? I leave the store
without the new glasses, but as I do, a flood of emotion washes over me

regarding the unsatisfactory communication with the agent. I suddenly understand how that desire for new sunglasses arose as a distraction, first masking and then at least attempting to placate my previous discomfort. Buying things: clearly another distraction habit.

This insight sheds more light on the instruction to investigate what I am trying to distract myself from, which in this case were unpleasant thoughts and feelings. Aha. Vigor is called for here. I do not want to ignore or push away every nastiness that arises. I also do not want to obsess about it because that would be like falling into the tar pit, sucked down and stuck there. I don't want to deny turbulent emotions are having an impact. But I want to see them clearly as just a natural response to what occurred, a response that is light enough to float into and then out of the mind naturally, if I don't grasp and invite it to stay. Instead of the distraction of buying a new pair of sunglasses, or getting enticed by the story I create around the incident, or rehearsing endless dialogue responses, what other choices might I have here?

I could focus on the quality of a response. Although I felt dishonored by this individual, I am clear I do not wish to respond in kind. And poof! That's it. The entire interaction, rehearsing for a second round, and even the urge to respond at all to the unkindness immediately dissipates, as does the urge to placate the discomfort with the distraction of buying or eating my way back to ease. Where and why the communication with this person went awry isn't the issue. I suddenly understand I did not cause or fuel this agent's anger. And although it took a while, and there are some lingering "this is unfair" thoughts, suddenly I can see an entirely new and different path. I can just walk away. And I did. And it worked. It was a tremendously freeing observation.

I am beginning to understand why viriya follows wisdom. Otherwise we might be out fighting windmills, battling the wrong adversary in our eagerness. Instead we should brandish our sword of wisdom with courage and stab holes in the real opponent, which is the habit of luring ourselves away from anything unpleasant with an enticing, soothing, pleasurable distraction.

Shortly before Joseph and I began this parami work together, he recommended me as a candidate for a prestigious scientific study entitled the "Well-Being Study," conducted by Richard J. Davidson, Antoine Lutz, and Giulio Tononi at the University of Wisconsin–Madison. The purpose of the study was "to examine the effect of long-term meditation practice on basic emotion and attention functions, sleep patterns, pain regulation, and social stress." They were seeking thirty individuals experienced in vipassana meditation, from around the country, for a study that would span eighteen months. In addition to being seasoned meditators (at least one of the participants was a well-known Tibetan monk), we also had to be willing and able to participate in a series of tests that included pain, socially stressful situations, and sleeping while wired up and observed in a lab. In fact we had to meet a very long list of criteria, including "not uncomfortable with small spaces."

Now, in the middle of this viriya month, I am lying very, very still inside a whirring, clanging fMRI (functional magnetic resonance imaging) machine. The irony of the timing does not go unnoticed.

I am packed in as tight as a sardine, arms pinned between my torso and the sides of the metal tunnel, pillows wedged tightly alongside my neck, holding my head rigid. I am swathed in blankets because inside the machine it is remarkably cold. I feel like a tube of dough, wrapped tightly then placed in the freezer. I have goggles on and am looking at horrific images while pain is being administered to my arm via a heat cuff or jolts of electricity through wires taped to my finger. I am continually being asked to rate how I feel about all this, responding with a light tap of a finger on a button taped to it. I am warned in advance when pain is coming, with plenty of time to contemplate its impact, my thoughts and emotions registering on a brain scan. Meanwhile the machine vibrates and groans and thumps, piercing through my earplugs like thunderbolts.

As I lay there, for almost two hours, I am fiercely calling on any and every morsel of viriya I can muster. This is ultimate warrior work. And I am *fierce* in this cold metal tube of pain. It takes tremendous strength to continually and repeatedly relax every muscle in my body as it screams for attention, for permission to wiggle. Vigor keeps me ultra-focused on the task at hand. There is no allowing the mind to wander, no daydreaming in this freezer. Vitality keeps me alert as I encourage myself to just keep coming back to this moment now, just this moment now. I will not allow any distractions or discomfort to cloud my efforts. Perseverance is called up in the last half hour as I suddenly and desperately need a bathroom break. But to ask to be taken out of the machine means canceling the entire session, and I am unwilling to let the team down. They hover just outside the machine, speaking words of encouragement to me between tests via an intercom. We have come too far for me to give up now. Throughout all the days and nights of testing for the study, courage was there, continually arousing the original purity of my intent to make a difference in people's lives. Viriya: vigor, vitality, perseverance, courage. I was committed to helping prove the value of meditation, something I had found so profoundly useful. And my efforts were stellar. I surpassed my own expectations. Viriya seeds had been sown and were already sprouted. I could do this thing, and I did.

As I consider the instruction on the four great teachings, I realize how much I was using this teaching in that freezing chamber of horrors. As I toiled to remain balanced and present, moment by moment, I was using one of the four efforts. I was keenly watching for a stray emotion or thought to cause a fidget or fuss—or worse, to cause me to give up. If an unsavory thought, body sensation, or feeling did get through the first line of defense, I focused all my energy on letting it go, escorting that unwholesome state back out of the tunnel. When the mind was calm and the body relaxed, I took strength from those wholesome moments and asked for that clarity of mind to continue, smooth and at ease. And especially in the most difficult moments, I remembered those wholesome moments of ease and endeavored to cultivate more of them. Now, as I recall those days, the lessons seem particularly well suited to unlocking and understanding more deeply this month's viriya. I have only to imagine myself back in that dark inhospitable machine to understand and recreate the wholesome efforts, the skills and wisdom I utilized to ultimately succeed.

The work with viriya continues back home. I reread the instructions. How, when, where else do I keep at it, do I keep pushing? I often tend to keep at something and push long past usefulness and certainly past enjoyment. When I do this, the quality of mind quickly becomes weary, with flashes of self-pity. A good example is when I am gardening. I begin with enthusiasm for the gloriousness of the day, the fragrance of fresh dirt, the sun warming my shoulders, the exercise. But if I don't continue checking in, paying attention to my attitude, I can easily breeze through grace and gratitude and wake up sometime later to find myself raking up a seriously bad attitude.

And so on Saturday, viriya, wisdom, and I go out into the garden to rake and clean up rubble after two back-to-back big storms. Although much more pleasant than an fMRI machine, still I keep checking in to prevent the arising of unwholesome states, which in this case would be pushing to complete the task and toppling into an unpleasant "woe-is-me" demeanor. When I feel the first indications of weariness, right then I decide it is enough. I am not finished, but I *know* it's time. And by doing so, I very efficiently and effectively stop the arising of the more habituated, but unwholesome, state of crankiness. I put away the gardening tools, gaze on my hard work with pleasure. Then, energized—not deflated, weary, and cranky—I go into the kitchen to prepare dinner. This switch in thinking, placing the importance on attitude and not completion, rattles me to the core. It is a fist from my childhood that still clings tightly to the old behavior. There were rewards, then, for a kid who raked the entire yard. But to walk into the kitchen now and season dinner preparations with a lousy attitude would be neither skillful nor nutritious. I am rooting up and tossing rotten beliefs I have stubbornly believed since childhood, and it feels swell.

———

At the end of the month, the Buddhist teacher John Travis joined Joseph, Ron, and I on our annual ski-week vacation. John, who attended boarding school in Switzerland, lives in the mountains. This is how we ski together: Joseph, Ron, and I begin our descent. At some point a flash of red whizzes past us through the trees alongside the ski run. That is John skiing with us. He is an amazingly gifted skier. We stop to watch, as do others on the slope. John is that good.

John is also very humble, waving off our praise and astonishment. But if we persist in asking, he will offer a suggestion on our ski technique. It is often just what is needed to ratchet our skill up a notch. On this day we have just finished lunch together at the top of the hill at Lake Tahoe's Northstar Resort and are outside buckling boots, getting into our skis and goggles and gloves. John stands patiently waiting. When we are ready, he suggests we try an advanced slope on a part of the mountain we have never skied. He tells us the snow and light now will be just right on this particular run. He assures us we can do it. Ron, the better skier, agrees immediately. Joseph also agrees. I am startled by this sudden change in our routine. We have not skied an expert run like this before. Seeing Joseph's instant willingness to extend himself beyond his comfort zone surprises me. He must feel some of the same trepidation I do. So I sign on too.

The three of us start slowly down the advanced run, the steepest part of which is at the top. John stays close by, offering tips and encouragement as we work our way down, stopping often. The sun *is* just right. No icy shaded patches. The slope is steep, but also wide and without bumps. The last half of the run is easier, the views from this side of the mountain, through heavily forested valleys, magnificent. We are enchanted, boisterous, thrilled to have skied well down the challenging slope. At the bottom, quickly, we decide to ski it again. The second run is easier, more graceful. It becomes a run we look forward to each day after lunch. And because we have successfully skied an expert run, we stretch and try a few more black diamond runs before the end of the week, even after John has left. This is viriya.

We generate energy whereby wholesome states arise naturally in the mind each time we sit down to meditate. This applies not just during the time of meditation but continues with us through the day, aiding our ability to stay mindful of the attitude in our minds. Of course all this investigating and trying out new habits definitely gives rise to more wholesome states. And they are, simply, more pleasant. Why wouldn't we want to pursue the effort? Why wouldn't we want more? This is wholesome desire. We already know we are good at fulfilling desires. Now, when we feel resistance arise and release it by not frosting it with a story or emotions, a rush of energy blows through our thinking like a clean wind. Joseph described how he celebrated those moments of winning. There *is* more freedom available, more choices that expand and nurture.

We are halfway through this work with the paramis, and with all modesty, I sincerely feel I am operating differently. I am more focused. I am especially keen on catching habits as they arise and investigating them for usefulness or not. I am more generous. I am living much more simply and with fierce integrity. I am committed to non-harming. I am wiser than when I began. And now I have a nifty new tool for working with that wisdom: viriya.

———

This willingness to stay with it is what
makes everything possible.
—JOSEPH GOLDSTEIN

We each need great honesty of introspection
and wise guidance from teachers.
—JOSEPH GOLDSTEIN

Check-In Conversation: The Valor of Truly Being Present

"OK," I say, shuffling through my notes as I begin my report to Joseph. We are sitting in two matching leather club chairs in the mountain cabin. John Travis has left, and Ron is sitting with us, quietly. After three rigorous days of skiing, we decide to ski just a half day today. It is late morning and we are still lazily lounging. This seemed like a perfect time for a check-in, coffee mugs in hand.

I read aloud from my notes: "So Joseph, you said, 'Viriya is challenging ourselves to play outside our comfort zone.' I found it was great to have this piece to work with right after wisdom. The insights I had working with wisdom gave me some rich material to go deeper with on a couple more subtle habits I hadn't really noticed before. I began with a list, of course, of my distractions." I chuckle. "And the first insight I had was noticing that I fall captive to the same distractions working from home that I do working in the office. I still get up from the desk, go to the kitchen, forage for a snack, look at emails, answer the phone, look out the window, chat with somebody. Just seeing all those ways I distract myself from doing whatever it is I've decided I want or need to do was a revelation. Even when I'm doing something that I actually love doing, like when I am writing at home, those same urges of distraction—old, old habits—still arise. That is amazing to see, because I love writing, and yet the habit of distracting myself continually arises." I groan. "But then, because I am intent on catching them arise, I am able to re-choose more quickly, before the whole notion gets out of hand. Sometimes I even remember to use your reminder, 'Not now,' as in, 'I really am enjoying writing right now, but thank you for checking in.'" I laugh. "And so then I summon up more energy and refocus again. Most important, after a while I feel the distraction prompts become less interesting, less enticing, and then, of course, they happen less often."

"Exactly," Joseph says, chuckling.

I read aloud from my notes: "'Viriya brings the fulfillment of all of our aspirations. It is the willingness to stay with what is that makes everything possible. When we use it, wisdom grows. The more we use it, the stronger it becomes. And as we use it, we're developing strength of mind.' I just love all that. It's so inspiring. So a question: you said, 'It's a powerful force that also needs a gentle touch.'"

"Yes. The Buddha used the example of tuning the strings of a lute. You know, they can be tuned too tight when we are using too much energy or effort. Or if you're using the word 'courage,' it could be reckless courage." I laugh at this. I know this place well. "Or our tuning of our lute strings could be too slack. So that's why we really have to be aware of the *quality* of the energy. Is it too much? Is it too little?"

"Tuning the strings is a great image. It's so obvious, because when they're too tight they do sound bad."

"Right. And when they're too loose . . ."

". . . they don't produce any music. Yes, that's a great reminder."

I must remember to keep a gentle touch. Tune my strings just right. Not too tight; not too loose. What might this mean? I can be so disciplined, too focused on perfection. Rigid scheduling both at work and on days off. Tuning the lute, for me, probably mostly involves lightening up. I am definitely someone who could benefit from loosening the strings of my lute.

"So there are aspects of working with viriya that certainly got me motivated," I tell Joseph. "You said viriya seeks out difficult situations, is energized by challenges, inspired by difficulties. And I know people in business who are like that. They'll say, 'Let me help. I'm happy to talk to that difficult client.' And they *are* happy to do it. They genuinely thrive on challenging communications and solving difficult situations. I am definitely not like that. But I am a risk taker. I do enjoy stretching myself. Learning new things energizes me, like skiing that new advanced run with John. That was exhilarating." We are all nodding heads and smiling, remembering. "Or like all the new real estate tech stuff. For someone who didn't grow up with tech, my first response can be resistance. There are *always* new systems for me to learn. So it's another great arena for working with a more welcoming response instead of hesitating and backing away from the new challenges. And when I can approach it from that place, I have seen how facing a difficulty head-on and persisting until I've got it can be inspiring. It's surprising, and true. That definitely feels like viriya at work.

"And avoiding unpleasant communications is still an area where I tend to retreat from difficulty. I think this is somewhat universal, and not altogether unskillful." I laugh. "I can watch a thought arise, like a criticism, or wanting agreement on something, and then often just let it go, without acting on it. That seems skillful. But I also see that sometimes there are conversations that probably should happen. I can think of examples with co-workers, and sometimes with friends. When I do initiate this type of conversation, often it can be productive and stimulating for the relationship. But most often, I tend to avoid difficult communications. Sometimes I retreat from the difficulty because I've decided it is not worth the struggle with this person whom I will probably never work with again. Or maybe it's an old friend who I don't think will change anyway—you know, our lives have moved in different directions over the years. Do you know what I'm trying to say here? Because I'm not sure I do. There's something I'm missing here."

Joseph is quiet for a while. "I think a part of this is the connection between the wisdom parami and viriya. It's the whole notion of clear comprehension, which is really an aspect of mindfulness. For example, if you are retreating from a difficulty and you see it, it doesn't necessarily mean that's exactly the right moment to move forward. You have to notice that thought, *Oh, I'm avoiding this*. And then there has to be a kind of wisdom or clear seeing that asks, 'What is the right way to do this? What is the right time to do this?' It's more nuanced than just retreating. There has to be an assessment, a clarity of purpose and of timing. In the example you gave, maybe the retreating is a sign that, as you say, paths are diverging. There's no need to hold on to that relationship. Or it could not be. It could be avoiding, where you really do want to keep a connection, and you are just avoiding a difficult conversation. So all of that has to be understood. There is an application here of mindfulness and wisdom in the effort."

"'Clear comprehension. More nuanced than just retreating.' Oh, that's good. I can feel the discernment in that, the wisdom in it even as you say it. Also the taking time with it, considering—I really like that."

"Yes. And remembering to ask, 'What's the right time? What's the right way?' Sylvia [Boorstein] has a great line. You know, when people come up to you and say, 'I have to tell you how I feel!' And she will say, 'No you don't.'" We both laugh.

"That's great. Sylvia has such an easy way of helping us to laugh at ourselves." I am quiet for a few moments. "OK, so you and I share the same battlefield of wanting mind. And we have spoken about it already several times. What are some other battlefields that are as mined, say, as this one? Anger maybe? Regret? You see a lot of people. What are some other areas that can tend to trip us all up?"

"Self-judgment. Guilt. Worry," Joseph says.

"Oh, not to say that I don't have those too!" We both laugh.

"All of it," he says, chuckling. "You can think of any unwholesome pattern of mind that has become habituated, giving rise to resistance or pushing. It takes effort to work with it. It is difficult because now it's a familiar, well-established habit. Just like with the habit of buying things, it could be the habit of self-judgment or judging others."

"How would you work with something like that?"

"Well, there you would have to be very mindful of its arising. You need to watch for and learn about the tapes that are playing in the mind. This really takes us back to the effort of being mindful."

"So with desire, for example, and investigating it while working with viriya, are you saying it's about addressing that first thought that comes up?"

"Yes. Exactly."

"And it would be the same with, say, self-judging?"

"Right," he replies. "You want to consider whether it's an action of body, speech, or mind. There are so many different kinds of actions. You determine what arena they are playing themselves out in. Then you apply viriya to that arena."

"In a way it seems easier to do, or at least see, when working with renunciation, right? Because when you don't spend money, you have a little win. You didn't cave in to the desire and spend the money. But you still have those wanting thoughts arising. You're saying *that* is really the battlefield? So then with self-judgment . . ."

"It is about whether you get lost in those thoughts of self-judgment or whether you are able to see them at play, as they are arising."

"Ah, and then whether you believe them."

"Yes. One's speech is a very fertile area to work with. There's a lot to observe with our speech, as you discovered. Do we say this or not? Are we gossiping? It's everything! Every pattern of our lives should be investigated in light of 'Is this wholesome or unwholesome?' Then we can apply the appropriate viriya to either abandon or develop what we see."

"Abandon or develop. Wow. So simple and yet so powerful. That clear understanding definitely feels like viriya." I ponder this for a long time after we speak that day.

"And I loved the four great instructions," I tell Joseph. "I remember hearing this teaching."

"Yes. This is the application of energy, or viriya, in all of these different areas. In some ways it is the framework for everything we've been talking about from the beginning."

"Yes. My mind is spinning out on that. It really is a good way to understand the work we've been doing on each one of the paramis. When you talk about the quality of one's effort, investigating whatever arises within this framework is really helpful. Plus it reminds me we are doing all this for the purpose of liberation for ourselves and for others. It's not just about catching the unskillful habits that arise, but also about cultivating wholesome ones."

"Right. This is a classical teaching."

Perhaps viriya, and this teaching on the four types of effort, really belongs at the beginning of this work. And yet, without wisdom, a generous nature, virtuous intent, and a vow of renunciation, the effort could be off balance, ill conceived. I had to remind myself often this month of Joseph's warning, "This is a powerful force that also needs a gentle touch."

Skiing down the expert slope with John Travis that first time took viriya. To do so also included letting go of too much effort, staying loose, embracing the challenge, continuously checking in, everything we have been working with this month. But that slope can appear steep from the top. Very steep. We have to ski it *with* our fears and doubts, not pushing them away, ignoring, or resisting them. We summon courage and we go for it, with the fears like little weights on a weight belt. Yes, in this case, it would be better without those little fears accompanying us. But there they are, tucked into their little habit pockets. Weighing us down but not stopping us. Do we welcome the old habits still hanging on? Maybe we are not there yet. Would we like to just toss them away all at once? Of course. But we still ski the advance run! And in the rush of adrenaline as we work our way down the hill, through a new challenge, most times we don't even notice the added weight of our resistance or hesitations. We are exhilarated. What if we had believed those fears? What if we had not taken the challenge and joined others in the adventure? What if we continue lagging behind our actual abilities?

I don't want to lag behind life, I decide. I want to consistently keep re-choosing. I want to discard outdated habits. Most times I can't change the conditions—a forbidding slope, ants in the kitchen, associates who don't act as I think they should. But I can change my response, up the viriya, fine-tune the quality of my effort. Skiing down an expert run is grand. Really grand.

"This was great, Joseph! We're halfway through the ten components of integrity already. I have plenty of material for working with this parami and the others. *And* I'm having such a good time with it all! Already I feel I have the tools I need to fend off the restlessness and dissatisfaction that began this work. Thank you, Joseph."

"You're welcome," he says, smiling and stretching his long legs out in front of him.

And now comes patience, the sixth parami, I am thinking as we rise and prepare to hit the ski slopes. Not my strong suit. Just as I see how viriya supports an intention of generosity, virtue, and renunciation, I intuit how patience could be still another crucial ingredient in this soup we are brewing. But reminding myself to be more patient has not been very successful over the years. Certainly telling others to be patient doesn't work very often. I am curious to see how Joseph will clear up any misconceptions I might hold about patience *and* enroll me in strengthening it. Perhaps the first step will be getting me to agree that patience is a virtue.

———

It is sometimes difficult to see and understand
that changing conditions are not mistakes. They
feel that way because we sometimes think that if
we were only smart enough or careful enough, we
could avoid all unpleasantness—that we wouldn't
fall ill or have misfortune. In fact, we usually haven't
done anything wrong, it's just what happens.
—JOSEPH GOLDSTEIN, *ONE DHARMA*

6 Patience

Patience is the ability to be with things as they are.
—JOSEPH GOLDSTEIN

The Sixth Parami: Patience

The Pali word *khanti*, which we translate as *patience*,
is used to designate the sixth parami in Buddhist
texts. It means forbearance, the ability to wait or
endure without complaint, as well as steadiness
and perseverance in performing a task.

Instructions: Short Moments, Many Times

Joseph and I are cruising the racks of a local department store looking
for a men's summer sports coat that can pack easily and also look ele-
gant for al fresco dinners. Joseph is staying with us for a few days before
he teaches a retreat at Spirit Rock Meditation Center here in California.
Immediately after the retreat he leaves for a ten-day bicycle vacation
through the French countryside.

I soon discover it is not an easy task, finding a jacket for Joseph.
This is not because Joseph is particular. He enjoys holding up possibilities for me to consider. But no jacket we like fits him properly. His
is not an off-the-rack kind of body. Probably he is used to this, but still
I am amazed at his patience. He tries on coat after coat. Sometimes we

giggle or laugh. Sometimes we find one we really like, but again, the fit is bad, sometimes very bad. Eventually an elderly salesclerk comes by and offers to help. She tells us they can alter any coat we select.

We explain our short time frame, our assumption that alterations would take too long. She assures us this will not be a problem. We take her at her word and show her the coat we like best. She pulls a larger size off the rack and puts it on Joseph, then painstakingly tucks and pins, tucks and pins. Joseph stands patiently as she works. When she has the jacket full of pins, we all agree he looks smashing. I tell him I can see him sitting with a glass of French wine on a stone terrace overlooking a picturesque valley. We are happy as we leave the store. The coat will be ready in ten days, exactly when Joseph's retreat finishes and a day before he departs.

Ten days later we return. We wait. Finally the coat is located and Joseph slips it on. Generally, the fit is good, with one glaring exception. Two inches of Joseph's wrists hang below the end of the coat sleeves! After all the alterations, it still looks like he has hastily borrowed a friend's jacket. Amazingly, Joseph is neither angry nor frustrated. I am both. Joseph turns to me, eyebrows raised, as if I will know what to do. But neither my entreaties to the salesperson nor an offer to pay more succeeds in getting the store to redo the coat in twenty-four hours. So instead I suggest we try taking it to the dry cleaning shop down the street from our house to see if they would be willing to do a quick alteration. I know the owner well, and she chuckles as she looks at Joseph standing there, still patient, still unruffled, still smiling, with his wrists dangling below the sleeves. She assures us she can fix it. "Come back this evening just before we close," she instructs.

When we return, the coat is perfect. She doesn't charge him. And Joseph flies off the next morning leaving behind no untidy emotions scattered on the floor of the men's department. It was not as if he somehow knew it would turn out satisfactorily. He was just totally at ease with however it would turn out, and exceedingly patient throughout the process. Suzuki Roshi, in *Zen Mind, Beginner's Mind*, says, "The usual translation of the Japanese word *nin* is 'patience,' but perhaps 'constancy' is a better word. You must force yourself to be patient, but in constancy there is no particular effort involved—there is only the unchanging ability to accept things as they are." The image I have of Joseph, standing in that coat, with the same peaceful demeanor through all its incarnations, becomes my visual example of constancy as I begin this month's integrity work.

Joseph's Instructions: Working with Patience

What we are practicing here is the mind of letting go. When the mind is tranquil, it is not impatient. Practicing patience leads to tranquility. The Buddha said patience leads to enlightenment.

1. We begin by tracking the number of times in a day we experience impatience. What type of situations tend to give rise to impatience for you? Make a list.

2. Next we expand our attention to what mind states might be associated with impatience, such as restlessness, rushing, frustration.

   • How are these mind states related to impatience? How and when do they arise?

   • Investigate carefully the different nuances and tones of impatience. On a grosser level you could ask the question, "What is my attitude?" On a subtler level, watch for what happens in the mind in the exact moment you ask the question. You may not need an answer, the mind already shifting from the restlessness or aversion as you ask the question. You see that you can move out of restlessness, even if it is only for a moment. And then restlessness returns.

3. Now we go deeper. Look for how impatience may arise from a choice in your mind, not only because of a specific situation.

   • You can decide to get into mental projections . . . or not. Watch closely for them—and remember, it is not necessary to act on them. Imagine you have a remote control and practice changing the channel.

- See if you can notice a pattern of particular things that trigger impatience.

Watch for the subtleties of impatience. For example, watch for impatience during meditation, which really is just a moment of impatience. It is not necessary to act on it.

4. Finally, it is important to also investigate the different nuances that arise when you are feeling patience, not just impatience.

   - Ask yourself, "What else is present?"
   - Is it patience or is it resignation? Patience is allowing, enduring—constancy, not resignation.
   - Pay attention to those times when you consciously decide to be patient or when you are just naturally patient. Investigate, become familiar with that quality of mind.
   - See if you can catch the moment when patience becomes impatience, and when impatience becomes patience.

For three months my fifty-six-year-old mother lay in the hospital in a coma. Every day she was there, I sat beside her. I was young and brokenhearted. I couldn't imagine, or certainly accept, life without her. I was angry. I pleaded with God. Nothing changed. I had spoken to my mother just before she was wheeled into surgery for a procedure we both understood was risky but might alleviate the unrelenting bone pain she now had from advanced cancer. It might also leave her crippled. I don't think either of us understood it might leave her comatose.

In my foolishness, on the morning of the procedure, I asked her if she was mad at God. After all, she was a minister. I felt she had earned special dispensation. This disastrous turn of events did not begin to fit into my concept of fairness for one so young and so devoted to a spiritual path, nor did it confirm the presence of a benevolent spirit watching over us.

"No," she replied, smiling weakly, gently. "I am at peace with God, and with dying. But I am sad I will not see how you all turn out." Those were her last words to me.

My last words to her while she lived, but now in a coma, were just hours before she died. It had suddenly occurred to me that perhaps, if this were even possible, she was delaying death for us, her children. I am the oldest of six children. Were our moping, hoping, fierce bedside vigils waiting for her to awaken somehow keeping her here? Foolishness? But what if she were holding on until she could see we would be fine? As soon as I had the thought, sobbing and alone with her, I told her I was OK, although it certainly didn't look that way. I told her we were all going to be OK and that she could go now if that was what she wanted. I said my goodbyes, went back to her house to sleep, and she passed away a couple of hours later.

I've always thought it was patience that kept me there, steadfast beside her through those long days. Certainly my love for her kept vigil. But I wonder now, was it more accurately impatience that sat so still? If patience is the ability to be with things as they are, well, I surely wanted things to be other than they were. I have undertaken this work with Joseph to strengthen the mind of letting go. I am very clear how ferocious the grip of wanting mind can sometimes be. I certainly don't know, and probably don't believe, that my words helped her to let go. But I can become that young woman in that hospital room and feel again the rawness of my yearning, the fierceness of my holding on to something that was already beyond returning.

What we are practicing here is the mind of letting go.
—JOSEPH GOLDSTEIN

Rushing this process can simply lead to confusion.
—JOSEPH GOLDSTEIN

Working with Patience: Floating Downstream

And so I begin, impatiently, to work on enhancing my patience. The first thing I write in my journal is that I am not as keen on this topic as the last several. I am often impatient. Then I feel impatience arise for my (wrong) view. So I begin again, just settle into observing where and when I am impatient. How many times do I experience impatience? Three arise strongly the first day: waiting in a slow-moving line for a lunch sandwich, sitting in stopped traffic, and someone stopping by my desk to chat while I am working. The next morning I awake with a vague sense that impatience was probably more prevalent than I had noted the previous day.

OK, what other types of situations give rise to impatience? I dig deeper. When I am rushing to dress, eat, pack up to leave on time for the ferry to work, everything else unplanned (sigh) becomes an obstacle. And "obstacle" then instantly gives birth to impatience. At the office, I find that writing down tasks to accomplish for the day can contribute to a mild but increasing impatience as the day progresses and goals set are not being achieved. Again, anything that arises unexpectedly and needs attention is accompanied by impatience. Well, this is certainly not being with things as they are. At noon I have a conference call and in the late afternoon a meeting with staff. Both times I come with an agenda of topics to discuss. Both times participants talk about off-topic issues, change a subject midstream, and chat idly. Of course they do! Yet I can physically feel the impatience as heat arising in my body as I struggle to keep the meeting on track. So what arises with expectations for, visions of, a smooth (different) outcome? Impatience. No surprise there!

As the week progresses, I watch helplessly as I tumble again and again into impatience. It is astounding and eye-opening. I had no idea. The list of triggers for impatience lengthens. Midweek I go to the hospital for my annual mammogram, always with some accompanying anxiety, and I discover still another impatience trigger, as in, "Let's just get this over with." Sure enough, impatience blossoms and grows as I am shuffled from one desk to another, one waiting room to another. Handling errands on the way home, I am brusque with a clerk in an electronics store who keeps cutting me off with suggestions that don't address the problem I am attempting to describe. Ah, an overloaded agenda can lead to impatience. Again, no surprise there.

A sudden glitch on my computer needs fixing. *Not this! Not now!* Ah, a preference for no glitches in life? May not be serving me well. The desire or expectation for ease—at work, at home, in relationships—toss it into the blender with a time deadline? Recipe for impatience.

This morning I add still another item to the long list I am impatiently keeping: feeling impatient with myself. All morning I have been consciously and deliberately choosing distractions instead of tackling the work spread out on my desk before me. I have made a list of dinners I can prepare easily from food I know I have on hand, saving myself a trip to the grocery store on the way home. Useful. Not what I need to be doing now. I have checked email. And checked again. I have manipulated my calendar. Repeatedly.

I am the source of these disruptions, and they are contributing to . . . you guessed it: a rising sense of impatience. The idea that I am the cause of my own impatience is not a pleasant revelation.

Finally I rise from my desk and practically run down the hall, grabbing my business partner for "a long lunch," I tell him. He is willing, and lunch stretches into two hours—time, of course, I had planned for many other tasks. I love and adore my partner, the perfect foil to my frustration. Two hours later I return to my desk relaxed and renewed, so full of appreciation for this friendship that I am no longer impatient regarding what will not get done. I feel content. I feel clear of mind and reenrolled. I understand those two gentle, fun hours were more important than anything else I will accomplish in the rest of the afternoon. And, surprisingly, with an aura of peacefulness I glide through the next two hours and accomplish everything! Reflecting on the day's events brings a quietness to my body and mind as I drive home. What if I could take that quiet, relaxed, and peaceful mind state into everything

I do? Suddenly patience seems a bit more enticing. So this is why the Buddha stressed its importance. It is only my preconceived preferences for something different than what is that is giving rise to these rattled mind states. This is indeed something I can change, through skillful mindfulness and patience.

Ron's tennis club has a new restaurant and begins to offer live music and dinner on Thursday evenings. We get a group together and go. The restaurant, which has been mostly undiscovered and half empty up to this point, is packed. The band begins playing. Standing room only now. We are happy to have a table and are drinking wine, chatting, listening to the music. It is some time before we realize we have not received menus yet. Then we notice people at other tables are awaiting meals, looking around with some frustration.

Ron wanders outside to watch a tennis match between friends. Periodically he comes in to check. Finally we get menus. Ron tells me what he wants and wanders back outside. No one comes to take our order. I notice that the fitness club manager, with an apron over his jeans, is helping to deliver food. His wife, who is not an employee of the club, is clearing dishes. One of our friends gets up and begins pouring water and lighting candles around the room. Clearly the restaurant was not prepared to handle a crowd this size. Someone finally comes to take our order, then returns, after more waiting, to inform us they have run out of many items we ordered. We arrived at 7:00. It is now almost 9:00. Some of the other patrons leave without eating, and some, it appears, without paying. The room is thick with impatience, and I do not tumble into it, repeatedly re-choosing a different focus, a different response. My efforts feel skillful and also keep my spirits buoyant. The truth is I am enjoying myself and really no longer care whether we are served food or not. Eventually we are served.

That night I was practicing everything I had been learning about patience. I just flowed with the current, allowing what was so to be OK, without lamenting or railing or even wishing otherwise. I certainly had no control over the situation. Rising up and waving my hand, complaining, insisting, frowning were all options I observed around me. I could have chosen to participate in any of these reactions. I felt them arise. I could also join my friends enjoying the excellent magnum of wine one had brought to share. I could talk in depth with several people I don't often get the chance to sit with. And so I chose to do that instead. I kept checking in and was surprised to discover I was not impatient. I was genuinely enjoying the evening.

What does patience feel like? Like Joseph standing, smiling, with his newly altered coat sleeves still too short. My choice that night felt very clear. I embraced the way things were and was able to simply enjoy an evening with good friends. The world, including our reactions to it, is not as solid as we often perceive. We have a choice—a choice to be unencumbered by any desire for a situation to be other than it is. This parami work may be significantly shaking up long-held, cherished concepts and automatic responses about the way the world is wired up. Each and every moment offers us a new choice: react, respond, or embrace. We do not have to be impatient just because others are or just because a situation is not ideal. We can choose the current with less suffering, paddling skillfully and patiently around the boulders. Can we discover patterns in what triggers our impatience? Yes, I think we can. For me it now feels exquisitely clear and simple. Impatience arises, almost exclusively, from the simple desire for whatever is arising in the current moment to be other than what it is.

It is Saturday, in the last week on patience. I am in the backyard on a crisp, sunny morning. A small table, newspapers, paint cans, brushes, rags, and gloves are spread out on the deck. I found an old table for our kitchen at a flea market. The size is perfect but it needs painting. I have sage green and cream, and visions of painting it to look like an expensive antique table I saw in a shop window. I begin. Birds sing. Sun warms my shoulders. Opera plays on my phone. I am almost giddy with visions of how my little craft project will turn out.

After two hours I have enough paint on the carved base and top to understand it is not going to look like the expensive table I covet. The colors look murky on the rough-hewn wood, even after a coat of primer. The ridges and hollows of the subtle carvings have mostly disappeared under the two coats plus primer. It just looks old, beat up, and dull. I groan. Stand up. Stretch tired muscles.

The birds have stopped singing. The sun is hot now, my neck prickly. I peel off the sweaty plastic painting gloves, wad them up, and throw them down onto paint-splattered newspapers. I turn off the music, roughly, and stand scowling at the table. Clearly the paint was a mistake. *This is why you shouldn't do crafts*, the nagging begins. *You're no good at it. And this old cheap table will never look like the one you really want, anyway. Give it up. Enough! Don't spoil a precious after-noon off work like you have already spoiled the morning.* Sigh. I would never speak that way to someone. Sigh. After painstakingly working hard all morning, I realize I now need to strip all this paint off, and do so quickly while it is still wet. *No. No. No.* But it is so. *Now* I recall the doubts I did have before beginning, the doubts I just rushed and pushed through. I grab a bag of chips, angrily crunching as I drive to the hardware store for paint remover. Dissatisfaction with what is? Impatience? You bet.

Soon I am back home again, painting gloppy, clearly not-good-to-breathe goop onto the table in a dripping frenzy, then scraping, scraping, scraping all the new paint off with a wedge. I am determined to finish—and committed to never, ever undertaking another craft project. My foul mood stinks worse than the toxic fumes.

But surprisingly, the slow, steady scraping begins to subdue the fury. The afternoon air is cooler now, pleasant. The simple lines and carvings of the table begin to emerge again from under its burden of a bad paint job. It is a sweet table, I remember now. I had thought so when I bought it. It is slow work, but at some point both a decent state of mind, and even a bit of patience, begin to return. I certainly can't say I am enjoying the process, but as I see this new approach beginning to succeed and that I just have to keep at it, I relax. In retrospect, I don't think I could ever have kept at it for as long as I did if I had not been focused, these past weeks, on investigating and strengthening patience. Once I was quiet again, patience began to arise quite spontaneously. I just carried on, with a long-enduring mind, and patience carried me, like the tortoise, not the hare, across the finish line. The next morning I oiled the table and . . . it was perfect. It was even better than the table I had coveted in the window. I cannot believe I did that. All it needed was a good coat of oil and a cheery disposition. I think of it now as my table of patience. It is a lovely reminder.

As we reflect on this month, what arises for me is the quality of mind in the moment of letting go. For example, letting go of that first knock of impatience at the door. The more often we can recognize it, the more easily we can allow it to just pass through and away, instead of corralling and feeding it. We don't own it unless we choose to. What a freeing revelation that is. Impatience is our choice to make—or not— each and every time it arises. That moment may be brief, but it is a solid moment of choice. Patience, not impatience. We can also look and become familiar with what other mind states might accompany impatience and gently see them out the back door.

When we meditate daily, that gap where choice is available becomes more evident, more prevalent, and suspended. With practice, patience becomes more readily available and achievable. We move through the day more pliable, able to switch gears smoothly and maneuver around the obstacles. I have heard this referred to as "bamboo mind"—a mind that is resilient and yielding but returns naturally to center. I also like the image of floating softly downstream, skillfully avoiding any unexpected boulders. During meditation, slowed down and hypervigilant, it is much easier to catch oneself falling into an emotion like impatience. Often we may even feel it physically as the body begins leaning forward ever so slightly. We can continue to watch for this subtle leaning forward into the next moment when not in meditation. Conversations and meetings are especially good for seeing this gentle wanting lean into and become an emotion. When we catch ourselves, we can subtly take a deep breath and settle back; the meeting continues, and most times the impulse subsides.

I am also still actively working with stretching and toning the renunciation muscles, periodically choosing to give up sweets or wine or shopping. After a while the mind really does soften and quiet down. The freedom here is profound. Without the yammering voice of desire, more space for patience and other wholesome responses arises. It is refreshing, this not wanting, as is the patience that slides in naturally to the space left by the departed craving. We see how closely linked one is with the other. Feeding the clamor of wanting mind significantly fuels the fires of impatience. I want something different, something more . . . now!

It also helps to remind ourselves that what we are practicing here is establishing a mind of letting go. It doesn't help to latch on—"Did you see that nasty boulder? Let me tell you all about it. It reached out and grabbed me, bruised me, frightened me. It had no business being there in my stream!"—because meanwhile we are still moving downstream with more boulders ahead.

There is a delicious freedom that comes from just doing the best we can in each moment, and reflecting back on that when worries surface and take the wheel. Stop. Ease back. Take a breath. Then we can respond instead of reacting to someone's words or to a troubling or heated situation. This is skillful. This is patience. For me it takes being attentive, recognizing the rising habitual reaction before it takes over and barks out the wrong instructions. Being curious also assists in this for me, as in asking, "What else is here?" or "What else could happen here?" I give myself a second chance to get it right. If we respond instead of hastily reacting, this often opens up an opportunity for new, different outcomes. The other person may also respond thoughtfully instead of immediately reacting.

I admit to a bit of weariness and discouragement at seeing this same root behind the unskillful behavior with each of the paramis. Enough! Simple, but certainly not always easy, as Joseph reminds us. Impatience, aversion, restlessness: wanting the next moment because surely the next moment will be better than this one! But our naive insistence on a more perfect now is counterproductive and fuels the disheartening feeling that we are not making any progress. The sheer magnitude, and stubborn persistence, of this desire for something different than what is can overwhelm us. It is clearly the captain of our ship when we are asleep at the wheel.

One of the great laws of the Dharma that I find myself
often rediscovering is, "If it's not one thing, it's another."
—JOSEPH GOLDSTEIN

Often we are discouraged by the enormity of a task,
or the length of a journey, and become impatient with
the difficulties we face. We lose faith in ourselves.
Patience reminds us that what is in front of us is just
this moment, just this step, just this breath. Patience,
the Buddha said, leads to nirvana (enlightenment.)
—JOSEPH GOLDSTEIN, *ONE DHARMA*

Check-In Conversation: Practicing the Mind of Letting Go

For my check-in this month I am calling Joseph midafternoon. I am seated in my living room, gazing down the hill to the bay. It is clear, sunny, and the windows are open to the first warm, fragrant hint of spring.

"Hello," Joseph says, then coughs.

"Hi, Joseph." I hear him cough again. "Are you OK?"

"Yes. I have a bit of a cold."

"Oh, I'm sorry to hear that. Are you up for this?"

"Yes."

"OK, but let me know if you need to stop. So I recently mentioned to a woman I work with that I was writing about patience. 'Oh,' she told me, 'hurry up and finish. I need to read it. I need more patience. Now!'" Joseph and I both laugh. "And that was exactly how I was feeling when I began this month.

"As you suggested, I began with a list: waiting in line, sitting in stopped traffic, someone wanting just to chat while I'm working. That was the first day," I say, chuckling. "Easy, I thought. Then I looked deeper. When I found myself in one of those instances again, like sitting in traffic, I found I could actually watch the impatience arising. There was a space created by my noticing wherein I could choose impatience and just watch myself give in. Or, increasingly, I could think, *This is a place where I can get impatient,* and then have a moment or two to consider an alternative response before tumbling in."

"Right. Right."

"I also wrote down that I am chagrined to see my impatience with Ron's impatience." Joseph laughs. "Yeah," I say, "Just to see it also makes me laugh, lighten up, let go. Other people's impatience. Or impatience with myself!"

"Right."

"How does that saying go? She who lives in a glass house should not cast stones."

"One aspect of impatience to watch for is that of judging mind," Joseph says after a few quiet moments. "We're not patient with how others are. We want them to change. The Dalai Lama said, 'Honor your enemies because your enemies teach you patience.' It is easy to be patient when everything is going well, but when not, particularly with people, we can recognize that this is a situation that has the potential to teach us about impatience. Use this quote from the Dalai Lama when you are feeling impatient with another, when feeling they are the cause of your impatience. Try instead to take the situation as a gift from them to practice patience! Thank them for the gift of the opportunity to experience patience," he says, chuckling.

"Oh, I like that. I also watched my expectations factor into the arising of impatience. You know, planning for a business conference call and having expectations for what I wanted to have happen, then noticing myself getting impatient when others talk too much or change the subject."

"Yes."

"And the same with going into a store and having a salesperson not listen. Also frustration or anxiety can give rise to impatience for me, as in, 'Let's just get this over with!'" I laugh. "And selfishness—that can really cause impatience to arise in me toward others. And of course, the main one I keep seeing as I work with each of the paramis is dissatisfaction, the feeling that I just want *something* to be different than it is right now. Anything! That certainly creates impatience!"

"Yes," Joseph chuckles. "One thing that I thought of when you first started speaking, something that I think would be worth exploring when we talk about patience as being with things as they are, is to explore the difference between patience and resignation."

"Oh. That's interesting. I definitely could feel that coming up."

"Because people could misinterpret this to mean you learn to just be with things as they are and then you never work to change anything. And that is quite a different thing. It is important to investigate that difference between patience and being resigned to something, where there is a kind of passivity and giving up. One of the phrases from the Chinese Zen master Xuyun is 'the long-enduring mind.' So in that sense patience can really be an ally in whatever project one is doing, whether effecting social change or some other endeavor. Accepting things as they are doesn't mean just resigning yourself. I think we may not always understand that patience can be a support for action, not only inaction."

"That is really interesting, Joseph. So you're patient with standing in a line, say, because you know you're getting a sandwich," I laugh, "and so you are not inclined to give up. But also patience can be a support when it is not as obvious as awaiting a sandwich."

"Yes," he agrees. "Like in a big undertaking. When something is of value, it doesn't always unfold the way we would like it to, and so one needs patience. One needs a long-enduring mind."

"I understand. Patience over time."

"Suzuki Roshi used this idea in his book. He used the term *constancy*."

"Yes, I've read that piece he wrote on constancy."

"So in whatever you're doing, try exploring that theme. Is this constancy or resignation?"

"'Resignation' is a very good word and mind state to watch out for. I can feel how easily one might slip into resignation and give up the effort."

We are quiet for several moments.

"Are you still feeling OK?" I ask.

"Yes, I am fine for now."

I tell him about the restaurant evening. "The analogy of floating downstream on a raft came to me, you know? It is peaceful, everything beautiful and calm and then 'Oh, look out, there's a boulder! What's a boulder doing here? There aren't supposed to be boulders here.' And you continue floating downstream crashing into one boulder after another, grumbling, complaining, waiting impatiently for unobstructed waters and being surprised every time, when the truth is . . . there are boulders in streams! And so just remembering that there are things that will come up."

"Exactly."

"Just understanding this helps me to relax when unexpected, perhaps unpleasant, situations do come up, like with the overbooked restaurant."

"Right. I think that is really important to see."

"That analogy works to help strengthen my understanding of patience. It reminds me I can't expect to just flow along. You know, 'Row, row, row your boat,'" I begin singing, and Joseph joins me, "gently down the stream, merrily, merrily, merrily, merrily, life is but a dream." We are laughing.

"Life throws boulders in your path," I say after a while. "It's like your mantra, 'If it's not one thing, it's another.' Which is also saying the same thing."

"Right."

"Tell me more about restlessness," I continue. "In that restaurant, so many people, myself included at times, seemed to be struggling with restlessness, which was fueling, or at least tightly tied in with, impatience. That is a very common and unwelcome mind state for me."

"Yes. Well, restlessness is not always associated with impatience, but it is quite common. What is most helpful to work with when experiencing restlessness is to focus on the attitude present in the mind at that moment. Because restlessness can be such an unpleasant mind state, if aversion is also arising and is not noticed, we can really spiral down quickly."

"Oh." I think about this. "As soon as you said that, I could feel that aversion is definitely mingled in there when I am feeling restless, or immediately thereafter. In fact now I'm thinking a lot of my suffering there is caused by the aversion to the restlessness, and not so much the actual restlessness. Interesting."

"Exactly."

"And then I noticed another trigger: rushing. When I'm rushing, *everything* makes me impatient. No matter what I'm doing. It's just a mind state wide open to temptation and unskillful response. I feel like an open doorway, you know, 'Bring it on, throw everything at me you've got!' And I bitch and complain about everything. Amazing. Setting goals for a day? Another huge cause of impatience for me. This is something I routinely do and then find myself becoming increasingly impatient as the day goes on because I never meet all the goals I've set. The day slides into anxiety, impatience, and then disappointment."

Joseph chuckles. "Did you try some days without setting goals?"

I laugh. "Yes, I did! Because of that insight. I guess you could say it's a work in progress. When I do, I coast more. I forget more. I tried something else new as well, when I got overly frustrated about all the things I felt I needed to do in that one day. This was at home. I did a forty-five-minute meditation, then forty-five minutes tackling whatever needed doing, then another forty-five-minute meditation, and so on. All day."

"That's interesting."

" Yes. I've done it two days, when I was just so caught up in the press of things, and feeling impatient, and lousy, about everything. Because I certainly don't feel impatient after sitting for forty-five minutes. It allows for more . . . ," I laugh, "I don't know. Slower breathing for sure. I don't know if I'm clearer or just more satisfied with what I've done, but I actually get more things accomplished than I think I would have while going about in a stew of restless aversion."

Joseph laughs. "Well, I think the mind *is* clearer, with the meditation interludes, and when the mind is clearer, it is also more efficient."

After a couple minutes of silence, and another check-in to confirm he is still OK, I tell Joseph about the afternoon refinishing the table. "But now," I say, "I'm not clear about something. I know we touched on this already, but I guess it is still lingering. I can struggle here. I will watch impatience arising, often from some dissatisfaction with what is, and your suggestion was to look for that moment when it switches. I don't know that I catch that. Like with the table, it felt more like a gradual subsiding. Should I watch for a moment as a pathway to more moments like that to follow?"

"Well, yes—but also it is about seeing clearly what it is that just changed. What just happened? You really want to notice, to understand what it is that allows you to go from impatience to patience. So you just observe what happened. Very likely it is the seeing and letting go of some wanting, I would imagine."

"Ah, I understand now." I am still thinking of the table. Once I let go of the misguided desire for it to look like something it wasn't, the impatience receded also.

"A good example of that," Joseph continues, "is when I'm driving behind a slow driver on New England roads."

This makes me laugh. "Yes?"

"As long as I'm wanting the situation to be different, as long as I'm wanting them to go faster, I stay impatient. And then, when I finally see what is happening and say," he starts chuckling, "'OK, let me not want to go faster or not want them to go faster,' then there is no impatience."

"I see, so by just recognizing the desire, even though you are still behind the guy driving slowly . . ."

"Or woman," he says.

I whoop aloud, and Joseph laughs.

"You sound just like Ron now. OK. Or woman." I am still laughing. "So then you realize that it's actually your wanting to go faster, your desire, that is making you impatient, and therefore causing you suffering."

"Exactly."

"So then there's that space where you can choose or not, right?"

"Yes," he says, chuckling deeply. "You can either go on wanting to go faster and be miserable, or not. People generally just don't watch their minds closely and explore, 'OK, what is the cause of the suffering here?'"

I am trying now to hastily complete my check-in with Joseph, concerned about his cold. "I did find once again, as with the other paramis, I was mostly focused on impatience, watching it arise and dissipate, instead of also investigating moments of patience." I sigh loudly, and Joseph chuckles. "So how do we investigate and practice patience? Do I just watch for when I do feel patient and then ask what else is present?"

"Well, that's one way. Also, try to see what the difference is when you go from impatience to patience. What happens in that moment?"

"Oh, that transition moment again . . ."

"Yes. If you watch, you can see it. Basically I think it will probably come down to a letting go of some kind of grasping, as we talked about, or aversion. It could also be a moment of aversion to how something is and wanting it to be somehow or in some way other than it is."

"Oh, yeah. And this is a small thing, but it's also interesting—I set my goal of not buying anything and after a few months now, the mind is quite different. All that craziness of, *Well, let's just pull in here or browse there*. Driving down the road now those thoughts aren't even arising. Those are also moments of the mind letting go, moments of not struggling with aversion."

"Yes."

"I always thought the mind was somewhat my enemy in this regard, but it's right with the program. It's like the mind is able to take a breath. 'Whew!' it says. 'Thanks for the break.' It is fascinating to see and feel how much all that craving really grips and can tire the mind."

"Yes, exactly. That's the whole idea, I think, behind monastic life. You just take yourself out of the realm of a lot of wanting. Not that they don't have their own wantings. But it reduces them a lot I think."

"I've always wondered about that. That was actually a good idea," I say to Joseph, "your suggesting I continue with my vow of not buying anything."

He chuckles. "When you say 'actually' a good idea, is that in contrast to all the other good ideas we just discussed?"

I laugh. "No, just in contrast to how I normally operate."

"Continue playing with it. You've already seen how it can quiet the mind that might otherwise leap to impatience, or whatever."

"I will do that. Anything else on patience? I really feel guilty keeping you any longer."

"Well, I would just do a little more work on distinguishing between patience and resignation, between patience and the sense of constancy that involves continually bringing energy to something. Patience does not mean withdrawing or apathy." Joseph begins coughing, his voice softer.

"I agree, patience does have a surprisingly energetic, uplifting quality."

"Yes. Where resignation is clearly the opposite," he says coughing again.

"And patience is also self-control," I continue, "like you are now with me, patiently answering my questions when you are clearly not feeling well." He laughs. I tell him that is enough for now, and he readily agrees.

I write down a couple more insights that occur to me after we hang up. A moment of impatience does not mean the next moment also must be impatient. We can look for the gaps, the holes in the net we are caught in. I used this often that night in the restaurant. I would look around yet again for the waiter, feel impatience arising, turn to my companion to continue the conversation, and impatience would pass on by. We just need to use the reminder gently. Another insight is that impatience is not ours. Impatience is arising due to conditions out of our control, *and* we can choose not to get all dressed up and join in. It has been extremely helpful to recognize certain key situations that give rise to impatience, and I commit to continue adding to that list. We may feel a habitual impatient reaction arising, but we can choose, in any and every moment, to simply change the channel.

When I was getting the annual mammogram, as I finally entered the examination room, for a third time I was asked for my date of birth.

"Wow," I exclaimed after giving it to the technician, my nervousness giving rise to chattiness, "I appreciate how careful you guys are. You're the third person to ask me for my birthdate."

As she busied herself getting the machine ready, she laughed. "Oh, you wouldn't believe it," she said, "the things I see here. I can go out to the waiting area and ask, 'Mrs Smith?' And three women will stand up. 'Are you Mrs. Smith?' I will ask one. And she will say, 'No,' and sit down." We laughed. "No one wants to be here," she told me. "In their anxiousness to be out of here, they stand up when any name is called."

I laughed, but as she continued to get everything ready, I thought, *Well, don't we often go through life like that?* Anxious to be done with something unpleasant, preoccupied with worry and anxiety, we can be pretty unconscious. If someone is not watching out for us, as this woman was, we can do some serious harm to ourselves.

The technician then asked me what I do. I understood the questions, the talk, were to help me relax, and it was working. I said that I had begun writing a book about creating a life of integrity.

"Well, that's timely," she said. "Everyone seems so preoccupied, so selfish these days."

I considered this, surprised to hear her say it: the connection between integrity and living less selfishly. I guess that is why the first parami is generosity. I felt a sudden burst of enthusiasm for this work we've been doing.

"You have certainly chosen a livelihood of service to others, an unselfish path," I said.

"Thank you," she said, pausing to look closely at me. "Yes, I feel I have helped save many lives." And she said this with pride, kindness shining. Then, with much patience, she guided me gently through the procedures, and with a matched and sterling patience, I endured the discomfort.

As the month of patience comes to its conclusion, I can't help thinking that patience just might be the most important step on this path to integrity. I have felt the same at the conclusion of each of the last five months. And you?

Freedom is not simply doing what we want when we want.
That is addiction. Freedom is the ability to choose wisely.
—JOSEPH GOLDSTEIN

7 Truthfulness

What's surprising is how difficult it is.
—JOSEPH GOLDSTEIN

The Seventh Parami: Truthfulness

The Pali word *sacca*, which we translate as *truthfulness*, is used to designate the seventh parami in Buddhist texts. It means acting and speaking in accord with truth and includes the qualities of loyalty, trustworthiness, honesty, and sincerity.

Instructions: Not Fooling Ourselves

Joseph and I are riding up a ski lift together. I ask him how he has been sleeping lately. Joseph can often have difficulty falling asleep at night, a condition his mother also had. Suddenly he begins to sing—loudly! "Some enchanted evening . . ." A few people below the lift look up as we pass over. "You may see a stranger . . ." He nudges me. I giggle, then reluctantly join in. ". . . across a crowded room. And somehow you'll know . . ." Soon I am laughing and singing, completely charmed by our shared silliness. We sing loudly and with boisterous enthusiasm until we run out of lyrics we remember.

"I have a little routine now," Joseph says. "I sing in the bathtub around midnight, just before going to bed. It is helping me to fall asleep."

I am not sure what to say to this. I cannot imagine how this would help anyone fall asleep. But now he grins at me as he begins singing again, and after another embarrassed moment, I join him.

"Moon river, wider than the sky. I'm crossing you in style some day." Skiers on the chairs around us, including Ron, turn around. I am still grinning, and still self-conscious, as we finish our robust duet. This public singing is from someone who, as a boy, was told to silently mouth the lyrics in school holiday pageants. Both Ron and Joseph share a knack for singing off-key. The difference is Joseph's response. No problem if folks laugh at him. He has discovered he likes to sing. So he sings.

It is a spectacular winter's day. Crisp. Sunny. Fresh snow overnight has bewitched the towering ponderosa pines. They shimmy and shine in dazzling, white-lace gowns as if they have been dancing all night and are reluctant to retire. I glance at Joseph, who is also gazing at the trees. He is wearing a gray and navy blue parka, black nylon ski pants, and a dark gray knit cap. He is a visually, but certainly not vocally, muted participant in the sparkling scene. I remember a line I heard once while on retreat. "What others think about me is none of my business." I wish I could, truthfully, live that way. I am deeply habituated to considering, worrying about, how my appearance or actions or words will be received by others. Exploring truthfulness this month will probably be an excavation calling for heavy machinery! In contrast, after fifty years of mindful living, Joseph's carefree lightness is intoxicating and inspiring. He doesn't care a hoot if other skiers think he is singing off-key or, worse, that singing aloud is behavior unbecoming for a mature man. The contrast between my mind and Joseph's mind continues to be striking. Am I catching up, I wonder? If not, I want to understand why. I want to uncover the untruthful components fueling my perceptions.

Joseph's Instructions: Working with Truthfulness

1. The first thing to consider, which underlies any discussion of truthfulness, is that of truthfulness as the antidote to self-delusion. Even before one explores right speech and right action, this parami includes being truthful about one's own mind.

- So we ask the question, "Are we really seeing *ourselves* truthfully?"
- Are we observing our acts of body, speech, and mind truthfully?
- Watch for habits that give rise to moments of "almost true."
- There is a lot to learn here about our minds. This is also sometimes tricky.

2. Now we go deeper by investigating:

   - Do we acknowledge the defilements of our minds, that which is unwholesome? They are greed, hate, delusion, conceit, wrong view, doubt, torpor, restlessness, shamelessness, and recklessness.
   - Try working with each of these separately. Watch for it arising. What are its habitual patterns? This can reveal a lot. Unwholesome patterns in the mind often go unrecognized. And then we must also ask, "Are we acknowledging that which is wholesome? What wholesome habits are at work here as well?"

3. Finally, you can also work with truthfulness by watching for unskillful patterns of speech, such as exaggerations, unkind humor, or participating in gossip.

   - Watch for the obvious patterns, but also watch in ordinary speech for the things you say that are almost true. Look really closely for the underlying motive. Investigate those motives when saying something untruthful in social situations. What is the motive behind an untruthful response at work?
   - Investigate recurring patterns and habits here.
   - The two most important aspects of this practice are investigating what is our motivation when we know we are not being truthful and becoming familiar with what habits may be at work or unnoticed.

———

Seeing unworthiness as a wrong view of ourselves
helps make it something we can work with. Instead
of thinking there is something fundamentally
wrong with the way we are, we see it as the very
thought of being unworthy that is the problem.
—JOSEPH GOLDSTEIN, *ONE DHARMA*

Imagine your thoughts are coming from the person seated
behind you, and then only keep those that are useful.
—JOSEPH GOLDSTEIN

Working with Truthfulness: The Antidote to Self-Delusion

Truthfulness with myself. Perhaps the time is ripe for plucking some spoiled fruit out of the bowl of habitual thinking. When I wake up feeling blue—or harried or overwhelmed or fearful—I can suddenly find myself mentally composing a list of all that is awry in my life. And I often begin with doubts about my abilities and a list of my perceived shortcomings. I literally ensure I am sinking, then cast off to face the day. It is akin to pulling every negative, familiar thought and emotion from the bookshelf and stuffing them in a now too-heavy backpack, which I shoulder, slumping, complaining, and miserable, into the day. Kind of difficult to look up and notice anything uplifting with eyes downcast, already weary. Ever been there? Why do we do this—make ourselves right about being so wrong about ourselves?

Fortunately I am generally prone to a sunnier outlook. Some of this is instinctual, some from my upbringing, and much of it comes from years of mindfulness. Now I understand we have a choice here. Now I much prefer hanging out with my happy companion rather than the grumpy one. I have learned I can change the channel. Even though it seems obvious that both perceptions about ourselves cannot be true, we *believe* each in the moment of arising in the mind. When I awaken blue, I listen to the voice of dismay like it is a radio broadcast direct from God. When I awaken pumped up and enthused with myself and life, I am so certain everything will work out that it often does just that.

Truthfully? Both perceptions are just something else to be noted, as Joseph would say. Both mind states ride on habitual thought and feeling trains, and we blindly jump on board. Neither is true. They are just long-established habits of thinking. And we ride around and around like little plastic figurines on a train set. Joseph is right. Before I investigate speech and actions with others, I need to look at what concepts I may be indulging in about myself. So I begin this month determined not to believe every thought, every emotion that arises. Everything must pass the truthfulness test.

Perhaps we fear that the excavation into the truth about ourselves will uncover bad news. Fears are like tiny, furry, sightless moles that if left to burrow freely can do damage. Tunneling beneath our best-laid plans, out of sight, they can quietly, steadily undermine our aspirations until the whole shebang collapses one day. "I knew it," we say, giving up. So the fear that the truth about us will be bad news? Just something else to be noted.

At this stage in wisdom development, I understand non-self as those empty, free moments when we are simply aware of being aware and (ideally) welcoming whatever arises. When resting there, we can genuinely feel the difference. I am discovering that truthfulness in action, for me, is clearly watching a sudden, predictable response arise from certain conditions. Those conditions? For example: I browse. I see something. I want it. Or I'm in my car driving when suddenly the cars around me slow, then stop, and I am present for that first habitual arising of impatience, then resistance.

Just the idea that all our cherished notions of who we are, are not always true can be both exciting and terrifying. If we are not the stories we tell ourselves about ourselves, then . . . you fill in this piece. When we live with integrity, with an aspiration of non-harming ourselves and others . . . When we don't believe or act out the stories we make up about ourselves and others . . . Then we stand a real chance of attaining the bliss of blamelessness. This is my aspiration, and nothing less will suffice.

I work with the Buddha's list of defilements described in Joseph's instructions, which are also translated as "the unwholesome roots." Perfect. I want to know what is at the root of the untruthful concepts and beliefs that bind us so closely to our suffering.

We are now in the middle of truthfulness month and well into our year of integrity. I began this morning writing reflections, and aspirations, and a few insights for each defilement. It was not going well. Suddenly I was weary . . . of reflections, of aspirations, of insights. I recognized boredom arising, and I set it all aside to go out for a run. Now returned and energized, in less than an hour I compose ten haiku for each of the ten defilements. It is fun, arousing my enthusiasm for this work again. Try it. I think playing with and teasing these bastards of defilement is an exceedingly skillful response. I call mine "Defying the Defilements":

> Greed: desire for more than one needs.
> But everyone else
> is doing it, buying it,
> and eating it now.

> Hate: wish to avoid, aversion.
> It's simple, she says,
> I take care to avoid all
> those unpleasant things.

> Delusion: mental disorder, misconception.
> This cannot be so.
> I awaken convinced I'm
> all wrong for this role!

> Conceit: exaggerated opinion of oneself.
> If I am not me,
> and you, not all what you seem,
> "we" could be untrue.

> Wrong view: not in accordance with previous intention.
> Selecting a goal,
> I watch for my progress in
> the rearview mirror.

> Doubt: lack of trust or confidence, wavering.
> Red cloud of finches
> swoops through my trouble bubbles,
> bursting every one.

Torpor: state of being dormant, apathy.
Safe in my burrow,
my illusions beside me,
I wait out all hope.

Restlessness: seeking change, discontented.
I wander, seeking
changes to, well, everything
that is so . . . so-so.

Shamelessness: brazen, impudent.
Brazenly she wins
the race for fame and fortune,
missing the sunsets.

Recklessness: heedless, headlong, rash.
Headlong into flames
I leap, but cannot sprout wings
without knowing how.

And then, because I am still soaring from the run and the fun of the poems, I craft one more haiku. The finches and the starlings actually appeared on the run (as did the idea of writing defilement poems), so I call this one "Gratitude":

Starlings whistle as
I run by. I fly up and
kiss each feathered smile.

In the third week working with truthfulness, I invite new neighbors to dinner. After the food, drinks, laughter, and kidding, one of them expresses her surprise to learn that Ron has been studying Buddhism longer than I have. I confirm this is the case, that Ron opened the door for me. And then I say, "and I rushed right past him." Everyone laughs, including Ron, but I instantly regret my words. The sting of those unkind words, said in jest, still ring harshly in my mind. Not a sterling performance. Also not truthful. Ron is very much right beside me on this path.

So watching speech for untruthful moments, and simply asking what that underlying motive might have been, is skillful. And then looking deeper—what emotion, undetected, might have fueled the untruthful response? I am also curious to watch for things I might say that are almost true. I suspect this might be a particularly fertile field.

Just before the month ends, I have a good test of my truthfulness muscle. For months I searched for the perfect small couch to fit my home office, then waited several more months for its delivery. I am watching as the delivery folks slowly unwrap the new couch. Quickly I see it is not what I ordered. Instead of a honey-colored finish on the wood, it arrives with dark, almost black trim. After they leave, I just sit and stare at it. Beside the wrong wood trim color, everything else about the piece seems wrong: the design, the size, the cushion fabric. In the large space where the old couch, now sold, had been, this ornate chaise looks too small, too fussy. I let the store know the wood finish is wrong, then spend much of the weekend rehearsing for the dialogue that will ensue when the representative comes by to see the piece. I am clear that I want to use the wrong finish as my reason to just return the piece and get a refund.

Each time I catch myself rehearsing for the upcoming dialogue, I gently remind myself of my intention to be truthful. Yes, I do have to continually remind myself. But I also feel a deep desire to proceed with truthfulness. Perhaps in the past I would have acted otherwise, perhaps not. But this time I am clear. I definitely want to return the piece for a full refund. And I will not lie to do so.

Monday morning arrives. I am nervous. The designer, who helped me select it and whom I really like and trust, arrives. She confirms the finish is wrong and assures me she will personally oversee its refinishing. I take a deep breath, then proceed to point out all the other ways the piece does not work. To each observation she gently and patiently offers another point of view. She explains how just the wrong color can throw the whole visual off. She repositions the piece, rearranges the other furniture in the room closer around it. She brings in items from other rooms—a pillow, a throw—to make the chaise appear more comfy, more at home in the room.

As she guides me, I do slowly begin to see past the obvious to what will or can be there. I have to work hard to stay open, and she is good! I sense her honesty and her commitment to my being fully satisfied. She is not just trying to convince me. I can feel how she really believes it is perfect in the room, and so I just keep listening to her and trying to see what she sees. I feel obliged to honor her effort. It took some time, but this morning as I sit working and looking at the refinished little chaise, I can now see what she could see and I could not. It looks just right there. Not just good enough, but really nice. And although I imagined another outcome as the successful one, in fact this is the real win. I now have a home office that is functional and beautiful. The relief at not having to begin the search all over again was much bigger than I imagined. Decorating is not a pleasant pastime for me. But most important? I was truthful in a situation begging me to speak with a subtle but clearly untruthful motive. One hundred percent truthful. It is a most uplifting reflection.

———

Remember to look with interest, not judgment.
—JOSEPH GOLDSTEIN

When in the presence of or considering wrong
speech, ask the question, "How does this serve?"
—Joseph Goldstein

Check-In Conversation: What's Surprising Is How Difficult It Is

I am sitting in my office after everyone else has gone home, rain streaking the window beside my desk and snarling the traffic just beyond it. I am waiting it out tonight—and, ensuring the wait will be productive, I am also checking in with Joseph.

"One of the things I often notice," he begins, "is that aside from times when I'm either meditating or working on something, my day will often be spent going simply from one sense gratification to another." He laughs. "You know, it can be *little* things. But that's really what's going on."

"Oh, I can so relate to that, as you well know."

"So the practice is really just to look. Truthfulness would be *just seeing oneself truthfully.*"

"But it can also be so hard!" I say. "For example, I might recognize thoughts that are arising to be impermanent—especially habitual, reactive thinking. But then I become aware I am also still holding it as 'I' doing the unskillful thinking, or 'I' seeing it with wrong view. Seeing it as a self who is misbehaving adds so much additional baggage to the mix."

"Yes. So that's its own defilement."

"Oh. Yeah."

"Well, that is part of what you're discovering working with this parami. People have different patterns. Some people can be so judgmental that they don't actually acknowledge what is good in themselves. You know, what is genuinely good. And it can also be the other way around," he chuckles. "People can have an inflated self-image, not acknowledging what is difficult, what is unwholesome. Not being really truthful with themselves. So there is this whole arena *before* speech, *before* acting on truthfulness with respect to another person. And that is truthfulness with oneself!"

"I love what you said, right at the beginning: 'What's surprising is how difficult it is.' And that makes me smile. Because it is. And it's tricky, working with truthfulness regarding oneself. You think you're being truthful, but there are so many times when you are not."

"Yes," he agrees. "Well, the first thing that comes to mind just now, which is sort of underlying all of that, is truthfulness as the antidote to self-delusion. Even before right speech, it's being truthful about one's own mind. We ask, 'Are we really seeing ourselves truthfully?' And that could mean, 'Are we seeing truthfully our acts of body, speech, and mind?' And there could be two sides to it. There could be the meaning, 'Do we acknowledge the defilements of our mind, that which is unwholesome?' And also, 'Do we acknowledge what's wholesome?'"

"Oh! Yes. I've had this thought more than once; I've definitely had the feeling arise that I might not be truthful with myself. That I might feel I am better than I am. And then, the very next day, I'm feeling I am entirely a failure at something! How would you go about working with that, seeing that? What questions might one ask?"

"Well, it's not so much telling as seeing. You might try just using the list of the defilements." He laughs. "Try taking one defilement at a time and just really keep an eye out for the arising of that defilement, whether it is wrong view or greed or doubt."

"Oh, this is good. Go on."

"For example, you could consider the conceit factor, that 'I am,' or the comparing mind, or the projection into past and future. All of that is just part of the conceit of 'I am.' I think we've talked about this before. 'I am' relative to another person or 'I am' over the course of time. It arises a million times a day."

"It sure does."

"But do we see it? Or do we delude ourselves into thinking it's not there?" We are quiet.

"This parami is interesting, Joseph. So rich. It was like working with the precepts. I feel I can continue working with this list, watching for the defilements to arise, catching them more quickly, letting them pass through instead of fouling up the day."

"Yes."

"Another entirely new concept to work with. See, that's why I feel this book is never going to get done, because you continue to have great new ideas, and I have new revelations or stories, and we just keep going deeper, getting wiser. At least I hope I am getting wiser. And I *know* you are. I have it on tape!" Joseph laughs.

"Cool. What else comes to mind?"

"Well," he speaks slowly, "it's funny because just as you began talking about working with the defilements, the first thought that came to mind was, as I said, truthfulness being the opposite of self-delusion. So we're just seeing what's there—both the wholesome and the unwholesome. Basically not fooling ourselves."

"Yeah. And it's tough!"

"It is."

"Because there's so much to be noticed and so many deeply ingrained habits!"

"Exactly."

"And then it's so hard, when it's going well," I start laughing, "not to take it personally! Right?"

"Well, yes, but that's just something else to notice. That's all."

"Oh, right. Just something else to notice. Just something else to notice." I chuckle. "Just saying that aloud is so calming, encouraging. And," I chuckle again, "so darn obvious! I should make it a poster in my room or a tattoo where I will see it all the time. Seriously." We are laughing.

"OK," I continue, "so I am also seeing how often I slap a concept on whatever is arising, which definitely clouds my understanding of what simply and actually just happened. I remember hearing you tell a story about going for a walk with friends when you were teaching in Russia. And you happened to walk by a vacant lot . . ."

"Right."

"There you were in Russia, everything new and different, and you were just seeing colors and shapes and beauty. It didn't register as the concept of an ugly vacant lot."

"Right. It was actually a lot filled with garbage," he says, laughing. "So from a conventional point of view, from my mystified friends' point of view, it was an ugly, vacant urban lot filled with trash. But in that particular moment I was seeing it more like an artist might. I was just seeing colors and forms."

"Ah."

"Then," he laughs, "it became quite beautiful."

"I understand. Sometimes I'll see things along the waterfront of Sausalito that are totally funky at best. But they can also become striking—the way sunlight is reflected off the water onto a rusting tin roof, or the moonlight on all the anchor-out boats . . . and suddenly it is beautiful. So seeing it with the eyes of an artist, beyond concept. That's a useful tool.

"And you suggested in watching ordinary speech to notice what habits are there. But then I discovered, sadly, that I aspire to a new habit, I do it, and as soon as I do, the mind jumps into planning mode, spinning out on all the ways to establish this new habit. It's almost instant, you know? I have the thought, *Well, this was a good way to handle that,* and boom, instantly the mind jumps in with suggestions: *Oh, we can do this, and then we can do that* . . . And so I went deeper with it and asked myself what mind state is present when this is going on, and I realized it's craving!"

"Yes. Yes."

"Arrgh! So what happens next? I am having a craving for craving?" I whoop aloud, seeing clearly, painfully, the dysfunction behind this pattern.

"Exactly," he says, laughing.

"Well, so then what?"

"Well, the first is to be mindful of this reflection, understanding that this can be the beginning of the proliferation of thoughts. So then you can begin to recognize that as it arises. Do you know the Pali word *papanca*?

"No."

"It is translated as 'proliferation.' The Buddha taught that there are three conditioning forces for papanca. One is desire. One is conceit. And one is wrong view. So any one of those three can get the papanca going. And it's helpful when you see the mind beginning to spin out, you might just begin to look, to investigate what is behind that beginning to spin out. Is it desire, as you saw? Is it wrong view? Is it conceit? Or is it some combination of them? So you're really just being mindful of the process, rather than being swept along by it."

"Which of course is exactly what I was just describing. Interesting! And so then to be able to catch that moment early, to be able to see that this is a time where instead I could just say, 'No thanks' or 'Not now' to that stream of planning thoughts?"

"Exactly."

"Oh, that really helps, Joseph."

"Yes, or another helpful phrase is, 'Is it necessary?'"

"Yes, you've mentioned that one, and I find it has been really helpful for the yammering, planning mind."

"Oh, yes."

I laugh. "Or one of my favorite reminders is your mantra "You can change the channel." I think of the yammering like a commercial, and I just select another station."

Now I am telling Joseph the story about my couch. "And you suggested watching for the underlying motive when you are not truthful. You said that in itself is tricky. In instances where you find you are not being truthful, or just not quite truthful, to investigate. 'What was the motive then? Why were you not a hundred percent truthful?' So I asked the woman I'd worked with to come over so she could see the new couch in the room. And before she came, I had a weekend to tussle with it, and I came to the conclusion that I also wanted her to see that it was wrong, not only the color, but the piece itself, which she had advised me on purchasing. And so based on the wrong color I could return it and get my money back. I did not want them to redo the finish. I wanted my money back. I was very clear that was what I wanted.

"But I also wanted to be truthful. That was also my intention. So sure enough, she got there and agreed the wood finish color was definitely not what we ordered and that she would take care of it. Then I began my little, well-rehearsed litany of everything that was wrong with the piece. And with each thing I said, she was able to listen without reacting and painstakingly help me to actually see that aspect differently. And by the end of a good amount of time, I saw it through her eyes and realized she was right, and it was right. Joseph, it was amazing. The piece slowly transformed before my eyes with just a different perspective, like a concept melting away. And the relief I felt, at not having to start all over, was bigger than if I had gotten what I thought I wanted, which was my money back.

"So, telling the truth and then being open to the outcome. I really held that intention. And I could not have envisioned or predicted that outcome. It was beyond what I thought I wanted. I couldn't get over it. It was great. I was elated."

"Right, exactly."

Joseph also had some rousing advice for Ron when they spoke recently. Ron was relating several troubling work issues he was dealing with that were generating worry and worst-case-scenario thinking. After a bit, Joseph interrupted him (or so Ron told me in relating the story) with the encouragement to "cut off its head, instantly." As soon as the leading-to-suffering thoughts arose, Joseph advised being ruthless. He called it being in warrior mode: vigilant for those thoughts and slashing them the moment they arose. Ron repeated Joseph's words: "Do not even start down that path." I remember this now as Joseph and I are speaking.

"The talk you had with Ron seemed totally transforming."

"Great."

"And tell me if this is right. When you were talking about the thoughts that arise, the worries and fears," I start laughing, "did you actually say to him 'cut off their heads'?"

"Ah," he laughs.

"Well, it's a very interesting way of describing that process of catching your thoughts, and he loved it," I say.

"Exactly. That's what I intended."

"But did you really say, 'cut off its head'?"

"Probably."

I laugh. "Well, that's wonderful. It's so empowering!"

"Right. We were having a very energized conversation."

When Ron and I discussed the conversation he had with Joseph, the energy, or viriya, in Joseph's suggestion invigorated both of us. Approaching one's fearful, doubting, or catastrophic habits of thought with sword in hand made the effort sound like fun. What a shift from feeling like the oppressed victim.

"So this ties in to a common misconception about Buddhism," I say now to Joseph, "the idea that Buddhism is about a passive response to life. But it's not passive."

Joseph laughs. "Not at all."

"It can also include going on the offense, right? I mean, in this type of situation, it's like going into battle."

"Yes."

"That element makes it very attractive to me because it's fun. It reminds me I am in charge of my reactions and can rigorously resist. I think that's something that is not very well understood about Buddhism."

"Yes," he agrees. "Well, you know, there are many different skillful means. It just depends on what's needed in the moment. Sometimes it's the warrior mode. Other times it's opening, becoming soft and accepting. There are different approaches depending on what the situation is. But I really felt that for Ron, he needed this approach right now."

"Yes, it's great. It's working for him, and for me too! Well, I think that's about enough. I have a whole batch of new stuff to work with. And that's perfect."

"Give my regards to Ron," he says, chuckling. "Tell him to keep it up."

I laugh. "Cut off their heads! OK, I will. Thank you, Joseph."

Now, as this month of truthfulness comes to its conclusion, I see I could have used more resoluteness, more warrior mode, at times in cutting off the heads of untruthful inclinations as they arose. Resoluteness is the eighth, and next, parami. I can see why truthfulness would come before warrior mode. It helps to not go forth fighting windmills instead of one's real battles. And the added element of truthfulness as one's target, aligned with an occasional warrior response, keeps it fresh.

Buddhism is not about suffering passively. It can also include a fighting stance, which I admit I take to eagerly. Viriya. This is not resistance born of ignorance or fear. This is going into battle armed with truth to ruthlessly slay as many of the unwholesome and unskillful elements of our thinking, speaking, and actions as we can. This is no passive undertaking. We are awakening. We begin by paying closer attention, moment to moment, to what is actually happening. We develop clearer comprehension. Sometimes this clearer comprehension may require us to be fierce. There is so much work to be done. I will also add that understanding how and what to do about one's suffering, *within what is*, is the most miraculous gift I have ever received.

Words used in powerful new ways have the power
to free us from limiting preconceptions.
—JOSEPH GOLDSTEIN

8 Resoluteness

Why not aspire to greatness?
—JOSEPH GOLDSTEIN

The Eighth Parami: Resoluteness

The Pali word *aditthana*, which we translate as
resoluteness, is used to designate the eighth parami in
Buddhist texts. It means determination in following an
aspiration, and is also described as unwavering, faithful.

Instructions: Buddhists with Biceps

"One example of this parami comes from the days when I was mountain
biking," Joseph says. "When I was just beginning, I would be biking with
friends that were quite a bit better than I was. We'd be going up hills, and
a lot of them I would have to walk up. They were just too steep for me.
And I really had a kind of . . . *dread* is too strong a word, but," he laughs,
"I did not like going up those hills. It was a struggle. Yet as I kept on and
got a little stronger, at a certain point the whole attitude changed, and
I began to actually look forward to the difficulty of going up the hills,
because it felt like it was strengthening and challenging. That change
of attitude about what was difficult is resoluteness—appreciating what
can be developed when something is difficult. There are so many situations like that in life. One of the meanings of, one of the qualities of,

the enlightenment factor of the fifth parami—viriya, or energy—is that somebody with viriya is somebody who is energized by challenge."

"Right. I remember it well."

"So it is that energy that is called upon in resoluteness, not being daunted by challenges. This is the same thing."

"In business you see this a lot. There are people that head companies, such as myself, who describe loving the challenges. They'll say to their staff, 'Bring it to me! Let me help. I'll figure it out!' They really love facing new challenges, like you describe with the steep hills."

"Yes. So it is that quality. And the good news is that we can practice our resoluteness. We can strengthen our resoluteness. Maybe we start with small things. Maybe we find ourselves walking up the hills. But what is important here is to really investigate that quality of resoluteness for ourselves."

"I see, because it's so easy at that point where it becomes challenging to say, 'Those guys are just better than I am. Here I am having to walk my bike up the hill. This is no fun. This sport probably isn't for me.' That can so often be our tendency when that first big hill comes up."

"Right. Exactly."

Joseph's Instructions: Working with Resoluteness

The eighth component of integrity, resoluteness, is also defined as tenacity or determination. Resoluteness includes the aspect of carry-through. It is connected to achieving one's aspiration. What is needed is to investigate what is required to realize one's aspiration.

1. Set one to five things a day, or a week, that you aspire to. For each aspiration, be as truthful as you can about what is needed to achieve it. We must be really honest with ourselves. There can be many misconceptions here. As the aspiration takes shape, precision and clarity are needed to see what is required to achieve it. And this can change over time. Periodically asking what is needed helps give focus to the mind state of resoluteness.

- So we ask ourselves, "What is this day's, or this week's, aspiration?"
- Then we ask, "What is needed or required to achieve it?"
- And we begin paying attention to what happens around that aspiration.

2. Another way to practice with this parami is to:

- Focus on learning to recognize the quality of resoluteness.
- Learn the ways you might manifest it. You must investigate this for yourself.
- When you notice you are experiencing resoluteness, pay close attention to the various ways it manifests. Become familiar with what can cause it to arise.

3. Now we begin to look at what can undermine our aspirations.

- Notice the times you do not follow through with an aspiration.
- Investigate what is happening here. If you do not achieve an aspiration, ask, "Why not?" What undermined the original resoluteness?

Parami = purification of the heart. The application of resoluteness can be practiced on a wide range of things. And remember: we can have all these good intentions, but what is important is

- the carry-through element
- not giving up
- understanding that difficulties are part of the path
- and when we do give up, simply beginning again

Joseph adds, "Remember, for something to be considered a parami, rather than just a wholesome state, it needs to be practiced with an aspiration for awakening. If the larger aspiration of enlightenment seems unworkable or overwhelming, work with these smaller steps. It is all related to one's clarity about the aspiration and about investigating what is needed to achieve it. Even if one is practicing resoluteness with small things, if done with an aspiration of awakening, then one is on a whole-some, skillful path, the path to enlightenment. For example, you can practice generosity as a wholesome state simply to achieve lightness and happiness, or you can practice it as a parami, a component of integrity, with the aspiration to achieve letting go of greed completely." He laughs. "This is a good practice for me because of my inclination toward ease."

There are times when I specifically choose the difficult
option as opposed to the easy one as an antidote
to my tendency, or as a way to explore new options
for relating to difficulties when they do arise.
—JOSEPH GOLDSTEIN

> What we are doing is seeing clearly into the cause
> of our suffering, so that the resolve to change
> habits of mind becomes spontaneous.
> —JOSEPH GOLDSTEIN

Working with Resoluteness: Set an Aspiration and Ask What Is Needed

And so I begin: setting an aspiration and asking what is needed. Aspiration sounds significant, and I really need to do my taxes today. Is this an aspiration? I struggle with definitions, then select three aspirations for the day:

Aspiration 1: Meditate. This is easy, because I already did.

Aspiration 2: Exercise. What is needed? Schedule it. I am overseeing the house being power washed today. I will go for a long run after they leave, late afternoon.

Aspiration 3: Do my taxes. Perhaps not a proper aspiration; it seems a bit mundane. But deadlines are pressing, and well, this is the day for it. I am stuck at home for most of the day with the power washing. OK, what is needed to achieve it? Suddenly I have an insight. What is needed is also what suddenly makes it feel like a more worthy, engaging aspiration. My third aspiration becomes "Enjoy doing my taxes!" What a concept. But it's true—this is exactly what is needed . . . for me. This is in fact the only way, truthfully, that I am going to get through it—if I am also enjoying the task. So what is needed to enjoy doing my taxes? Now this is certainly a more uplifting question. And my answer? To *enjoy the process, not complete the project.* It is a revelation.

I set up everything on the dining table, where I can gaze out over the water, and put on some sing-along music. I certainly don't need a lot of concentration to add up numbers. I have a piece of chocolate as a reward upon completing the itemizing of checkbook entries. I follow that with a cup of chai after tallying the credit card statement. And I am also *enjoying the process.* So, no surprise, I keep at it. When interrupted (water suddenly blasting in through gaps around an old window, the

161

CREATING A LIFE OF INTEGRITY

painter with questions, a phone call) I remind myself the goal is to enjoy, not complete. Interruptions are clearly out of my control. I would only be adding suffering into the mix if I made completion the aspiration. The realization that I am doing the best I can under the present circumstances is tremendously energizing. Yes, it seems obvious now, but I am clear my normal process would have collapsed by the third interruption. It is much easier to achieve the aspiration to enjoy the process, and so I just continue. I keep checking in on the attitude, reminding myself I don't need to rush or complete. I just need to muster resoluteness and carry on. I am enjoying not pushing. I watch restlessness arise briefly with each interruption, then somehow just drift away as I turn back to the task.

And I do it! I actually enjoy working on my taxes, the task goes remarkably smoothly, and I finish the project just before 2:00 p.m. I feel splendidly, massively resolute. Wow. If I can *complete and enjoy* doing my taxes in one morning, with interruptions, what else can I accomplish?

I begin the second half of the month considering, *Do I follow through, and if not, why not? What undermined the aspiration?*

It is Wednesday. Last night I was sitting at a table of women from our tennis club. The topic was untidy spouses! One woman's husband had recently retired. We were all laughing as she described coming home from work each day to find little cast-offs of his day spent at home—a mug in the guest bathroom; a sweater draped over a dining room chair; newspapers, magazines, books on tabletops. I offered that Ron says he doesn't understand why we have to keep the house so neat when we are not expecting anyone. "Because it soothes my soul to have it that way," I say to the group. "It's not just about having guests over. It's for me!" The women nod, understanding.

This is true. And because it is more important to me, and Ron and I have shared a home for twenty-five years, I just tidy up things I feel need tidying up for my own peace of mind. Ron definitely does his share of chores around the house. It may be a universal conundrum, but as I sit listening to the criticisms, I am inspired to summon resoluteness and be kinder with my spouse. I don't want to sound like these women, complaining. I understand I can do better here, and we will both be happier for it. I often say I don't know what God was thinking when she thought men and women could live together. She overlooked, it seems to me, some significant tweaks she could have easily made early on.

Does having a relationship with someone automatically dictate we must abide by, adopt, and embrace the other's preferences? Does it include the right to blame or cajole or get angry at them for not doing their share of something we want done? I think not. Again, another's willing participation lies out of our control. It only causes suffering for everyone when we insist on their seeing the situation as we do. It is our problem, not theirs. This is not the outcome I had envisioned working with this resoluteness aspiration. This feels like all the paramis at work: a generous spirit, an ethical striving to be honest, renunciation of my own tight-fisted desires, wisdom, viriya in looking more deeply under the muck, patience with myself, and understanding that these thoughts and feelings are impermanent—not mine, not even true! Then we just season the mix with enough resoluteness to carry onward with a cheery disposition. This is investigating with an intention for awakening. And enlightened is exactly how I feel right now. I stand leaning on the broom I am sweeping with outdoors, grinning at the results of my hard work— a clean-swept yard *and* mind. It really is a beautiful day to be out of doors, released from a constricting attitude.

As mentioned, that steadfast, perseverance quality is one I have an abundance of much of the time. Mostly my edge is not pushing a task into drudgery. Still, I can also begin projects that appear simple, then add a (strong) preference for perfection into the mix, stir madly, and soon find myself overwhelmed, sliding toward crankiness.

This Saturday I decide to further hone my resoluteness understanding and skill by tackling a long-avoided project: my bookcases. I now have books stacked on top of books. There is not one book-sized hole left in which to wedge one more book. Shelves supporting solid, hardcover books on all four walls of my little home office, weigh heavily on my mind as I sit quietly contemplating where and how to begin. I would surely die under a giant mound of books if I am in here during an earthquake.

And so I begin, as usual, with great energy, enthusiasm. Windows open to spring, birds singing, opera on the stereo. I am lighthearted, my mind bedazzled by glowing visions. I even have a few magazine photos of how to arrange things in the open shelving I will soon have. I also have asked, in preparation, "What could undermine this resolution?" And my answer was "Zealousness." That should have been my clue, the caution flag waving. But no, I tumble in with fierce gusto and totally unrealistic expectations.

I shouldn't, but I take *all* the books off *all* the shelves, slowly placing them in teetering stacks by subject. No more searching for books. Hours later I collapse on the floor of the hall, as there is now no floor space left in the office to stretch an aching back. Books are heavy! I may have begun this project with shining visions of a well-ordered library, of gleaming open space on the shelves, but now I am stuck fast in a goopy tar pit of lethargy and doubt. For a while I lay on the floor of the hall totally unwilling to even look at the chaos I've created. And then after a while I do get up, go back in the room, sit on a stack of books, look around. New fiction. Classics. Buddhism. Poetry. Health. Gardening. Reference. *Whose crazy idea was this? What was I thinking? This is taking order to the extreme. I'll never finish this. How many Saturdays will this take?* But now, of course, I can't abandon the project. Other things begin tugging for attention. *I need to buy groceries. Return emails.* I literally just sit and watch myself turn cranky.

Now I remember that resoluteness included an understanding that zealousness might undermine it, and that my practice also was to include periodic check-ins on current state of mind, which of course has been sliding into fatigue and overwhelm for some time now. I trampled right over the initial squeals of doubt from a tiring mind. The magic ingredient, so clear to me now, is stopping to ask, "What is happening? What is needed?" in the moments *before* overwhelm and disillusionment. Didn't we just go over this? Sigh. This was profoundly obvious, and successful, when doing my taxes. Here I could have paused many times, gazed out the window, stretched my back, called my sister for a chat. I could have started with one wall of books. Yup. And I didn't. Can't help but love a mind so full of enthusiasm, like we had at the start.

Something to appreciate there, I think. That spirit of resoluteness. And so sometimes, as now, resoluteness entails gently turning away from the chaos. I leave the room, close the door, and go for a long run.

Several hours later I return to the stacks of books, body refreshed, mind still reluctant, but clearer. I see I can make the job much easier by selecting which books should go into the donate-to-the-library boxes. And I just begin again. Did I complete the project that Saturday? Oh, no. I lived with stacks of books on the floor for several days. It took two Saturdays and a bunch of evenings to complete the task. But I did place clean books onto polished shelves with a wiser mind. Slowly. And now? I know where any book is when I want it, and I found lots of interesting new books to read in my own little bookstore that I had forgotten were there. I also donated over three hundred books to the Sausalito library. They were thrilled. I am thrilled to see my walls again. I now have family photos among the bindings. It is lovely and comforting to sit at my desk and gaze around the room. Resoluteness and wisdom accomplished this, any lingering untidy mind states swept away with the dust balls. I honestly feel the spaciousness of the room mirrors a new spaciousness in my mind as I regard my handiwork. I promise myself that I will listen more skillfully, and I honestly believe I understand how to go about it now.

Buddhism offers the possibility that very ordinary everyday tasks and conversations can be undertaken with an aspiration for enlightenment. This understanding can be a source of much joy and much ease. I have been inspired by this aspect of the teachings for many years. I believe it is a significant contributing factor in the lighthearted, carefree nature seen in people such as Joseph Goldstein and the Dalai Lama. The idea that *it is enough* just to attend to whatever is up at the moment with attention and a welcoming heart is so awesomely radical to one who can tend to press long after my welcoming heart has had enough, closed down shop, and gone home. Could this really be what's important? Not completing the task? It sounds so simple, so easy . . . and so compelling!

The Dalai Lama says, "My religion is kindness." We can be intrigued and inspired by just the possibility that this could be true. The idea that attending to the moment with a welcoming, kind heart, including for ourselves, is really all that matters can offer us tremendous relief from our tendency to discount our efforts, minimize our worthiness. I can also confirm that living this way is not always simple or easy. Still, I have found it to be powerfully good news. And I have tasted its sweetness again and again. We all have experienced this when we respond simply with an open, loving heart to whatever is arising. In those moments, when we can remember, *Ah, this is all there is to be done,* we may feel remarkable peace. For me the idea has been life-turning. It's not the grand stuff. And we know it. It's the everyday stuff that nicks and scratches and dents us, entangles us, brings us down from loftier aspirations. This is where a life of integrity gets crafted—moment by moment, day by day, strengthening each of the parami factors of integrity, of freedom. And this is where the bliss of blamelessness arises. This is the source of that carefree, joyous, and kind response that is, for most of us, our deepest yearning.

What is important is not giving up. And there will be
times when we do give up. Then we just begin again.
—JOSEPH GOLDSTEIN

What's needed is to continually reflect on and check
in on what is required to realize the aspiration.
—JOSEPH GOLDSTEIN

Check-In Conversation: A Vision of Where We Are Heading

Once again I am chatting with Joseph after dinnertime on the East Coast, in what has become our customary check-in time. This time, Ron and I are up in the mountains for the weekend. Joseph is at home in Barre.

"OK," I begin. I am stretched out on the couch watching snow-flakes gently floating down from clouds that seem to be perched in the treetops. This is a surprising late spring snowfall, and it is particularly entrancing. I pull my gaze from the dance out-of-doors and direct it onto my page of notes.

"So I decided to work with being resolute about doing my taxes, which of course I had been putting off and putting off, probably like most everyone else. It definitely felt like a project in need of some resoluteness to get completed. And I asked myself what was needed. And I decided I needed to set up a time I would do it, be prepared for interruptions, and reward myself for little bits and pieces as I finished them. But I was still doubting the aspiration-worthiness of doing my taxes . . ." (Joseph laughs) "until I had the idea that the most important piece was not saying 'getting my taxes done' but saying 'doing my taxes and enjoying the process.' Now *that* was an aspiration I felt I could get myself enrolled in. I was clear there were a lot of other circumstances that could contribute to not completing them that were outside my control. But I did feel I had control over enjoying the process, not to mention the better chance they would get completed if I were enjoying the process!" I laugh. "For some reason, which sounds a little silly as I am telling it, that aspiration felt more worthy, as in using wisdom to create a way that I would be more willing to stay the course. And in fact I did enjoy doing them, and I did finish! Was that skillful?"

"Well, I think what you're describing is an individual component of aspiration and resoluteness. This addresses the point that each person needs to discover their own individual aspects. So I wouldn't make your insight necessarily universal. That's what you discovered for yourself was needed to achieve your aspiration. Maybe for somebody else the satisfaction *would* come from getting it done."

"Ah, yes. And they wouldn't need it to be fun, or need to have the aspiration to try to make it fun."

"Exactly."

"OK. That's a good distinction. I can see that."

"Right. Again, it is different for different people. That is why it is so important to really investigate this for oneself."

"I do love the word 'resoluteness.' I like it a lot. I don't think it has much excess baggage, you know, like 'determination' or 'tenacity.'"

"Right, it doesn't have negative connotations," Joseph says.

"And it also doesn't have an overly aggressive tone. It feels more like an inner strength, an inner process."

"Right. And resoluteness includes the quality of carry-through, which is an important piece to remember."

"Yeah. You once mentioned that it isn't your strong suit, but you said it's my strong suit. And it certainly is. But for me the edge is not pushing too far too long, you know? It feels like I can tend to be *too* resolute. I can get all enthused, hurl myself forward, then keep at something without much investigation, perhaps pushing long past the value in it. I especially like how you tie resolution into aspiration. Being really clear before one begins."

"Right. What's needed is to continually reflect on and check in on what is required to realize the aspiration."

"Oh, yes. This was very much on my radar both the times I remembered and continually checked in and the times—much later—when I discovered I had not checked in and barged right through into fatigue, unclarity, and then ill humor."

"Yup," he says as we both laugh.

"There is another unclear and tricky edge in here for me: discerning the difference between making anything I am doing fulfilling by merely being present versus working skillfully with a more worthy aspiration. Because in so doing, I can find myself, sometime later, blazing blindly down a path that perhaps is, or has become, not ultimately worthwhile. Do you know what I mean? Help me here."

"Yes, well, one of the measures for that assessment is to investigate if what you are being present for is *onward-leading*. Is it cultivating the paramis? This is a big one to ask oneself, to check in on. A key here is wisdom. When one is holding the highest aspiration *and* is being present with whatever one is investigating, this leads to the development of wisdom. A criteria for onward-leading can be to ask, 'Is development of wisdom present here?' Go back to our notes on working with the wisdom parami. Explore how to work with developing wisdom while cultivating resoluteness. You can do the same with the other paramis also."

After a long pause, he continues. "One basic understanding that can also be useful is that of the three characteristics, which we discussed previously: impermanence, suffering, and selflessness or non-self. For example, you could be working on strengthening your generosity, but without wisdom present, you could tumble into a lot of selfing. You know, 'Look at what a generous person I am.'" We laugh. "In meditation, people often don't notice that wholesome mind states are also arising and passing away, that they are also impermanent and therefore ultimately unsatisfying. We can all be seduced by the wholesome states."

"Oh, now I'm thinking about rewarding myself at certain junctions in the tax preparation . . . not so much wisdom there."

He laughs. "Rewards can give rise to more greed. You don't need rewards. The parami work itself purifies our motivations."

"I remember you once spoke of the way people approach meditation practice, depending on what they want out of it. If they just want to chill out, that equals a certain amount of practice; if they want deep concentration, that is a different amount of practice; and if they aspire to awakening, that's still another amount of practice. Does that sound right?"

"Well, the amount of time and effort extended is a factor, but of course the quality of that practice is also a factor."

"Yes. So with each aspiration, then, quality would mean being honest and truthful about what is needed?"

"Right. And there can be many misconceptions here. As the aspiration takes shape, precision and clarity are needed to see what is required. Asking what is needed really helps give focus to the mind state of resoluteness."

"I find myself wishing I'd had this parami at the beginning! It's so helpful to have resoluteness as my focus when working with an aspiration, any aspiration, or with any of the paramis, like an aspiration to be more generous or more ethical. That critical step of asking what's needed is so crucial. Previously, I might have an aspiration, run after it, not check in, get off track, run out of steam, become totally discouraged . . . and quit."

"Right. Right."

"So that piece has been really important for me. I keep imagining you pushing that bike up the steep hills."

He laughs. "Yes."

"OK, Joseph, asking what's needed was key. And then also to investigate—if I didn't follow through with something, to ask, 'Why not? What undermined it?'"

"Right."

"And I think, like you said, it feels important to discover and understand that for ourselves. It can be so different for one person than for another."

"Exactly."

"Also watching closely for what might undermine the aspiration. I would ask your question, 'What is needed?' Then I would add, 'What might undermine it?' Because after a while I knew only too well what might rise up to undermine the original intention. It was abundantly, almost ridiculously, clear."

Joseph laughs. "Yes."

"And I found that working with resoluteness in those really ongoing, active ways was energetic, with very clear comprehension. Really no doubts. And that pursuing and succeeding at the aspiration brought with it its own satisfaction. So I admit you're right. Looking back, I see that I didn't need to reward myself."

"That's good," he says, chuckling.

"You also said that it's good to awaken in people the idea that the ordinary things we do can be in the service of liberation. I just continue to love that concept. It describes so well what we're doing with the paramis."

We are quiet for a while before I speak again. "So I have another question. We have talked about this so much that I hesitate to bring it up. For something to be considered a parami, instead of just a wholesome state, it needs to be practiced with an aspiration for awakening, even when practicing with the smallest of things. You used the example of how one can practice generosity to achieve lightness and happiness or one can practice it as a parami and achieve letting go of greed."

"Right."

"So I continue working with desire. I stopped for a while, but this month seemed ripe for doing so again, resolve being such a good support for renunciation. I'm now almost a full month into a new aspiration of not buying anything," I sigh, "and no surprise, it continues to be a juicy path for me. This time I used the questions and asked what was needed. No browsing was the first answer, which I discovered previously. So I have not been browsing. I don't put myself in temptation's claws. But now, up here in the mountains for the weekend, Ron suggested we cruise the village, which you know I love to do . . . especially with you!" Joseph laughs. "And Ron looks in a store window and says, 'Oh, you should try that on. That would look good on you.' And so I did, and sure enough, it looked great. But I felt *no* interest, no desire. Very curious. Not buying is my aspiration, and it seems to be working. And this is really different for me, as you well know!" Joseph laughs.

"What was your feeling when you let go of the wanting?" he asks.

"Uh, the wanting never really arose . . . or at least that is how it felt to me. It was curious, and certainly different. In answer to what is needed, for me," I say, chuckling, "in addition to no browsing, clear comprehension is needed. I was standing there considering *the impulse to buy*, not how great the coat looked on me! The coat looked great. I imagined it hanging in my already full coat closet. Wearing it. Loving it. And then the eventual passing of its allure. I saw very clearly the impermanence of its allure. From beginning to end. And I understood I already have enough! *Impermanence* and *enough*. Two words that helped me hang the coat back up."

"And how did that feel?"

"Oh, I felt tremendous relief! To just release the impulse to buy, let it float away and not continue to gnaw on it as we kept walking through the village was awesome and uplifting!"

"Yes."

"There was a little pride in there too, of course, but mostly relief. I felt I was able to browse—you know, throw myself into temptation's lair—with a clear mind. As we continued, I'd see a store and think, *I know there's probably something I might like in there.* And then I could feel I didn't even want to go there. Not just into the store, but into desiring."

"Right."

"And get all caught up . . ."

"Right. Exactly."

"And la-di-da, la-di-da," I say, laughing. "I adored just floating on by, not ruffled, not caught in any sticky desire."

"Maybe you should make it more than a month," he says, laughing.

"Yeah, I actually feel right now that that would be fine."

"Yes. It's more peaceful not to want than to want."

"Oh, infinitely."

"And that, I think, is what you've been talking about," he adds after a few moments. "That's the point."

"I see that. I was holding the aspiration of not getting caught up in desire, in the larger context, in the context of liberation and purification of"—I make choking, gasping sounds—"the stranglehold of desire."

He laughs. "Exactly."

"It's just been the best, Joseph. I keep working with each parami like using another key, each unlocking a different aspect of my nemesis desire, and I can really feel a loosening happening. A much clearer and deeper understanding is maturing here. And then even when I forget and tumble back in, I am also watching the way that works, how desire unfolds, grabs, lingers. In a way, I'm choosing to . . . choose it. I am not being sucked in. It is amazing and getting richer and deeper all the time."

We are quiet for a few moments, a pleasant ease between us, both greedy types, understanding well this dance with desire.

Then I continue. "I'd also like to ask for clarification: You said one can practice with small things, you know, like to have the aspiration to have one cookie instead of two, or really big things, like enlightenment. And I think you said something like small aspirations over time can lead to enlightenment and big aspirations over time can lead to enlightenment. Is that what you said? Because of course I thought," I am laughing now, "*Well, if that's the case, I'm just going to go for the one cookie over two as my aspiration. Forget the tougher, bigger aspirations!* I think I might have something wrong here."

He laughs. "Well, in a way that example ties in to the renunciation parami we were just discussing. You know, like not taking the second cookie or not buying something new. If one is really conscious of the force of the desire, of the *wanting*, then when the wisdom mind comes in and says, 'No, I don't need this,' one actually lets go of the *desire*, not just the cookie or the coat. There's awareness of that whole process, as you were just describing. So then I think that is in the service of the higher aspiration of liberation."

"Ah. Of course, the awareness . . . like browsing a store, watching desire arise, and then simply passing on as if walking past a barking dog."

"Right. It's more than just not taking the second cookie."

"So with that awareness, with that understanding present, it doesn't really matter what the thing is you're doing."

"Yes. Exactly. It is utilizing all of these everyday situations in the context of really understanding what's being developed in the mind and what's being abandoned in the mind."

"I can feel that. There's real wisdom there," I say slowly.

"Oh, yes. Indeed."

"You used another example, which I think is a little different than what I was describing with my library. On retreat when you're having difficulties, you have said to yourself, 'Joseph, just sit (meditate) and walk. Just sit and walk."

He laughs. "Right."

"You said to yourself, 'Surrender to the Dharma. Just do it no matter what.' And that's a little different, don't you think, from what I was describing? It's doing it in spite of or no matter what else arises."

"Right. That is the persevering aspect of resoluteness. As you said before, not giving up. Just doing it, even if one is not seeing the results right away."

"I guess that would be like living with the stacks of books on the floor for days until I finish. That is skillfully resolute."

"Right." We are quiet for a while.

"And then there have been those times," he says, "that have been so vivid and alive that I didn't want to waste a moment. Those are moments of pure resoluteness."

"Ummm, yes, I think I know that place. Where you're in the groove. I've experienced that in concentration practice, especially when on a retreat, where I don't want to get sucked out of that deep concentration state into *anything* else that might be happening around me. No interest. *I'm staying right here!*" I laugh. "Right?"

"Yes. And it can be with anything. It can be with the concentration practice. It can be with the moment-to-moment continuity of mindfulness. Clearing books out of a library. Or anything. Just really staying on track."

"As with renunciation of desire!" I add.

"Exactly," he says, laughing.

"So I also found that what seemed particularly useful was asking what was needed. Simple. But I'm used to setting lots of resolutions and never following that up with the idea of asking what is needed. I really love that. It really helped to clarify the resolve—asking what was needed to achieve it. It strengthened not giving up at the first difficulty, while also recognizing there will be times when I am irresolute . . . and not giving up then either!" I laugh.

Joseph adds, "Or then, just beginning again."

"Ah. That's better."

"I mean, there *will* be times when we *do* give up."

"Oh, yeah."

"But," he says slowly, "the important thing is recognizing that, and then when we do recognize it, and the energy is there, we just begin again. That is also a very important part of resoluteness."

"Yes. Which would certainly not be giving up."

"Right. But it's not giving up in the more macro sense, because there might be sittings, or situations in our daily lives, where we do give up—for a period of time. We notice this, and then we don't let that be discouraging. 'For whatever reason I did give up, but I'll begin again now!'"

"Oh! I don't think I'm always that kind to myself. I love that. Sometimes I may just need to step away, refresh the mind, and then begin again. Like I am slowly doing with the library. It is wonderful in ways I never could have achieved even had I pushed to do it all in one day."

"Exactly," he says, chuckling.

"So not changing the channel, but just doing something else for a while, while holding it within the scope of the aspiration. That's a little different spin on it, but it allows me to return to it refreshed, renewed. You're saying that would be skillful?"

"Oh, yes. Definitely."

"And here's my last question." I sigh, and Joseph chuckles.

"Yes?"

"This is something I struggle with sometimes: Can you talk about expectation versus aspiration?"

"Well, expectation is feeling that things in the moment should be a certain way. You know, we can have an expectation of a concentrated sitting, or whatever. But," he laughs, "things are largely out of our control. And so expectation is a setup for disappointment."

"Oh, for sure! I know this one really, really well."

"Whereas aspiration," he continues, "sets up a larger goal, or vision, of where we are heading. But still, in that journey," he laughs again, "there will be a lot of ups and downs, things that we might not want or appreciate, but that are there nevertheless. It doesn't have to deflect us from our goal or aspiration. But if we have an expectation that it should be one way or another, then it is a problem."

"So an aspiration would be more like . . . not a goal, but something that almost doesn't have . . . ?"

"No, I don't have a problem with the word 'goal.'"

"Oh, OK."

"I think aspiration is a goal. But some people have a hard time with that word 'goal.'"

"They do! Aspiration is a much better word, I think."

"I never understood why the resistance to the word 'goal,'" he says, "but you can use that word, or you could use the word 'vision,' or 'aspiration.'"

"Hmm, 'vision' is nice, but I think 'aspiration' is such an uplifting word."

"Yes, right. That's why I use it. It implies a bigger picture. Expectation has to do with some kind of immediate result that we want. And so that's just a very different thing."

"Yes, and like you say, it doesn't take into account that we don't have total control over what's going to happen next."

"Exactly."

"So an aspiration might be to meditate daily. Right?"

"Yes, or one might have an aspiration to develop loving-kindness . . . or to get enlightened! Or to make a lot of money! I think people have all kinds of aspirations. And from day to day, people will be more or less successful, but that has nothing to do with the validity of the aspiration."

"Ah. That deeper understanding, that perspective, is what helps one stay encouraged."

"Exactly."

"And that takes resolution. I got it. OK. We did it. Resoluteness manifested. That's awesome, Joseph."

He laughs. "I like the spontaneity of these conversations. We sit down and I have no idea what I'm going to say and it all comes out and I'm surprised at how easily it flows out."

This makes me happy. I hold an aspiration to contribute to Joseph's well-being and happiness. This aspiration arises quite spontaneously when I am with him.

Just as the word 'mindfulness' has infiltrated our daily language, so too has the word 'loving-kindness.' The Dalai Lama, Western Buddhist teachers, scholars, and now many self-help book authors use the term freely. We know the feeling of loving-kindness that can arise, quite spontaneously, in response to another's suffering. Loving-kindness is our next parami. *I could have used a little loving-kindness for myself and my foolhardiness*, I think as I remember walking into my small office and stepping gently around all those piles of books

---

Without integrity, mindfulness is morally meaningless.
Without integrity, metta is wishful thinking or a spiritual
bypass. Both mindfulness and metta require the actions
of conscience motivated by an ethical barometer.
—LARRY YANG, *SPIRIT ROCK NEWSLETTER*
(SEPTEMBER–DECEMBER 2019)

9 Loving-Kindness

People who practice *metta*
sleep peacefully,
wake peacefully,
dream peaceful dreams.
People love them,
angels love them,
angels will protect them.
Poison and weapons and fire won't harm them.
Their faces are clear.
Their minds are serene.
They die unconfused.
And when they die, their rebirth is in the heavenly realms.
—TRADITIONAL BUDDHIST VERSE

The Ninth Parami: Loving-Kindness

The Pali word *metta*, which we translate as *loving-kindness*, is used to designate the ninth parami in Buddhist texts. It means benevolence toward others and is commonly understood as showing kindness, affection, or love for others.

Instructions: Don't Throw Anyone Out of Your Heart

"There was a time I was in Burma when I was doing loving-kindness practice intensively for a couple of months," Joseph tells me as we begin this month with his instructions.

"Oh, a couple of months!" Loving-kindness practice is a structured meditation. The process is to silently repeat phrases of loving-kindness, directed at oneself and others, over and over and over. It can be tedious. It can also give rise to soaring moments of open-hearted bliss, deep contentment, and feelings of loving-kindness toward ourselves and others. It can also bring insights into the truth of our relationships with others and with ourselves. I have often practiced loving-kindness meditation while on retreat for one or two sitting periods. I have also done a half dozen metta-only retreats. It is hard for me to imagine doing the practice for months. It can be frustrating as one struggles to stay focused on the phrases, hour after hour. Aversion can arise, and distractions beckon.

"And there were two ways that I kept checking my mind," Joseph continues, "ways that were not that wholesome. One was looking into my mind and asking, 'Am I getting more loving? Am I getting more loving?'" We both laugh. I know that dance well. "And that then would become the primary thing, that checking in, rather than staying in the feeling of wishing well for the other person. So it is important to realize: it's not about me, it's about them!"

"That's very tricky. I agree. I have certainly observed this in myself as I send loving phrases silently to another, then check to see if I am feeling any kinder yet!"

"It *is* tricky," he says, "because on the one hand we're doing it in order to develop loving-kindness, so that is part of the motivation. But if we're continually checking in," he laughs, "then we are actually coming out of it. That is how the ego creeps in. So it is good to reflect on that. This is not about ourselves. This is not about what we are getting out of it. The challenge arises because we do get something out of it, *and* we have to watch closely for greed arising. It can be subtle. We need to use the wisdom parami to investigate with clear comprehension. True loving-kindness is not about me! In that moment of checking in to see if we are feeling loving-kindness, we are not actually cultivating it."

"Well, that's for sure."

"And it can quickly become more ego-striving. And because this is also a concentration practice, I found myself doing the same thing with that. I would also be checking in continually and asking, 'Am I getting more concentrated?'" We laugh again. "It was the same process."

"Yes, it is interesting. On that very first retreat I did with you, you had one sitting of metta practice in the afternoons. And each afternoon, after the loving-kindness meditation, I would go up to this little special place I had discovered outdoors and away from everyone. And I would have these wildly blissful times there, every afternoon. I was up on a hill, looking down and feeling tremendous love for all my fellow yogis doing slow walking meditation below. And the birds and the hills and the trees and the sky were all so overwhelming beautiful that I was in love with everything, so high and so blissful. I would run up there every day after the loving-kindness meditation and just wallow in love.

"So then, for several years after, I would go on retreat looking for those blissful afternoons after the loving-kindness practice. Just as you describe, I would be continually checking in, continually wanting, continually trying to duplicate the previous experience. All self-directed. Naturally I felt, instead of the prior bliss, disappointment and doubts."

He is chuckling. "Right."

"Or, if I did experience some bliss, then I would think, 'Oh, I am having those blissful moments again.' And then I would feel good about myself and my practice, thinking I was doing it correctly and was a loving-kindness kind of person again."

"Exactly. So all of that is just ego stuff."

"Sadly, yes."

"So what is important here is just to be clear about what is happening. It's not that it's not going to happen. But rather we want to recognize it when it does happen, so we're not deluding ourselves. We need to realize it's actually taking us out of the loving-kindness we are working to cultivate."

"Yes! It is definitely counterproductive. I hadn't thought about this, but clearly it is. You have that feeling of unbridled love for everybody and everything, and then you stand back and think, 'Oh, look at me, I'm having unbridled love for . . .'" We are laughing.

"Exactly," he says.

Joseph's Instructions: Working with Loving-Kindness

Loving-kindness is always about our relationships with others. We can use every relationship, every meeting, as our laboratory. "One of the first things to do, which will be easy for you," Joseph tells me (and I cherish the compliment), "is to really pay attention when this feeling is present."

1. To begin:

   - Be exact and clear in recognizing this quality.
   - Get to know it. See it clearly. Investigate it.
   - When loving-kindness is present, we want to highlight it.

2. Then continue:

   - Pay attention when meeting people throughout the day.
   - Notice when loving-kindness arises and when it doesn't.
   - What obstructs loving-kindness when it does not arise?

3. Next, go deeper:

   - Notice when attachment is present with loving-kindness.
   - Notice when expectations are also present with loving-kindness.
   - How does this feel?
   - How is this mixed feeling different from pure loving-kindness?

"It is good to discern when loving-kindness is mixed with its near enemy, which is usually attachment," Joseph explains. "Loving-kindness and attachment are often mixed, but they are very different. Love is offering. Attachment is holding, which is the opposite. In a situation where you can feel a sense of attachment, such as within the context of a relationship, pay close attention. All the problems of relationships, such as fear, possessiveness, and rejection, can be seen here, arising from the root of attachment. Use each interaction to investigate deeper. The tricky part is recognizing each, because they are so often intermingled. Watch for the attachment in all situations. Ask where it is present, then notice how it feels. Expectations can also be mixed in."

4. Finally:

- See if you can discern a distinction in the way you interact with the different people you meet.
- Look for when pure loving-kindness is present.
- Look for when it is mixed with attachment.
- Become familiar with the differences.

———

The best portion of a good man's life: his little, nameless unremembered acts of kindness and of love.
—William Wordsworth

Like all qualities, loving-kindness can be
strengthened through practice.
—JOSEPH GOLDSTEIN

Working with Loving-Kindness: What Obstructs Our Loving-Kindness?

When I remember that suffering is a natural part of life, I can relax. "I" didn't mess things up. And when I remember that most of us just want to be happy and kind, my heart opens wide. Certainly we may have different approaches and desires and hopes and dreams and plans and points of view about how to achieve happiness for ourselves and others. But just looking at another with this understanding allows me to hold them as family. From there it is easier to expand loving-kindness to others sharing this planet. It is believed that animals experience happiness. Dogs smile. Cats purr. Birds sing. And although we may not be able to distinguish a smile on the faces of slugs and spiders, who knows? As a young child I heard about a study where plants wired to a sensor trembled when someone approached with a pair of scissors. Whether it is true or not, I have never forgotten it. I confess to murmuring reassurances to plants before pruning. I am not alone. I once saw a gardener, not knowing I was watching from a window, bow silently to a tree he was about to cut down and remove.

One of my favorite ways to work with loving-kindness I learned years ago on retreat. Loving-kindness practice can include the repeating of phrases directed to a specific person or group of people. Over the years I have used different phrases. Right now my four phrases are:

May I/you/we all/ be safe and protected.
May I/you/we all be healthy and strong.
May I/you/we all be happy and contented.
May I/you/we all live with abundance and ease.

At work I often walk to lunch by myself. Because I interact with people all day, the quiet, solitary, out-of-doors break is a welcome one. As I walk, knowing it will cheer me up, I sometimes zap the people, dogs, birds, and squirrels I pass with a loving-kindness phrase (silently). "May you be safe and protected," I might say as someone drives by. I direct the thought like a laser beam into their car. "May you be happy and contented," I say silently to one of the neighboring Pixar employees who passes me on the sidewalk without looking up from her phone. I use the phrase I think is most needed, sometimes tailoring it with extras. I wish a street person good health and a bed tonight as I put a dollar in his bowl. I wish safety for a bird flying by.

Joseph would probably say my motivations are mixed, and this is true. Doing so inevitably lifts my spirits and that is part of my motivation for doing it, I discover. I enjoy the game of it. But I also like to think that directed prayers, such as this practice, do have results. The idea that I might be contributing to another's well-being is uplifting also because I do genuinely want others to be safe, healthy, happy, and content. I also do it while running, driving, or waiting in a line—sending my little anonymous missile of goodwill to whomever seems to need it. And of course, passing out dollar bills with a silent loving-kindness phrase attached is now a generosity habit.

This week I make a dedicated effort to engage in the silent phrases, and I add the aspiration to investigate the quality of loving-kindness that arises, to explore more deeply its origins and nature when present, as well as what arises to undermine it. So I purposefully play the game and then just watch with mindfulness. First I notice how quickly I can slip out of open-hearted kindness into stories about the person or situation. And after a short time I become quicker at catching myself, quicker at the return to the practice. This, I understand, is useful practice for many endeavors. Sending out the silent phrases, genuinely inspired, I can feel the warmth of loving-kindness arise and then flow through me like a river of well-wishing from my heart to another, as trite as that sounds.

One day, I returned to the office totally refreshed. Within an hour, because I am the sales manager, I was engaged in a challenging communication with another agent who vented his anger about how he was treated by one of our other agents. Quite spontaneously (after doing the practice frequently all week), I suddenly found myself silently sending out the phrases to him as he was talking. They just began spontaneously playing in my head, directed at him, as I had done with other unsuspecting recipients. I was still present. Still listening. *And* I was directing loving-kindness toward him until, totally spontaneously, I smiled! The effect was amazing. He literally stopped midsentence. Looked at me. And smiled! And when he began again, I knew we both had felt the shift in the air around us. The adversarial vibe that had been present just a moment before had somehow evaporated, and we quickly arrived at a solution comfortable for him. It was quite remarkable. Wow, I thought. This practice is powerful.

I continue keeping watch for what obstructs loving-kindness. I heard it said once that everything other than loving-kindness is like stale frosting on a moist cake. After a couple of weeks focused on keeping my heart open, the stuff that obstructs it does indeed feel like old news, stale frosting. All that goodness inside, trapped there by old, constricting beliefs, expectations, clinging. It doesn't really matter what I'm clinging to—an opinion, a desire, a preference. When I am clinging, it is difficult to access loving-kindness.

It is 5:00 p.m. on Friday, and I am driving down the coastal highway to Pacifica, a small beach town on the opposite side of San Francisco. I have opera CDs as traveling companions as I anticipate a commuter-laden, slow trip across and then out of the city. But I am mistaken. I encounter no slow traffic and arrive almost an hour early. Bliss! So I park on the beach, roll down the windows, and just gaze at and listen to the waves while watching the surfers, seals, and gulls, a salve for the heart and for the sadness that awaits. I am here for a memorial celebration of the life of a woman who worked with me for many years. She was forty-five years old when she died, suddenly and very unexpectedly. I am here for her spouse, parents, siblings, friends, and associates, and to say my farewell. Her sister also worked with us. Her mother once led our whole company on a whitewater rafting trip. Three hundred people are attending. Many of them are my tribe, as I call them. Family. Others are extensions of that family, associates I have not seen for years. As I sit gazing on shimmering waves, the thought arises that this, surely, will be a good opportunity for observing and stretching loving-kindness. With a heavy heart and curious mind, I arrive at the event.

It is a wild affair. My friend was a woman of many talents and interests. She was a woman fiercely on a spiritual path, something we shared and often spoke about when working late together at the office. The evening begins with Goddess trainees leading us in chanting and dancing to Indian music. Then my friend's belly-dancing troupe performs. Her family, her friends, and her real estate co-workers share tearful memories that make us laugh and cry. We are packed like anchovies into the Pacifica Community Center, folks standing at the back and even out in the hall, peering in. The evening stretches into a third hour of ceremony and sharing, the room heating up. When we finally tumble out of the tight chairs and move around, mingling, grieving, laughing, eating, and drinking together, I feel seared on the outside, raw on the inside. My response is only loving-kindness now, everything else wiped away, nothing left to obstruct its free flow. The evening is all about Stasi and her tribe coming together to honor her and send her our love. Compassion, love, kindness, tears, laughter swirl within and all around me. Even chatting with an associate I have tussled with or with another that, perhaps, I have regarded with less enthusiasm, none of that past aversion seems at all relevant or even true now. I greet everyone as a dear friend, as the Dalai Lama suggests, and for the entire evening I genuinely feel this is so, without exception. Around midnight I float out of the hall feeling transformed by the understanding that we all have a capacity for loving-kindness that far exceeds any puny belief we might have previously entertained. Remembrance of death is the silent, oft-forgotten yeast that can make loving-kindness rise and abide.

And then, so quickly, it is Monday morning, and I arrive at work to a surprising, viciously worded email from a co-worker. He is very upset, his words accusing and combative, stating I had overstepped my boundaries and made a couple of decisions he felt he should have been consulted on. A wash of emotions surges as I sit at my desk, shell-shocked after reading his message. I am actually trembling. I watch anger arise. Righteousness. Hurt. Embarrassment. And sadness. This co-worker and I have always worked together easily, enjoyably. After steadying myself for a few moments, I feel bits of loving-kindness, like snowflakes, swirling in the morass. The thought comes to investigate. What *had* my motive been? Was I attached to something—some point of view, perhaps, on what should be done—and then made an end run around him? No. I am clear that was not the case. In my enthusiasm to solve a problem that had suddenly arisen, I had simply overlooked the fact that he might feel left out of the process. It was an honest mistake. I am satisfied there was no underlying dishonest motive on my part.

But clearly my co-worker has a different viewpoint, a different interpretation of my motive, and is angry and hurt. So I take a few deep breaths and call him. As soon as he answers, I apologize. I do not say those little zingers that let the other person know you are apologizing even though you do not think you need to. I do not say I had not intended to hurt him or that it was an honest mistake. I understand we are discussing his reasons for his response and anger. I don't believe he cares to hear what my motive had been. If he is right, then I have to be wrong. And I am, shocking to see, at peace with that. I want only to add no fuel to the raging fire. So I just let him talk, let him vent. I repeat my apology. I ask what I can do to remedy the situation. After hanging up, I feel a mix of pride for my wise response and also my genuine compassion for his suffering. I am shaken, yet remained openhearted and responded with genuine loving-kindness to his pain. This is different for me, and quite amazing. After several weeks of focusing on and strengthening loving-kindness, it was . . . *almost* my first response. And a situation that could have blown up in any of several ways quietly faded away. Neither of us spoke of it again, and our relationship eventually returned to its former ease.

It is loving-kindness final week. We are about to have the house repainted, and I have been organizing pieces of this project for weeks. Repair carpentry, power washing, sanding, and deck refinishing are all parts of the task to be bid, scheduled, and overseen. Today a carpenter is here repairing some rotted wood trim. The painter is scheduled to begin tomorrow, but my calls over the last five days have gone unanswered. Feeling tired and overwhelmed, my mind rehearses dialogues with the painter, and I have left messages that probably sound increasingly frustrated. This morning, once the carpenter is settled into the work, I call again, trying to be uplifting in my message. And it's a miracle. The painter calls back. He tells me that his mother is in a hospital in Mexico, gravely ill. I feel the angst dissipate instantly, no sense of urgency now as I listen. He chokes up, he apologizes, then tells me that after a small routine operation his mother has contracted an infection while in the hospital and is in critical care and heavily sedated. They have already amputated a finger in an attempt to halt the infection and are considering more dire actions. His sister in Mexico has been trying to get her moved to another hospital. He and his brother, who also lives here, are deciding, depending on her fluctuating condition, when they will fly down to assist. As we talk, I feel the loving-kindness and compassion flowing from me through the wireless airways. We decide I should find another painter. I tell him about the bedside vigil with my own mother. I tell him I will pray for his mother. We are both choked up. After, I remain seated and say the prayer for his mother. I will begin again the long process of interviewing, bidding, hiring, scheduling, waiting for the house painting. All the previous reasons that the house had to be painted now just totally evaporate. The feeling I have as I slowly rise, I understand, is pure loving-kindness.

Loving-kindness is accessible when we remember that it is.
—JOSEPH GOLDSTEIN

Covetousness keeps the mind agitated and unhappy, far
from contentment . . . We shouldn't underestimate this
habit of the mind, which unnoticed can easily lead to the
suffering of envy, jealousy, and endless dissatisfaction.
—JOSEPH GOLDSTEIN, ONE DHARMA

Check-In Conversation: Am I Getting More Loving?

Joseph and I begin the monthly check-in. I am sitting in the backyard,
listening to the fountain splashing and gazing over my just-raked garden. Muscles tired. Mind content. Loving-kindness practice did not feel
like work. Could this be the result of all the previous months' work coming together now as support? And I have enjoyed the focus on opening
up, as opposed to changing things and letting go. Energetically, loving-
kindness feels like opening to the beauty here, right now, as contrasted
with my previous efforts to rake and weed out unskillful thoughts.

I begin by describing the loving-kindness affirmations silently sent
out to passersby. "How about this?" I ask. "You see someone on the street
and you're inspired to give them something, a feeling of generosity and
loving-kindness arising spontaneously. And there is anticipation of the
pleasure, for yourself and for them, that you envision the act will bring.
Those are the original motivations arising, it seems to me, from a place
of loving-kindness and generosity. But if you then have the understanding, at some point along in that process, that really what you're doing is
working to free the mind from greed, which of course I *really* want . . .
is that still OK?"

Joseph laughs. "Yes. In the first and more mundane part, I understood it was more than just, 'Oh, if I give this, this is going to come back
to me.'"

"Right. That's right."

"That would not be the simple appreciation for the pleasure of giving in the moment. I don't think there is necessarily much attachment
involved in what you're describing. The attachment comes in when one

has the motivation, 'I will do this, because then I'll get something back in the future.'"

"But I know when I walk down the street with dollar bills in my pocket and loving-kindness phrases in my mind, I'm going to feel happier when I get to the end of the street. I was thinking that perhaps that was not . . ."

"Well, basically, again, it depends on the motivation. Are you doing it *because* you'll feel happier? Or are you doing it out of care for the other person? Those are two very different motivations. And too often mixed. But again, it's not that we need to have or will have total purity of motivation. What is important is at least to be clear." He chuckles. "This can be a very interesting investigation—to watch the complexity of our motivations, to see them clearly."

"Yes, and it can just," I snap my fingers, "so quickly switch, then switch again."

"Yes, it does."

"That's good. I think I understand now that subtle discernment."

Recalling the night we honored Stasi, I tell Joseph, "For that entire evening, I felt a spontaneous and genuine loving-kindness for every person at the memorial. I entered that hall with a fierce intention for loving-kindness to be my focus, my first response. I wanted to just be present, to really be with everyone I connected with." I laugh. "Only later I had the thought, just imagine proceeding through life, beginning every day with that intention, that understanding. That is behind the devotion I feel from the Dalai Lama, and Dipa Ma, and Mother Teresa—just pure open heart, pure loving-kindness, regardless."

"Yes." We are quiet.

"Certainly the nature of a memorial helped reinforce the aspiration. I also found that, even with the inherent sadness, the loving-kindness and the engagements with everyone were deeply satisfying. I felt sad and also so full, so completely content. Of course this is all I ever really need to do—go forth every day with an intention for loving-kindness." I pause. "And this month I also resonated, just naturally, with a lot more of the suffering all around me."

"Yes, because as you observed, you were paying attention more."

"Just paying attention. Isn't that amazing? So when one is not feeling loving-kindness, just paying attention . . ."

"A comment here," Joseph says. "What you are describing is the relationship, the segue from loving-kindness to compassion. In other words, when the basic ground is loving-kindness—which, just as you said, has that interest in others—then we're much more open to the suffering that's around us, which then naturally leads to compassion."

"Oh, yes, I understand."

"Without the feeling of loving-kindness, we're less likely to be open."

"I see. Yes, compassion does seem to arise naturally from that quality of being open, from that place of genuine interest and caring." We are quiet for a few moments. "I am thinking of the woman, Julie, I met on the street. I was genuinely interested in her, in finding out what her life was like. And as we spoke, compassion did just naturally and spontaneously arise and flow through me, through my words."

"Right. Right."

"So I have a question here. I'm not feeling it now, but I did when I was going through my notes. What should one do when not feeling loving-kindness?"

"Well," Joseph laughs, "have a drink!"

I whoop in surprise and giggle.

"There are two factors that can be helpful here," Joseph continues after a bit. "One is realizing that, like everything else, loving-kindness is a conditioned state, which means that it arises out of certain conditions. And when the conditions are not there, loving-kindness is not there. So it's not surprising. And then it's just to consider, 'OK, what are the conditions needed for loving-kindness to arise?' And one of the most basic ones is seeing the good parts of people. Sometimes that can be one's intentional focus."

"Yes, I try to do that a lot. Or gratitude, right? That can be a condition for loving-kindness to arise."

"Right. In fact, in one way, an interesting exercise is to notice when you are feeling loving-kindness, just noticing it in your own experience. And then to ask, 'OK, what brings this feeling about?' So that it is not theoretical. One can really learn from one's own experience by asking the question and seeing what arises. 'When I am this way, then loving-kindness arises.' So people can discover for themselves—whether it is gratitude, whether it is focusing on what's good in people, whether it is seeing the universality of our condition. Whatever it might be for us. I think it's good for people, as you did, to really explore it for themselves."

"Oh, that is especially helpful! And what is also so wonderful about all of this is that there is a way to go about it. We can actually practice and strengthen our loving-kindness muscle, like practicing scales on the piano. We're not stuck with whatever inherent loving-kindness we may feel we possess. In fact we can change it, expand it, deepen it at any time, in any moment, and over time. That was what was so uplifting for me at the memorial, to witness my own enhanced capabilities—after just one month of focusing on it."

"Yes. Exactly."

Next I describe the angry email and then the phone call with my co-worker.

"So there I was," I am telling Joseph, "totally lambasted and also unfairly blamed. But instead of getting as immersed in it as he was and responding in kind, as I might have before—you know, defending, denying, getting hot, feeling righteous—I just listened and apologized, with no attachment. I was clear about my motivations, and also clear I surely didn't need to go there, squirt lighter fuel on his rage. And I felt that was loving-kindness, a kind of loving-kindness for both him and myself. To be able to take that one step away from my own selfish need to be right felt hugely different—invigorating and also kind. Any resistance seemed totally pointless, and also not compassionate. He was truly suffering."

"Yes. Yes."

"And the exchange was remarkably open and quickly over. Amazing. So then I tried extending that dynamic into other areas, like letting go of my own interpretations or preferences. Just playing with that. If someone had a different preference, I would respond, 'You want to go there? Great. Let's go there. You want to do that? Let's do it.'" I am laughing. "'Sure, it's fine. Everything's fine.' And . . . surprise! I genuinely felt like that, for a while anyway. You are so often like that. You have a genuine willingness to accommodate others' preferences. It is admirable." Joseph laughs. "Anything else you want to add here?"

"Well, in that respect, I think that it works both ways. I think that loving-kindness helps you be aware and open to more, but also I notice that when one is just practicing awareness, mindfulness, and one is in that place, it's as if awareness itself contains loving-kindness. That is my experience. The heart and mind are just naturally very open when one is aware, so one's relationship to things has that flavor of love. Dipa Ma said something about that. I don't remember the exact quote, but she said she no longer saw such a difference between mindfulness and metta. She said, 'When you're mindful, aren't you also loving? And when you're loving, aren't you also mindful?'"

"Oh, that's lovely. And inspiring."

"Yes. So just to see how the two really can be sides of each other."

"And part of, just naturally, who we are. Right? What comes up for me is that when we are on retreat, we spend so much time and effort being mindful that soon this blissful, loving spaciousness opens up within. Just from spending all that time paying attention, as you're describing."

"Yes, but just a note of caution here. Not everybody on retreat feels that. A lot of people struggle for some time until they get to that place. So you don't want to be cavalier about it."

"Oh, OK. Got it. But that *is* what happens?"

"At a certain point, yes. For some people it is quicker, and for others it is much longer."

"I understand." We are quiet for a few moments before I speak again.

"Now, this is changing the subject a bit, but it relates to experiencing loving-kindness, experiencing it, and then not noticing when it has dissipated. You told me a story once that was really great. You said something like, 'When I'm teaching, in a question-and-answer session, I may feel loving-kindness arising. I get into a loving exchange with a yogi (retreat participant) and it becomes, over some time, a kind of loving bantering. Then I notice I like that feeling. Then I notice sometimes I'll continue the banter for the enjoyment of that feeling, and at that point it ceases to be loving-kindness for the other person.' Could you say that again in your own words? Because that's really good. I think a lot of people have that experience in different ways."

"I could," he says, laughing, "but I think you just said it. I don't know how I would say it any differently. You captured that sequence well."

"Thank you. All right. Then to follow on that, to me it feels like pushing loving-kindness beyond what it is until it's not true anymore. It's not authentic anymore."

"Exactly. We're just trying to extend our own good feeling, and now attachment is mingled in with the loving-kindness."

"Ah, attachment, that pesky little sucker fish that just won't let go. So then it becomes no longer about the other person, like when we were discussing sending the loving-kindness phrases out to others while checking in on our own developing loving-kindness."

"Right. This type of progression probably happens a lot. But if you notice it, then you can press the 'reset' button."

I laugh. "The reset button. I like that!" *I just need to locate mine,* I'm thinking, *and then remember to carry it with me.*

Finally, I tell Joseph about our painter and his critically ill mother. "Another example of loving-kindness naturally and instantly arising," I say. "No wonder I love working with this parami so much. I did also watch for that subtleness you described where you think you're feeling loving-kindness for people but then realize you're having loving-kindness only for people that you like! That's why the call with the painter and the altercation with my co-worker were so startling. I could feel the difference. Different indeed."

"Right. Exactly."

"Is there something to help us more skillfully discern, and to help us *remember* to discern?" I say, laughing now. "For example, I admit I have trouble understanding what would be so wrong with affection that morphs into loving-kindness!"

He laughs. "Well, I think you just have to look to see whether in the affection there's attachment. It's pretty slippery the ways we use words, and people may use the word 'affection' in different ways. But if the ideal of loving-kindness is universal, then unless the affection is universal, it is not loving-kindness."

"Oh, now I can feel that difference."

"So then it's just to explore that difference for yourself."

"Hmm. Like Dipa Ma or the Dalai Lama."

"Yes," he agrees. "You don't get the sense that it's personal, even though it's expressed personally. You know that they feel that way toward everybody. There is a quote I love by Montaigne that I took from an article in *The New Yorker*. I think it exemplifies this pure aspect of loving-kindness, especially in relationship with others: 'In a truly loving relationship—which I have experienced—rather than drawing the one I love to me, I give myself to him. Not merely do I prefer to do him good rather than have him do good to me, I would even prefer that he do good to himself than to me. It is when he does good to himself that he does most good to me. If his absence is either pleasant or useful to him, than it delights me far more than his presence.'"

"Oh, I do love that," I say. We are quiet.

"One more thing to mention here," Joseph continues. "As with the other paramis, it is important to continually investigate one's motivation. The challenge is understanding that all these states do bring benefit, but that is not the motivation for doing the practice. For example, I may be considering a specific act of generosity. In my mind I know it's a good cause. I want to make a contribution. I also know I'll get something good out of doing it. The wisdom piece is understanding that the action itself is also beneficial. So we make the donation. The generosity aspect is our genuine desire to help. The wisdom piece is understanding that action does have a karmic result. So then we need to look closely at our motivation. If we are doing it for that karmic benefit it will bring, and not out of a genuine desire to help, then our action actually weakens that benefit! It does get very subtle here, because part of right understanding is the understanding that wholesome actions will bring good results." Joseph pauses, then begins laughing. "Actually this is something I was just writing about in my book. So when we do a meritorious or wholesome action, it can be done for the sake of worldly merit, which is connected with attachment. And it is still wholesome, but there is also a wanting in the mind for the good result. Whereas there's another kind of merit that is a more wholesome action, which is pointed in the direction of freedom or liberation. And within the appreciation of the wholesome action, we also see and understand that it's about the freedom of the mind letting go. It's not about what we're going to get from it. It's about the purification of the mind and really seeing the non-grasping. So it is both a different motivation and level—there are two different levels of understanding how our wholesome actions work."

"Yes, I follow that."

"And one final piece to that. In an act of generosity we are weakening the defilement of greed because we are letting it go. We understand this weakens the defilement. If our motivation is to weaken the defilement, that is wholesome. But if, again using generosity, we are doing it to bring about abundance, then that is not a wholesome act. Our practice is discerning the difference. So continue to look back to the original motivation. Strengthen that original purity."

"I totally can feel the difference you're describing. And I can also feel the subtlety, so easy to overlook. And I honestly don't think I have understood that subtlety. Thank you, Joseph. I think that's it. You know, I am feeling all the paramis are getting strengthened together now. Each of them is so closely tied in to the others. It feels exciting, invigorating. Thank you so much!"

"You're very welcome," he says, and we say our goodbyes.

My first thought, as we hang up, is *I can't believe we are almost through all ten paramis*. It seems as if we were just beginning, with generosity, last week. It also seems like we have been working on our generosity for lifetimes, which perhaps we have.

Joseph's distinction is important and can be a tricky edge to watch for and remember as we continue our practice of loving-kindness. It is not about us. We can feel good about ourselves when we respond from a compassionate heart. But when we catch ourselves checking on or delighting in our own loving-kindness, we must just begin again. When we do, we find loving-kindness is often—not always, but often—our natural inclination, our first response. Without affection or attachment, the response is simply open loving. It is not us practicing loving-kindness, but all hearts open to the world's suffering, responding spontaneously. Our part is, simply, to be present. I am reminded again of the lunch with Julie. Once I let go of the fears and doubts and resistance and just listened, just opened to her, loving-kindness flowed freely. There is nothing else needed. Nothing else to do. Just be open, with a friendly heart, to every human being.

———

The challenge is understanding that all these states do bring benefit, but that is not the motivation for doing it.
—JOSEPH GOLDSTEIN

10 Equanimity

The great lesson here is that it is not what is happening
that is important, but rather how we are relating to it.
—JOSEPH GOLDSTEIN

The Tenth Parami: Equanimity

The Pali word *upekkha*, which we translate as *equanimity*,
is used to designate the tenth parami in Buddhist texts.
It means non-reactivity and even-mindedness toward
phenomena and is more commonly understood as
the quality of composure—an evenness of mind and
temper, the ability to remain calm and undisturbed.

Instructions: Path to Peace

"I don't know if you remember," Joseph says, "but I often tell the story of two neighbors here in Massachusetts. They were building a house in the woods, in a location where there were a lot of blue herons. When they finally moved into the house, they heard a faint chirping in the unfinished basement area. And they were so happy because they thought the blue herons had somehow made a nest down there. Not wanting to disturb them, they did not venture into the space for several days. Every time they heard the chirping, it brought them much joy. Then one day the contractor came by. He went down into the basement, then came back up and told them, 'Your smoke alarm down in the basement is broken and chirping. You need to get a replacement.' After that, they got totally annoyed every time they heard the chirping noise—the very same sound that had brought so much happiness just the day before! These are concepts, obscuring equanimity, obscuring our ability to be with things as they are."

Joseph's Instructions: Working with Equanimity

1. First, notice what it feels like when equanimity is present. Then, watch through the day for whenever you have a reaction or desire arise that pushes away equanimity.

   • When you see equanimity is not there, investigate why it isn't there. What just happened?
   • Practice when on the receiving end of speech. Watch for little reactions while listening that might push away equanimity.

2. Next we begin investigating what is beneath initial reactions/ responses: See if there are certain conditions that automatically tend to give rise to reactivity in small or big ways.

   • One way to investigate this is when you notice you have a reaction to something arising, work with letting it in.
   • Watch for how the equanimous mind is a support for this process.
   • Also watch for how the equanimous mind is a support for work with other paramis.

3. Now we go deeper: When you notice you are not impartial, investigate further. What is the idea or concept you may be holding that gives rise to the reaction you are experiencing?

   • Explore the relationship between those concepts and equanimity using the various sense doors.
   • Where does the mind tend to get caught, preventing equanimity from arising spontaneously?

4. And finally: Watch the mind's relationship to pleasant and unpleasant.

- Is the mind impartial, equanimous with each?
- Try observing this in response to others. Am I responding to everyone equally?
- And if not, why not? Where do I tend to be impartial?

"This quote from Ajahn Chah describes the process well," Joseph says. "If you let go a little, you will have a little peace. If you let go a lot, you will have a lot of peace. If you let go completely, you will have complete peace. Your struggle in this world will have come to an end."

———

Our practice is not to follow the
heart; it is to train the heart.
—AJAHN SUMEDHO
(IN JOSEPH GOLDSTEIN'S *A HEART FULL OF PEACE*)

Working with Equanimity: We Ask, *What Just Happened?*

I have experienced deep states of concentration more profound than the blissful states that precede them, a tranquility so complete that even to take a breath feels like adding something more than what is necessary. It is sublimely peaceful to rest here, quintessentially content. I access this place through meditation. I would like to have more access to it in daily life. Maybe not a tranquility as lucid and fulfilling as can be found in deep meditation, but more than I am experiencing when I am suddenly whipped off center by life's inevitable surprises and setbacks. This is what I hope to achieve this month working with equanimity.

And so I begin. I am attending a meeting of the Spirit Rock Meditation Center Capital Campaign Committee. This is our first such meeting to discuss raising funds to build several new structures at Spirit Rock. There will be a presentation, but mostly, because it is our first meeting, there is time to socialize and get to know other team members. I arrive with an additional agenda item—investigate my equanimity. As I chat casually, and especially as I listen, I watch for those little non-equanimous reactions. I find many arise from wandering attention, unrelated to the person or the conversation. I smell food: curiosity then desire arise, and I glance around for the appetizers. I am enjoying a conversation, but I am also looking for the next person I want to speak with before the presentation begins.

Curiously, each time my focus wanders away from the person I am speaking with, so does my equanimity, my open mind. Surprise! I watch as I slide into desire. One or two distracted moments and suddenly I want something. I want something else. I want something different than the conversation I am having. Refocus. I continue watching reactions, feelings, emotions, and desires arising as I am speaking and listening to the other person. I decide they are using too many words to make a point and I fade out, eavesdrop on a neighboring conversation that is much more animated and looks like fun. Or I notice the person I am speaking to is looking over *my* shoulder at someone else! Or I hold an opinion different than the one they are articulating and I tune out while rehearsing my response. In fact, a fountain of unskillful, disheartening, but also familiar reactions continues to arise as I work my way around the room. Not all of the time. But much more often than I had imagined.

As the presentation begins, slides are shown with renderings of the new buildings drawn into the existing landscape. Also depicted are ethereal, white, translucent figures wandering the grounds, sitting at picnic tables, standing on a bridge together, and gazing toward the hills. I guess this is how architects depict humans in the future, but I do think they looked enlightened, and appropriate, gracing a place offering the possibility of transformation. They look heavenly but also insubstantial. Our strong fog winds would surely blow them all away. And then I smile, recognizing the same insubstantiality in my earlier stumbles and reactions. It is simply behavior habituated after years of often tedious business cocktail parties. I remind myself to just begin again, and settle back into my chair to do just that. Relaxed and open, I welcome back equanimity with renewed aspiration.

I think of equanimity as that deliciously languid place where I feel everything is just as it should be. Everything is fine. I am working easily within what is. Often in meditation I find this quiet serenity. Cooking— just chopping, mixing, sautéing—can bring it on. I am tranquil and content. This week, I am eager to watch for where and how I can slide out of that wondrous feeling that nothing arising has the potential to disturb or ruffle me. And then, right on cue, I take a call from upset clients, or I am missing a key ingredient for the dish I am making and need to go out to get it. Instead of just habitually reacting and then toppling further into desire for something different, I try to catch that dynamic in progress, determined to see if and how I can respond differently. I want to learn how to open to what is not in my grand plan for life and practice how to stay in that beguiling open place of equanimity.

I am very busy at work this month, and life is piling up on itself— rescheduled meetings, pressing calls, appointments, reports, emails, plus home chores and family responsibilities. I am experiencing many periods of feeling overwhelmed by all the commitments, and then more overwhelmed at the idea of investigating overwhelm as a concept perhaps up for some scrutiny. Overwhelm is simply another restrictive perception that if allowed to fester unchecked can add more misery and unclarity to a currently difficult moment. We can get trapped inside a mind of delusion. Joseph has told me the feeling that "this is too much" is a signal the mind is not equanimous. So I try working with opening to and allowing the situation of "too much" to just be what it is. Then I stretch to letting it all in by dissecting it into its pieces: the overwhelm, resistance, discouragement, panic, and so on. This questioning and breaking it into pieces, surprisingly, I find immensely refreshing. *Oh, it's just this. Just that. I can handle this quickly now. I can tackle that tomorrow.* The overwhelm dissolves into the pieces that fueled it, which seem much easier to address and tackle individually. Sylvia Boorstein says, "May I open to this moment fully. May I greet it as a friend."

I wait. Take a breath. Wait. A couple more slow breaths. Look again, more deeply. I wait until I feel a moment of balanced, equanimous mind. Then I ask—very cautiously, very gently, with curiosity—"What just happened?" Again I find just the willingness to *make* the inquiry brings respite. Now I am the one outside, investigating what is transpiring inside. Reaching this place of serenity, if only for a moment, *within* tumultuous emotions, feels empowering. I have the thought that before I tumble into the next unguarded moment, I want to look around here. I want to anchor this place and program the route.

Just those few moments, and more like them repeated throughout the day, begin to genuinely shake up a seemingly solid, unsatisfactory, and very familiar mind state, allowing for clearer comprehension and an opening to options I had not seen. When we pause and step outside a habitual reaction, wisdom helps us see that overwhelm is just another painful but untrue concept, a story we are painting and then stuck in. Just seeing that, if only for brief moments at a time, begins to crack its solidity. After a while, continually feeling (choosing) a response of overwhelm begins to seem just a tad indulgent, and that woe-is-me syndrome a bit old.

Another morning, while showering before work, I play with labeling whatever is arising. Pleasant body sensations are present, warm water massaging my scalp, tight calves, sleepy face. I linger, indulging in the pleasant sensations. Thoughts drift by. I chomp on some, let others pass. Planning thoughts, of course. But as soon as I use the label "planning," the thought dissolves in the steam. I am getting quite skilled at heading planning off at the pass.

We can also use the loving-kindness phrases, repeated a few times silently, to help balance the mind, bring it back into equanimity. On clearer days, we may find the loving-kindness phrases arising unbeckoned as we begin to drift out of balance. Then, resting in equanimity again, loving-kindness just naturally becomes our response to whatever is happening. We can also add viriya energy into the pursuit—asking the question, listening, opening again. So many shiny new tools we have assembled for ourselves.

Dropping a concept = equanimity. Equanimity = no concept. I am in the kitchen getting breakfast when I slowly become aware of a whining noise. What new construction device do they have now up the hill? It continues to get louder, and I, more annoyed. Then I see the street cleaning machine go by. Oh! Instantly I feel my shoulders drop as I perceive the noise as welcome instead of unwelcome. The street needed a good washing. Concepts—so pervasive, so restrictive, so blinding. I'm suddenly reminded of Joseph's beeping smoke alarm story. One of his famous early talks was entitled "Concepts and Reality." Notice he didn't call it "Concepts versus Reality." Just one and the other.

We have a choice. We can watch helplessly as we tumble into a concept, or we can remain in an open, easy, welcoming awareness of every piece as it arises. *Ah, concept. Ah, reaction. Ah, aversion to reaction.* And so on. Sounds, smells, sights, thoughts, concepts arising and passing away. The choice to make up a story around them is ours. You may find, as I did, that it is not as difficult to be open and equanimous as it is difficult to *remember* to be, especially as our tendencies can be well habituated. But each time we are able to recognize the tendency and still remain equanimous, we widen the pathway, broaden our chances it will appear as an option, not a given, the next time. We do not have to be swept away with the hubris.

Last night I watched a documentary entitled *Wagner's Dream*. Have I mentioned I love opera? The movie was about the process of producing the New York Metropolitan Opera's first *Ring Cycle* in over twenty years, a production that included a massive new machine designed to serve as all the sets. Just the visioning, designing, and production of the machine alone was filled with confusion, missed deadlines, and failures. Once it was miraculously installed on stage, rehearsals were filmed, many with machine-related mishaps: a terrified Rhinemaiden frozen in place on a tilted piece of the machine; a star singer stumbling and falling during a rehearsal and proclaiming he would not return; the machine failing during the grand finale on opening night.

Throughout, the producer, the stage manager, the opera general director, and the technicians were incredibly unruffled and composed. I was struck by their response of calm curiosity as various mishaps were presented to them. Did they become this way gradually over years of dealing with the turmoil of live performances? Did they work on achieving that steadiness, or were they just born with it? The even-mindedness they brought to each challenge, each discussion, and each mishap certainly looked like equanimity to me. Their continued open response and curiosity were inspiring.

Naturally, as has happened in so many previous months, the perfect foil to my best-laid equanimity aspirations arises in the equanimity month. We have a new neighbor, something rare in this close-knit neighborhood of longtime residents. And she has quickly become a serious obstruction to my aspiration for expanding equanimity. The weather is warm now, and we sleep with the bedroom windows open. Our bedroom is on the back of the house, and the new neighbor's house and outdoor parking space are across a small lane from us. Suddenly we find ourselves being awakened most every night between 2:00 and 3:00 a.m. by the sounds of her coming home. She drives up the lane and into her driveway with music blaring, then sits in the driveway, music ripping holes in the quiet. Finally she exits her car only to, repeatedly, open and slam the car doors shut, music still rocketing through the night. Twice already this week I have to restrain Ron, who wants to jump from the bed and go out to the street to speak to her. I lay awake, long after it is quiet again, with visions of recruiting all the neighbors to stand silently together, in our pajamas and bathrobes, in the street. This, of course, is not a response I would characterize as compassionate.

Ron and I have worked hard to get along with all our neighbors, but this new neighbor is now a serious challenge to that aspiration for equanimity. Last night we heard a neighbor yell out into the darkness, "Turn off the fucking music." I feel she is unaware of her impact, but I am also loathe to be the one to say anything. Ron feels she is inconsiderate and that the issue needs to be addressed, although he, too, hesitates. He also appreciates that we are friendly with everyone. This has taken some effort, and some restraint, over the years.

Then something curious happens. I am having breakfast in the backyard, Ron already at work, when a tow truck backs up the small lane and stops. At the edge of our backyard is a two-story-high, thick bamboo hedge—great for privacy but not as a sound barrier. I can clearly hear our new neighbor speaking with the mechanic. Her car has a flat tire. The mechanic is talkative, friendly. I hear him ask her what she does as he drags equipment from his truck to change the tire. And I am fairly certain that her answer is "rock star."

Now my first (yes, non-equanimous) thought is, *Who would describe themselves as a rock star, even if that is what they do?* Musician, maybe. Singer. Performer. I have seen her only once, briefly, from afar, but I do suddenly remember the barely-there jean shorts, cowboy boots, and wild, curly blonde hair. As soon as I hear "rock star," everything falls into place. Her appearance fits. The late nights fit. The music and unloading of the car fit. Even the gravelly voice, now, clearly resonates as a singer's voice. I am not sure I overheard her words correctly. But still . . . rock star? Really?

They continue speaking about recording studios and bands, and I figure I must have heard what I heard. Now I am pretty certain she may not be aware of the impact her late night arrivals have on the rest of us, and my resistance dissipates. When I tell Ron what I overheard, his response also now becomes one of more equanimity. We laugh. Suddenly she is no longer the Inconsiderate One. She is the Inconsiderate Rock Star! We did eventually see her on the street and expressed kindly our feelings about the late night music. She did promise to turn the music off as she entered the street, and did so, but within a couple months she had moved on. We heard other neighbors were not so kind.

As I complete this last month's parami work, many times throughout a day I will feel all the paramis working together like a symphony. Sometimes it is the violins, loving-kindness, sweetly and softly gladdening the heart. Sometimes the drums predominate; that would be viriya. Equanimity feels like the conductor, from whose direction all the players know when to enter, when to play, and when they have a solo.

———

Of course, there are moments when I do get angry, but in
the depth of my heart, I don't hold a grudge against anyone.
—THE DALAI LAMA

Look at others, remembering everyone wants to be happy.
—JOSEPH GOLDSTEIN

Check-In Conversation: The Essence of the Path

"Hi, Joseph." I am calling on a lazy Sunday afternoon, from my bed, having just attempted to nap away the resurgence of a cold.

"Well, hello, Gail."

I cough several times, then sigh. "I seem to have caught your cold," I say, which makes us both laugh, as we have only spoken by phone since he had a cold.

"Oh, that's too bad," he commiserates.

"I am definitely under. You know, I heard myself boast to you about not having been sick for three years, and I think it was less than a week later . . ." I laugh.

"Uh-huh. That happens to me, too," he says. "I have the thought, *Oh, I haven't been sick in a while*, and then . . ."

"That's it!" I say, laughing, then coughing. "Last night Ron said to me, 'How nice it must be to just lie around the house all day, because you can't do anything.' And I said to him, 'No, no, no . . . don't go there. You're going to be sick next!' But actually, it has been rich territory for investigation of equanimity while feeling so lackluster now at the end of the month."

"Oh, definitely."

"I've now added being sick to my list of places where I don't always feel equanimous."

"Yes, and that's an important practice."

"It took me a couple of days to see that, however," I say, coughing again. "OK, so my report on equanimity. You said equanimity means non-reactivity. And I found that really useful, because equanimity is kind of tough to recognize in daily life. But that quality of being non-reactive I can definitely feel."

"Another good word I like for it is 'impartiality.'"

"Mm-hmm, that's good too." I am quiet while considering this. "Again, using sickness as the arena, that would be like saying, 'OK, just this cold now.'" I laugh, feeling how untrue that is for me in this moment, coughing, trying to focus, trying to sound like I have properly completed the homework. Clearly I am not impartial about being sick. "Being impartial. Tough."

"Right."

"First, I admit I am a little unclear about exactly how to work with or differentiate equanimity from loving-kindness or compassion."

"Well, compassion is actually a more active state. It's the movement *toward* the suffering, followed by the motivation to do something about it. That idea is behind Thich Nhat Hanh's phrase 'Compassion is a verb.' You know that one?"

"Yes."

"Which really implies, 'How can I help?' So that is different than equanimity. And it is different also than loving-kindness, because loving-kindness focuses on the good qualities of others. It is the feeling that arises from that place. Equanimity just sees everything as it is. It's not particularly focusing on the good or the bad. It is seeing everything just for what it is. I know you're familiar with the equanimity phrase 'All beings are the heirs of their own karma; their happiness and unhappiness depend upon their own actions, not upon my wishes for them.'"

"Yes! I loved that phrase the first time I heard it from you, years ago. My heart relaxes each time I hear it, and I say it to myself often, like when I am frustrated with another's . . . stubbornness," I say, chuckling.

"That is the wisdom mind of equanimity. It is bringing understanding, through equanimity, to that level of understanding, that of the karmic unfolding."

"So it is equanimity first, then, that opens us up for a response of loving-kindness or compassion?"

"Yes. Exactly."

This is a new and useful idea, I'm thinking. It seems obvious that equanimity, that state of just being OK with things as they are, is the starting point for the heart to open with loving-kindness, or with compassion, or both. They would naturally be our response when we have no preconceived notion or concept or desire or aversion.

"Then, watching myself through the Spirit Rock event, for example, whenever I had a reaction or desire arise that was pushing away the equanimity, that was pretty easy to see," I say.

"Right."

"Also watching for all the little reactions that were happening as I listened. I guess everyone has that experience of listening while watching those thoughts and feelings and reactions arising uninvited as someone is talking."

"Yes."

"OK. A question. I am feeling a bit dull, but here goes: Is working with equanimity more about investigating why or when one is not equanimous, thereby opening us up to its natural arising? That feels very different than doing something, as with generosity or loving-kindness or renunciation. In other words, it doesn't feel so much like a process of doing; it feels more passive. Is this right?"

"Well, I think that, in one respect, one could say that. But it is also, as you know, something that can be practiced. So in that sense there could be a doing aspect to it."

"I guess that's what I'm a little unclear about. How exactly does one practice strengthening equanimity, as opposed to watching for its presence or absence?"

"Well, for example, when you are doing the equanimity meditation, repeating the phrase, you are cultivating the quality of equanimity. It's a state, just like all the others, that can be cultivated."

"But in daily life, when you are practicing or working with it, it seems more passive. Or is it the quality of noticing when it's not there?— First you notice that it's not there and then, by paying attention, you are able to choose to just drop into it?"

"Well, but remember," he says slowly, "that process you are describing would probably take a little investigation . . ."

"To naturally drop into it?"

"To recognize that equanimity is *not* present. That recognition. When you see it's not there, then you ask the question, 'Why isn't it here?' You have the recognition it's not there and then ask the question. So all of that, you could say, is a kind of doing."

"Ah. That's true. I'm with you now. And then, by actively watching for those times when equanimity is not present, we begin to see if there are certain things that habitually give rise to reactivity, in small or big ways. Or certain groupings where we are less than equanimous, like cocktail parties! And that is a process, a strengthening of our skillfulness. That's basically how I've been working with it. I see."

"Yes, exactly."

"To which I have now added being sick! This has been several days now," I laugh, "and I find 'Enough already!' often arising and clouding the equanimity."

"Yes," he says, chuckling.

"OK, Joseph, watching for how the equanimous mind is a support for the other paramis—for everything, actually—was very insightful, because I found it went from theory to actually something specific for me to focus on and work with. It was especially insightful using it as an investigation of all the crap arising . . ." Joseph laughs. "I mean all the unskillful mind states that arise while I'm sick. It is really a bounty of new behaviors to investigate, when I'm not totally lost in the 'poor me saga,'" I say, laughing.

"Oh, yes."

"You mentioned that one of the useful ways to investigate here is, when you have a reaction to something arising—especially if it's something complex, like the concept of "overwhelm"—to work with just letting it in. Opening to it without preferences or aversion. So that would be equanimity, right? To actually embrace the feelings of overwhelm? You know, 'Oh, there's Gail toppling into overwhelm again. No worries.'" We laugh.

"Right," he says.

"I don't think I've explored that dynamic with the other paramis. And I can see now how valuable that could be."

"Yes."

"So if one is experiencing an equanimous state, the mind balanced and open, we just naturally respond with compassion. But when we don't have that equanimous mind that's balanced, then we can struggle just to let something be, to let anything in, right? I think that's really helpful to understand."

"Right. In our vipassana tradition, when we talk about the *brahma-viharas* (or four immeasurable attitudes), when we study them, we always begin with loving-kindness. In the Tibetan scheme, when they talk about the brahmaviharas, it is my understanding that they always begin with equanimity. And I think for just that reason."

"Oh. Because it *is* a good basis for opening to everything else."

"Yes. It's just what you're talking about."

"That's interesting. And it's funny because when we were working with resoluteness, I felt certain we should have started there, that resolution should have been the first parami, because it gives you the energy and the carry-through aspect to better succeed in this work. But in fact each parami is so different, and the way to work with each is so different. You just can't push," I say, laughing. "Before you can know what to do with it, you've got to first notice *what* is arising, and that understanding really comes more easily from a balanced place of equanimity."

"Right. Exactly."

"So I was just thinking equanimity should have been the first factor, and now you say it is in the Tibetan teachings."

"Yes."

"That is interesting to me. OK, so here's another challenge to my equanimity that I am struggling with. I, oh so lovingly, call it the "Leaf-Blower Rhapsody." You probably don't deal with this much, because your house is set off apart, but you know how close the houses are here. Every day there's a different gardener in a different yard with a different leaf blower. Or so it seems, especially being home sick this week and wanting to nap! It's terrible. Really. It's obnoxious, loud, annoying, and irritating. So working with it . . . any suggestions for being more equanimous with leaf blowers?"

Joseph is laughing. "Well, this will be coming up a lot in the next three-month course here at IMS, because we're going to be doing construction of the new building. So what we're planning to do, actually, is to use the basic instructions of a big mind meditation, you know, where you *start* with sounds. You open to all the sounds around you, open to them simply as sound. And then that in itself becomes the meditation, so that you are not struggling. You're not trying to keep out certain sounds. You're letting everything in, from the very beginning. Construction work becomes just another sound in space. And there can be a lot of richness and depth to explore here. There can be equanimity present, in making that very sound the object of the meditation. It's the same thing, as we discussed, when one is feeling sick. If one has decided this is an unpleasant feeling, then the tendency is to contract. The practice of equanimity requires that we just open to a sound the same way you described opening to the unpleasant sensations of not feeling well. When we can do that, we will find that the mind just relaxes. It's just hearing, that's all it is. Sounds are not inherently annoying."

"Hmm. I can feel what you're describing. Yes."

After a few moments I start laughing. "Joseph, I remember another story you tell—the one about a Colgate with Gardol commercial. The Gardol ingredient worked as some sort of invisible shield that wouldn't let the bacteria in. You used that commercial as an example of a more fixed, stable mind. And I think people who meditate have probably experienced this, where one gets deep enough that things going on around them just aren't as engaging or intrusive."

"Right. But keep in mind . . . you probably have this in your notes somewhere. The near enemy of equanimity is indifference."

"Oh."

"I think it is important to make that distinction, because equanimity is very different from indifference. Indifference is a non-caring."

"And equanimity also implies some activity."

"Right," he agrees.

"One of the bad raps Buddhism has, I think, comes from that misunderstanding of indifference."

"Exactly. That's why I also like the word 'impartial,' because it implies an openness to, rather than a withdrawing from."

"Oh, yes. Impartial. Letting one know they are fine either way. It is an opening word. I like that." We are quiet a few moments as I look through my notes, still feeling woozy.

"OK, so I've also been working with the concept of *concepts*," I say, "with leaf blowers, construction noise, noisy neighbors, whatever. Trying to remember that they are concepts, labels, and not what is actually happening. Like last night there were howling winds, but the howling was also somehow kind of cool. Ron and I both thought so, even though the winds were also disrupting our sleep."

"Right."

"It certainly wasn't a particularly pleasant sound. But it was easier to lie in bed without cringing or complaining when I could recognize it as just another sound to be listened to. It would do no good to step outside and yell at it to stop. I remember you told me a story once about when you first started teaching. You had a preconception about what to say, what to do, what to be. And that now, you just trust your response in the moment will be skillful. Now your teaching and your speaking is open and easy. That would be a form of equanimity. Right?"

"Ah, yes, I guess you could say that."

"At least in the moment, as you are present with whatever is arising?"

"Yes. That openness allows for creativity and intuition because the mind is not caught in anticipation or reactions."

"It also takes a big level of trust," I say, laughing, "that you're going to have something to say!"

"Well, either that or trust that it's OK to say nothing." This makes us both laugh.

We are quiet for a while. "Wow, that would take some trust," I agree.

"Yes, it would."

"And equanimity for one's ego," I add. "Joseph, ever since beginning to work with the concept of *concepts* during truthfulness month, I continue to hone my discernment there. It was your suggestion, when you notice you are not impartial, when you feel a reaction arising, to investigate the connection of that reaction with the idea of a concept you may hold. That did it! That was it for me. I got it. In a way it makes it more impersonal and therefore a little easier to open to and work with. It's very good. I think that really says it all about equanimity."

Joseph laughs. "Did you come up with examples for that?"

I start by telling him my insights after watching the Wagner movie. But as I am speaking, I keep stopping, coughing, sipping water. I am unwrapping a cough drop when I see it and begin laughing. "Wait! Yes, actually I can come up with a really obvious one," I say, coughing and laughing. "Right now is a perfect example: I am not impartial or welcoming or equanimous to . . . drumroll here . . . the concept of being sick anymore! Especially now that this is the fourth day. Not at all. The reaction coming up is a combination of self-pity . . ."

"Yup."

". . . and impatience and aversion, and and and! Still another piece of that unwelcome concept of being sick, something further feeding all that turmoil, is the aversion or the notion that I am a healthy person. *Why am I sick? You know, me of all people!*"

"Right," Joseph replies, laughing.

"So the conceit of that is really sobering," I add.

"Yes," he agrees. "And you can apply this with any of the paramis, but in the example of being sick and focused on equanimity, the equanimity makes possible the understanding of the selflessness of the process. The body is not always amenable to our wishes. It follows its own laws. This is a transforming insight." He begins that low throaty chuckle, and my ears perk up. "*And*, it is an insight you have to learn over and over again. The non-identification with the body becomes clearer when there is equanimity present."

"Ahhh, and especially as we get older."

"Exactly. The body is clearly out of our control," he says, laughing. "That's another meaning for *anatta* ('selflessness'). The idea that the body is ungovernable."

"Oh, it certainly is! Most times I feel I've forged a decent relationship with my body. We have conversations, I listen, and I certainly treat her well. It's not her fault she got sick."

"Exactly."

"It's just what happens."

"Exactly."

I am coughing and laughing. "Actually, what I am most interested in right now is this idea of an open mind, a mind free of all the limiting concepts. The instant I see something, I realize I have already categorized it into some concept I hold. It's amazing. I can sense the equanimity that lies just beyond those initial, immediate concepts. Oh, I want to go there," I say, laughing again.

"So, Joseph—paying attention, taking the right action, and then letting go of any attachment to the outcome; would that be a more active version of equanimity?"

"Yes."

"Looking at people and remembering that all beings want to be happy, as with our neighbors and co-workers—that too is equanimity?"

"Yes."

"That simple thought has been helping me release the initial irritation or anger that may arise first as an unconscious, habitual reaction. When I remember that—even when the other person may not be acting wisely, from my perspective, if I can just come from that understanding, that wisdom—it allows me to be open and not so attached to my preferences for their behavior. Especially when I feel they are going about things in all the wrong ways," I say, laughing.

"Right. I think that particular understanding can be used in support of all the paramis. Reminding oneself that everyone wants to be happy can be a cause of loving-kindness or generosity, certainly ethical conduct, and so forth. I think it can be used with any of them."

"Yes, I see that now. And one final question. I have heard you mention there are two types of equanimity, and that either one is fine. One is the fixed and stable mind state equanimity, in that case being a deep-in-the-marrow-of-the-bones tranquility."

"Right."

"And then the other type of equanimity you mentioned is a vipassana mind state, open and spacious like you might have walking through a forest or looking up at the stars, being mindful from a place of *everything is OK just as it is.*"

"Yes. This can also be an advanced meditative state in vipassana practice. In that vipassana stage, it has the quality of openness you describe, but it is also a very refined state. So that is very different than just ordinary equanimity."

"Would it be, for example, that feeling of equanimity one has just coming out of a retreat?"

"No, it's more. It's the equivalent, in vipassana, of the equanimity of deep concentration states. There's that depth to it. And that is different than a more casual meditation. So that's all. We have been talking about equanimity in our ordinary lives, working with and cultivating equanimity there. And there is also a state of equanimity to be found in deep meditative states. This is not the thrust of this work, but equanimity also refers to these more refined meditative states."

"Good. I find that distinction helpful."

"Yes, it's the understanding that equanimity covers a broad spectrum of experiences, but all with that same quality."

As Joseph and I reach the end of our check-in, I drift again to discussing being sick, probably because I keep coughing as we chat.

"When I was meditating this morning, the mind was yammering, yammering, and then there would be moments of this incredible surrender. It was really sweet. I'm not sure why. The mind yammering, and then the sweetness, and I thought, *Let's have another long sweet breath of surrender,* then off the mind would wander again, yammering. That was about all I got, but it was remarkably peaceful when I let all the chatter about being sick just go, pass on by as just another thing that was arising."

"That surrender you are describing is really about the willingness to open to unpleasant feelings."

"Oh."

"Our whole conditioning is avoidance of unpleasant feelings."

"It's so true!"

"Oh, yes."

"That is exactly what was going on! I could open to feeling so miserable, even for just a few moments, a few breaths. I surrendered. I just let it go—all the complaints and aches and disappointment about being sick. I just sort of set them aside to open to a few clear moments of peace, peace with and peace within things just as they were."

"And that is the essence of the path," he says softly. "The Buddha said, 'As long as there is attachment to the pleasant and aversion to the unpleasant, liberation is impossible.' This points to the profound nature of equanimity in terms of liberation. It is a very powerful practice. What you just described is really the essence of equanimity."

"Perhaps that's why it felt so sweet, because it was so clean and clear."

"Exactly."

"That's really great, Joseph. Thank you for that last bit. I can feel the difference. And I think I'll end this lovely conversation for now." We both laugh.

The next day I wake up feeling much better. And then . . . a neighbor's leaf blower begins. So I try just letting the sound of the leaf blower blow right through this mind of equanimity. When it rattles my bones, I toss in some loving-kindness. I say the phrases to the laborer, who is just doing what he thinks is best, what he is being paid to do. I add the high-pitched whine as background to the crows' harsh cackles, the fog wind slamming a window shut, the construction clatter nearby. Sometimes it works. Applying the wisdom of impermanence, remembering the blower will round the corner of the neighbor's house and the sound will become dimmer, also helps. And sometimes, well, it still sounds very much like an annoying whine. There is a marvelous poem by Billy Collins entitled "Another Reason Why I Don't Keep a Gun in the House" that addresses the attempt to incorporate a nuisance sound, his neighbor's barking dog, into his listening to a Beethoven symphony. He imagines the barking dog as one of the musicians in the orchestra, not always playing on cue or in tune. Leaf blowers—just another instrument playing in the symphony of a Sausalito morning.

I open the newspaper and immediately try extending equanimity to what I feel are, at best, misguided politicians. This troubles me deeply—the dug-in positioning and posturing of the current political arena. And not just ours. Europe's keenly crafted alliance is also teetering because of an either/or mentality and finger-pointing. It is a dismal mirror to our own system, mired in antagonistic barbs delivered over thick walls of innuendo, mistrust, and downright stubbornness. It is disappointing and worrisome. It sounds naive, but if I can find a way to get along with my neighbors' leaf blowers and continual construction projects, why

can't the folks whose job it is to negotiate, do so? Isn't remaining equanimous when negotiating with the opposition a worthy endeavor? Isn't it
part of what they vowed to do when they promised us they would operate with integrity? Wasn't our support based on their promise? Even
with my friends, I hesitate to repeat a wise or thought-provoking comment said by an "opponent" because the comment can provoke a spirited, not always equanimous response. How did Gandhi and Mandela
and His Holiness the Dalai Lama find the strength to walk their paths
with such searing equanimity and loving-kindness and wisdom? Can
you even imagine a political arena, a country, a world populated by such
valor and truthfulness? I wish I could.

This verse by Atisha is a useful reflection, a final instruction on
equanimity:

> Consider all phenomena to be dreams.
> Be grateful to everyone.
> Don't be swayed by outer circumstances.
> Don't brood over the faults of others.
> Explore the nature of unborn awareness.
> At all times, simply rely on a joyful mind.
> Don't expect a standing ovation.

Conclusion:
Final Thoughts on a Life of Integrity

The key to our freedom comes from two essential things.
First, we make an effort to stop causing harm through our
speech and actions . . .
and second, we learn how to relate skillfully in the present.
—JOSEPH GOLDSTEIN, *INSIGHT MEDITATION*

"Do you want to go first?" I ask Joseph.

"That's OK. You can go." He smiles at me.

Joseph and I are standing at the top of a ski run. A steep ski run. Much farther down the hill a ski instructor is waving a pole, indicating we should come down now. I can just see him through thickly falling snow and fog.

"You can go first," I say.

"That's OK. You can go." We grin. Down the snowy steep slope the instructor turns from the conversation he is having with Ron to peer up at us. He waves his pole again, a bit more forcefully. We have been learning to carve turns, ride edges, shift our weight, lift a ski. The challenge has been for Joseph and me to follow Ron, the better skier. All afternoon we work to keep up. We are both exhilarated at learning new moves, and exhausted. The instructor directs his suggestions and drills to Ron's level of expertise, the two of them having a wonderful time discussing subtleties, showing off for each other. The lessons have become increasingly more difficult, while the snowfall, and our strug-gling limbs, have become increasingly heavy.

The drill now is to ski down the slope backward! Did I mention it is a steep slope? We are to feel each ski carving a wide circle as we lift and shift our way down. First the instructor demonstrates. Beautiful. Ah, so easy. Then Ron, who is not only a very funny guy, but also a gifted ath-lete and eager to try, executes beautiful wide turns, smiling, dancing to show off as he faces us while skiing backward down the run. We laugh. But now it is our turn. Still we hesitate, look at each other.

"You can go first," Joseph says, chuckling.

"No. You go." We both start laughing. The instructor raises both poles. Ron also waves a pole. Joseph peers down the hill, then turns his head slowly to me. "You know," he says, "I don't think I've ever had the desire to learn to ski backward."

It's too much. I lean over my poles, giggling, then reach under my goggles to wipe away tears with a crusty glove. The goggles fog up immediately. I look in Joseph's direction. He is just a dark blue shadow. Joseph is right. The truth is I also have no desire to learn to ski back-ward, however it may contribute to my skills. It is cold and very dif-ficult to see. Both the wind and the snowfall are fierce, biting. I don't want to be the last one up here. My goggles now clear again, I look at Joseph. He looks at me. We nod and, without a word, ski together facing downhill to where Ron and the instructor await. We are both grinning as we rejoin them. I don't need to ski backward just because others do, or it looks cool, or it is someone's good idea to improve my skill. I don't schuss, I don't jump, I don't ski backward. I just hadn't thought to check in with myself, as Joseph had done. Tip #1: *Check in with yourself first.*

Quite early in my integrity work I caught myself lying to a friend on the phone about a "prior commitment" in answer to her invite. This was not an uncommon occurrence as I endeavored to schedule some quiet time for myself each week. When I hung up the phone, my stom-ach felt queasy. My radar activated. Lying to someone is certainly not speaking with integrity. Never mind the "reasonableness" that most of us have attached to the little white lie. I still remember the moment. I just stopped. Cold turkey. That day. And now? The tell-a-fib impulse rarely arises. Yes, I felt awkward and apologetic in the beginning. Now I think I'd be awkward trying to lie and then remembering the lie. Tip #2: *Choosing integrity is not always the easiest path . . . at first.*

This past Christmas I worked swiftly to bake cookies, then clean the kitchen thoroughly before the winter rains that would probably bring in the ants again. But it is now late January and we still await our winter rains. Good news: no ants. Bad news: no rain. We do see an occasional ant scout headed into our shower! Also looking for rain? Tip #3: *Count on things changing.*

Ron scraped the side of his car on a neighbor's wooden post while maneuvering to park curbside. A colleague told him he was "friendly" with the insurance adjuster and could get his entire car repainted, paid for by the insurance company, with a wink and a story of an unknown drive-by scrape. Ron decided he did not feel good about the proposal and paid someone else to just buff it out. Tip #4: *Working with integrity rubs off on and inspires others.*

There is hunger worldwide. The affluent hunger for meaning and contentment, continually reaching out for more but never satisfying the hungry ghost inside. Comfort foods, new clothes, houses, and well-paying but unsatisfactory jobs temporarily ease the longing. Meanwhile, the poor hunger for basic necessities in a world that has enough to go around if everyone shared. Lynne Twist, in her book *The Soul of Money*, says, "Mother Teresa once noted what she called 'the deep poverty of the soul' that afflicts the wealthy, and said that the poverty of the soul in America was deeper than any poverty she had seen anywhere on earth." Tip #5: *We hunger to live a noble life.*

We know there is a better way. We know overeating and overin-dulging do not appease the hunger of our hearts, nor our yearning to live impeccably. Instead of feeding our dissatisfaction, we need to listen to it. We must investigate the hunger that drives us to relentlessly gorge and then regret, the aversion that keeps our minds riled, our hearts bound up tight. The world desperately needs our skillful, compassionate voices . . . perhaps now more than ever before. The path is simple: mind-fulness. We need to have moment-to-moment awareness in order to see clearly the truthfulness of things as they actually are in a moment, in our speech, in our actions, in our hearts. We now know that path. We now know the wise response that also honors and fulfills our deepest yearnings. We yearn to do better and now we know that we can! We need to fight for what is right for our own peace of mind, for all humanity, and for our planet. Tip #6: *We must live true because we know now that we can, and we are needed.*

This morning I read a story about a local man tragically killed in a taxi in Asia. His friend said, "He was the most honest guy I've ever known. I don't think he ever even told me a white lie. He stood for everything he did. He believed in the truth." If you died suddenly, would this be what is written about you? What would you like to be said about you? Our last words should be, with a blissful smile, "Done is what needed to be done." Tip #7: *Start now.*

Casey Schwartz, in the January 2012 issue of *Newsweek*, writes, "The lurid headlines of the past year—cheating politicos, lying coaches—are enough to make you think morality is a thing of the past. If you ask Joshua Greene, a leading researcher on morality and the brain, he might say the tools most of us use to navigate moral conflicts are outdated, too. Ultimately, this is Greene's great quest: to help people understand that moral progress only becomes possible when we don't believe everything we immediately think." A brochure for a continuing education course, offered by the Institute for Brain Potential, arrives in our mail. The title of the course gives me pause: "How the Brain Forms New Habits: Why Willpower Is Not Enough." The first topic of the course is testing automatic thoughts for their accuracy! Tip #8: *We are not our thoughts. Go deeper.*

By now, if you have been diligent with this work, you will have experienced moments of the bliss of blamelessness, the reward for our mindful commitment to do the right thing. As we begin to notice and then trust that our first response may often be truthful and compassionate, a deep relaxation arises. Confidence and contentment bloom. When we encounter a rough patch and stumble, recollections of our past solidly good efforts arise to cheer us and keep us focused and committed. We notice less interest in the siren song of overindulgence. We are not so easily distracted, entranced. There is less need to placate a yearning heart. The heart is full. Habitual responses now skillfully satisfy inner longings to live more kindly. Understanding we are solidly on a path of integrity, we are more playful, like the monks at the seashore, like Joseph catching himself in an unskillful moment and laughing in delight. Knowing we are on the path, knowing we are doing our best, our mistakes, too, are more easily forgiven. Tip #9: *With understanding, trust, and a light heart, we naturally just begin again.*

Joseph's suggestion for investigating one's motivation is to ask ourselves, "Is it onward-leading?" I love that and use it often. Again: simple, but not always easy. And when we do stray from our onward-leading endeavors? Kelly McGonigal, PhD, a health psychologist at Stanford University, counsels in her book *The Willpower Instinct: How Self-Control Works, Why It Matters, and What You Can Do to Get More of It*: "Has beating yourself up ever helped you stick to a diet or stay within your budget? Probably not. You may even have ended up indulging more. Instead, ask yourself this: 'When am I likely to err again, and how will I prevent that from happening?' Once you've figured out how to avoid the problem in the future, let it go." Tip #10: *Investigate, then just let it go.*

Remember the Mars Exploration Rover? When it was on the back side of Mars, all communications would cease. Only the little rover knew what was going on internally and what it was seeing externally. Those who had watched and cheered its progress now had to sit and wait for it to communicate with them again after its personal odyssey through the dark side. We will all take journeys through the dark side. We, the rovers, can only keep moving onward through the darkness and trust that if we just stay on the path, eventually we will arrive once again into the light. Tip #11: *Trust yourself more.*

Joseph is about to begin a retreat of many months, meditating alone and without contact with the world, in his home. We are having our last conversation before he turns off phone and email.

"You're really going under tomorrow?" I ask.

"Ah, yes," he says, chuckling.

"Are you excited about going into such a long retreat?"

"'Excited' is not the right word . . . but very happy."

"Well, I'm excited now," I say, "about continuing to work with the paramis and beginning to draft a book on it. But I also notice I'm feeling a bit nervous too. I have your reading list, but it's not the same as consulting live with you." Joseph laughs. "So I did have one last question that came to mind this morning. May I?"

"Of course."

"Did you ever do any practice, specifically with the paramis?"

"Yes, yes, I have . . . and I continue to work with the parami of *dhana*, of generosity. That is an ongoing practice for me. Really looking for opportunities to give, and responding to every situation that arises. So that's in my mind a lot. Bringing this practice into daily life. And one of the interesting things about it for me has been that being receptive to being asked, in one way or another, opens me a little more to the range of need in the world.

"Oh. Yes."

"So instead of holding a preconception of where I might want to give, or might devote my energy or resources . . . I'm practicing just being responsive to whatever comes my way. It doesn't mean I'll necessarily respond to everything that comes. But I consider it all. Then I become more aware of a lot of different arenas, not just with generosity but also with many of the paramis, that need help. And it's interesting. It expands one's consciousness out into the world. This is a whole other dimension to this work."

"That *is* interesting. I don't think we've talked about that. So still another interesting way to practice with all of this."

"Right. So have a good few months," he says.

"Thank you, Joseph. Thank you so much."

"You're very welcome. And . . . we'll be in touch."

"All right. I hope to make you proud. Have a wonderful retreat. Both Ron and I send our love." Sadness wells up. I so often feel this after speaking with Joseph. Now he will be unavailable for months. I am on my own. Will he like what I write? How to know? All this is tumbling about in my head as I hang up the phone on our last parami conversation.

Shortly after this last check-in, in January, I go for a follow-up mammogram. My first, in November, had been abnormal. Because of the holidays, this had been the earliest re-exam the clinic could offer. That wait, through all the holiday festivities, became a real test for watching and working with the mind. Just this moment. Breathe. Then the next. Fear. Breathe again. Just this moment. Release. More fear. Breathe. Let it go.

Awaiting the exam now, I sit in a rumpled hospital smock in a little green-and-coral-walled waiting room with a small group of women who have also been called back in for a second mammogram. Stoic and silent, we sit together with heads bowed, looking into magazines none of us are reading. Our fears are probably so thick it is a wonder the attendants can walk between us. We are young and we are middle-aged. Asian. Latina. White. Black. One of us at a time is called out for the imaging, then returns to wait for the results. After some time that person is called out again. I am sitting next to the entrance into the hallway. (Hoping for a quick escape?) I can hear what is said to each woman as she is called out of our little room of impending doom. "The doctor will meet with you here. Do you have your insurance card to schedule the biopsy?" I begin to get nervous. Arm-pit and palm-sweating nervous.

I had decided it was fortuitous this was scheduled on what would have been my mother's birthday. Somehow she would be more available, the reasoning went. As I sit here now, nervousness twisting the insides of my stomach, I call her in, I pray, I plead for her help, for anyone's help, for everyone's help. This is the first time I have called on my mother like this in years, and in the compressed, stifling little room, I suddenly feel her with me.

Finally it is my turn. During the painful examination I feel my mother with me, her presence like the warm blanket she would tuck in around us when we were children and sick. Then back to the little waiting room I am led. When I am finally called out again, the young woman who escorts me is smiling as she leads me down the hall. When we reach an empty room and enter, I am not surprised when she turns quickly, handing me a form and speaking fast. My second test is clear. "Good work," she says, which seems completely nonsensical to me, as if I were in charge here. But she seems so genuinely happy for me that I reach out and hug her, which I think pleases her. Surely she must be the bearer of frightening news so much of the time. She probably looks forward to these rare opportunities to deliver good news.

As I walk down a rainy sidewalk, then begin the drive home, I keep looking for relief to arise. I keep waiting for the ebullience of the young woman to flood me too. I thank my mother, God, Buddha. Still no gladness arises. Perhaps I have lived with the fear so long that relief will take a while to sink in, I think. Perhaps it is just the gray day.

I am almost home when the tears begin. I have to pull over, they are so consuming. I am not driving home, I realize. I am still sitting in that room of gloom with the other women. I am waiting beside each of them, sharing their fear, their pain, their worry. I yearn for their prognosis to be all clear, as mine has been. I *am* those women. I am also the husband sitting with folded hands in the outer waiting room, there when I arrived, still there, sitting in the same pose, when I left. I am so much a part of those women that my good news is not something to celebrate. I ache for them and with them. So instead, I sit in my rain- and tear-swept car and do all I can think to do, which suddenly is to say the phrases of loving-kindness aloud, as a prayer of health for each of them. I am those women. Their fibers are my fibers, their hearts beat in my chest. I grieve with them and worry with them, just as I know they are happy for my good news. Eventually, as I restart the car, I suddenly understand that this is new for me. This depth of my compassionate response, this inability to exalt when others are suffering, arises from a new and deeper capacity for understanding. It is a natural wisdom, arising spontaneously from a heart already open and receiving, born of this hard-fought parami work. "It's working, Joseph," I say aloud in my car. And then I open the window and shout into the rain, "I live with integrity now!"

Tip #12: *From commitment to integrity, compassion arises, and with it the greatest happiness, which is peace.*

Acknowledgments

Thank you to my mother and Unity minister, Glory, for guiding me and my five siblings onto a spiritual path. We all remain deeply connected. Thank you to my father, Arne, Norwegian at birth, American veteran and pilot of three wars, who lived with sterling integrity and deep love of family.

Thank you to all my spiritual teachers: Swami Muktananda, who pointed to me in a vast, crowded hall and asked, "Why have you waited so long to come see me?" (I was only twenty-two), and then visited me that night in a dream—and I was launched. His Holiness the Dalai Lama, whose giggles intoxicate me when I hear him teach, and whose faith and deep commitment to the possibility of one's enlightenment is palpable. Jack Kornfield, one of the founders of Spirit Rock, my spiritual home, for his teachings, for the family he has created at Spirit Rock, and for his books—so clear and touching, inspiring and fun! Sylvia Boorstein, my dear friend, travel companion, and writer of many charmingly accessible books, whose daily life is a living demonstration of love and commitment. Like Joseph, her wisdom is so deep that our time together is a blessing I never take for granted. Guy and Sally Armstrong, friends, teachers, vacation buds, and two shining examples of what living an awake life together can be like. James and Jane Baraz, single-handedly awakening joy around the world and living it with a deep commitment to teaching, sharing, and giving back. Kamala Masters, whose retreats with Joseph I have sat for almost thirty years. Her genuine, soft response to daily living is inspiring. Thank you all for your teachings, your wisdom, and your support in reading this book and offering your kind and moving endorsements.

Thank you to the colleagues, friends, mentors, mentees, and partners I have come to love in my many years of San Francisco real estate.

You are the audience I imagined as I created this book, working with the monthly integrity instructions in our shared business community.

Thank you Sandy Boucher, Buddhist teacher and author, for offering to look at the first few rough chapters and assuring me it was worthwhile pursuing. Thank you Kim Baker, friend, therapist, and longtime Buddhist practitioner, for offering me the opportunity to try out the first chapters on your therapy group. Their eagerness to take these instructions into their daily lives and then return to share their stories with the group was an inspiration.

Thank you Wisdom Publications for the truly amazing work you do and the gifts you offer to our world. I am deeply grateful and totally smitten to have you as my publisher and be included in your family of remarkable teachers and writers. Thank you Andy Francis and Laura Cunningham for seeing in my rough draft what now is available to everyone, thanks to your early, gentle suggestions that made it all come together so beautifully. Thank you Mary Petrusewicz for stepping in so smoothly, midstream, and gently nudging it along to a timely completion. Thank you Josh Bryant for the beautiful cover design that everyone loves. Thank you Ben Gleason for moving the manuscript through production so effortlessly, and Brianna Quick for patiently teaching me how one markets a book. I have loved working with everyone at Wisdom and thank them deeply for their kindness.

I feel honored to know each and every one of you and to learn from you personally, as we share this life together. This is a blessing I would not have envisioned for myself, and I continue to be awed and deeply grateful for the opportunity.

And thank you to all of you who are reading this book and working with your integrity. Those efforts are no small undertaking. Ah, but the bliss of blamelessness is no small achievement.

About the Author

Gail Andersen Stark has been quietly infiltrating the San Francisco world of business with Buddhist teachings for thirty-plus years. Cofounder of a highly regarded San Francisco real estate company, she has guided and mentored hundreds of new agents and clients, gently utilizing the concepts of integrity, kindness, and grace. Her passion is to help make these ancient principles available and accessible to a world in need. She lives in Sausalito, California, with her husband Ron.

What to Read Next from Wisdom Publications

Wholehearted
Slow Down, Help Out, Wake Up
Koshin Paley Ellison

"Intimacy is based on the willingness to open ourselves to many others, to family, friends, and even strangers, forming genuine and deep bonds based on common humanity. Koshin Paley Ellison's teachings share the way forward into a path of connection, compassion, and intimacy."
—His Holiness the Dalai Lama

Free Yourself
Ten Life-Changing Powers of Your Wise Heart
Carolyn Hobbs

"Carolyn Hobbs offers readers a guide for awakening heart wisdom that arises from her years of healing work with others—and her own deep understanding. *Free Yourself* will help us to inhabit our lives with the fullness of loving presence."
—Tara Brach, PhD, author of *Radical Acceptance*

Business and the Buddha
Doing Well by Doing Good
Lloyd Field

"Field offers an inspiring perspective on Buddhist principles and their ability to transform our traditional capitalist system from a greed-driven enterprise into a humanistic and compassionate endeavor."
—Gary Erickson, owner and founder of Clif Bar & Co., and author of *Raising the Bar*

A Heart Full of Peace
Joseph Goldstein

"In this short but substantive volume, Joseph Goldstein, who lectures and leads retreats around the world, presents his thoughts on the practice of compassion, love, kindness, restraint, a skillful mind, and a peaceful heart as an antidote to the materialism of our age."
—*Spirituality & Practice*

The Magnanimous Heart
Compassion and Love, Loss and Grief, Joy and Liberation
Narayan Helen Liebenson

Narayan shows us exactly how it is possible to turn the sting and anguish of loss into a path of liberation, moving from the "constant squeeze" of suffering to a direct experience of enoughness—the deep joy, peace, and happiness within our own hearts that exists beyond mere circumstances.

About Wisdom Publications

Wisdom Publications is the leading publisher of classic and contemporary Buddhist books and practical works on mindfulness. To learn more about us or to explore our other books, please visit our website at wisdomexperience.org or contact us at the address below.

Wisdom Publications
199 Elm Street
Somerville, MA 02144 USA

We are a 501(c)(3) organization, and donations in support of our mission are tax deductible.

Wisdom Publications is affiliated with the Foundation for the Preservation of the Mahayana Tradition (FPMT).